16

PARALLEL MOTION

PARALLEL MOTION

A Biography of Nevil Shute Norway

Storytelling was his genius . . . and he had a profound
faith in the abilities of the dedicated man.
                                        —Eric Linklater

John Anderson

The PAPER TIGER®

Published by:
The Paper Tiger, Inc.
722 Upper Cherrytown Rd.
Kerhonkson, NY 12446
(845) 626-5354
website: www.papertig.com
email: FredWeiss@papertig.com

Cover design by Linda Robinson
Book layout by Mark Van Horne

ISBN: 978-1-889439-37-2

This book is dedicated to the memory of
Mike Meehan

Nevil Shute Norway Family Tree

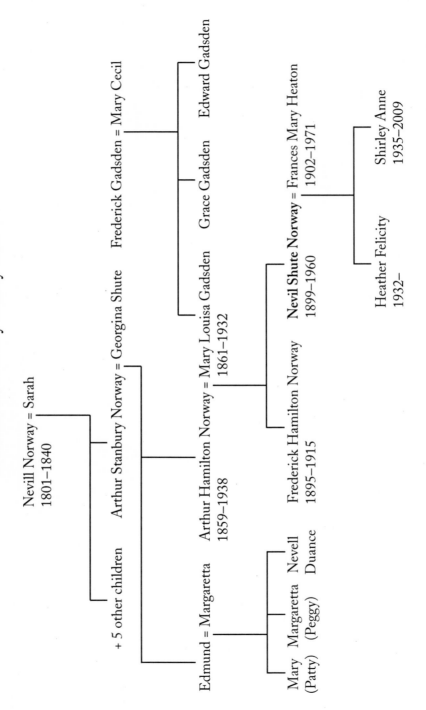

Contents

Foreword

John Anderson has done something that should have been done decades ago, and done it very well. He has written a biography of Nevil Shute, the engineer/author, who wrote in the mid 20th century.

He has brought to life not only the author, but also the times in which he lived and worked, starting with his childhood, and the effect that his stammer had for the whole of his life, continuing on to his school life at Shrewsbury in England, his participation as a 17-year-old in the Easter Uprising in Ireland in 1916. He follows him to Balliol College, then to his early working years at de Havilland, his work on the R.100 airship, and his start up of Airspeed, his own aircraft company, all while in his 30s, and beginning to write the novels for which he is now remembered. He writes about his wartime service with DMWD, (Department of Miscellaneous Weapons Development), and his working with the Ministry of Information, while he still continued to write novels.

Finally, John relates his journey to Australia and back in 1948/9, the flight of fancy, with Jimmie Riddell, another author. They flew in a Proctor aircraft, taking 2 months out, 2 months in Australia, and 2 months on the return trip, all the while meeting many very fascinating people. As a result of that voyage, Nevil Shute moved out to Australia, taking his family with him. He settled on a 200 acre farm south of Melbourne, where he continued his output of best selling books. He suffered a stroke there, and died in Melbourne on January 12 1960, just short of his 61st birthday.

John has done a tremendous amount of research into Nevil Shute's life, and has written a well balanced and eminently readable biography of this truly exceptional man whom I'm proud to call my father.

Heather Mayfield
December 2010

Preface

The path to writing this book began when I went to the Nevil Shute Conference in 2003. Richard Michalak from Australia, a long time researcher into the life and work of Shute, told me that there were 40 files relating to Shute's wartime work at the National Archives in London. He wanted to examine them but didn't have time on that visit to England. Also at the Conference Dan Telfair, founder of the Nevil Shute Norway Foundation, presented a paper entitled "In Search of Nevil Shute", in which, with the help of the audience, he built up a picture of Shute based on the characters in his novels and his own interviews with those who knew Shute.

This Conference inspired me to discover what else might be available from U.K. archives. Over the next few years, together with other Shutists, I delved into archive materials at the National Archives and elsewhere. The more we looked, the more material turned up. The results of some of this research were presented at subsequent biennial Nevil Shute Conferences and intermediate gatherings.

I had absorbed Shute's own autobiography, *Slide Rule*, and the biography written by Julian Smith. *Slide Rule* finishes in 1938 when Shute left Airspeed but the majority of the book is about his work on the R.100 airship and the formation and early years of Airspeed. Whilst he wrote of his childhood, schooling and Oxford, there are only passing references to his wife and children. Julian Smith's biography covers all of Shute's life but his emphasis is on the literary analysis of his novels.

I came to believe that there was room for a biography which told his whole life story, complete with the details that could be added from our researches. It would tell the full story of this remarkable man, a successful aeronautical engineer who became one of the best selling authors of his generation. As he matured as a writer he had an extraordinary ability to weave his own life experiences into wonderful stories. It is my hope that this biography will show the reader just to what extent he drew upon the people and events he encountered during his lifetime and how his skill as a storyteller developed over the years.

An explanation of the title, Parallel Motion, is perhaps in order. Shute did not live to write the second part of his autobiography, which would have been called *Set Square*. A slide rule and set square are tools that he used as an engineer. A parallel motion is a system of wires and pulleys that are used on a drawing board to keep the ruler parallel as it is moved up and down the board. It is a device that Shute would have been familiar with during his own working life in engineering. It also has a connotation of his parallel careers as an engineer and writer.

The person who encouraged me to begin writing this book was my friend Mike Meehan. I first met Mike at the 2003 Nevil Shute Conference. We became great friends and shared many enjoyable research expeditions as self-styled "Dust Pirates". He was as dedicated a Shutist as they come, possessed great enthusiasm, a wonderful sense of humour and steely determination in the face of illness. He also had an almost encyclopaedic knowledge of aircraft from his own long career in aviation. Sadly Mike passed away in December 2009 and this book is dedicated to his memory.

John Anderson
December 2010

1
Born with Aviation

In the last novel, *Trustee from the Toolroom*,[1] completed before his death in 1960, Nevil Shute has the main character living at number 56 Somerset Road, West Ealing. The house is described as "a tall thin slip of a house . . . built at a time when English architecture was going through a bad patch." It was in this house, in reality number 16, that Nevil Shute Norway was born on the 17 January 1899. He was the younger son of Arthur Hamilton and Mary Louisa Norway. His older brother Frederick Hamilton Norway (Fred) had been born in the same house in 1895. Their father was a civil servant, at that time employed in the Staff Branch of the Post Office in London.

Although he was to become one of the best-selling writers of his generation, Shute did not earn his living from writing until he was in his late thirties. Even at the height of his popularity as a novelist, when he had written best sellers such as *A Town Like Alice* and *On The Beach*, he regarded himself more as an engineer who wrote novels than as a novelist in his own right. He was trained and graduated as an engineer and spent almost the first twenty years of his working life as an aeronautical engineer, writing in his spare time. He was to make his mark in the worlds of both aircraft and airships and in a real sense he was born with aviation. The year after he was born the German *LZ1* rigid airship made its maiden flight. When he was four years old the Wright brothers made their famous flights and by the time he was ten Blériot had crossed the channel and A.V. Roe and others in England had made pioneering flights in heavier than air machines.

On his father's side of the family his roots were in Cornwall, for several generations of the family had lived and worked in that county. Shute's great-grandfather Nevill was a well respected timber and general merchant who frequently attended markets in Bodmin. He went to market on 8 February 1840, concluded his business and set off, shortly before 10 o'clock at night, to ride the nine miles home. Later that evening his rider-less horse arrived at his home. His wife raised the alarm and a search party set out to look for him. Early the following morning Nevill's body was found, face down, in a stream and it was apparent from the scene that there had been a desperate scuffle before Nevill had been killed by blows to the head with a blunt instrument. The hunt was on for the killers, and a detective, Charles Jackson from London, took charge of the investigation. On the evidence of a witness at the market two brothers, James and William Lightfoot, were apprehended and charged with Nevill's murder. Their trial took place at Bodmin in April 1840 where, it transpired, William Lightfoot had dragged Nevill from his horse and fired a pistol twice, but it did not go off. After beating him to death and robbing him, William and James had dragged his body across the road and rolled it down a bank into the stream. They were found guilty and hanged on April 13, with, it was said, a crowd of ten thousand assembled to witness their end.[2]

There is another story about Nevill's brother Edmund, who was in command of the merchant vessel *Orient* in the South Atlantic off St Helena the night Nevill was murdered. He told the second officer, Mr Wren: "I had a dreadful dream. I dreamt that my brother Nevill was murdered by two men on the road from Bodmin to Wadebridge. One fired a pistol twice, but I heard no report. He then knocked my brother from his horse, struck him several blows about the head, then ran away and left him." Wren advised him: "Don't worry about it. You West Country people are too superstitious." On 9 February 1840, just a day after the murder, Captain Norway recorded his dream, and the conversation with Wren, in the ship's log.

Nevill's widow Sarah was left with six children under the age of nine. As she was left in the most straitened circumstances, a collection was made for them in Cornwall, and the very large sum of £3,500 was raised on their behalf. However Sarah died the same year and her sister Maria assumed charge of the children. Later Maria married Edmund Norway, the ship's captain. By the 1850s, after Edmund had retired from the sea, he and Arthur Stanbury, Nevill's eldest son, were in business together as E & A Norway, wine and spirit merchants in Wadebridge.

It was in connection with this business that Arthur Stanbury travelled to Liverpool to visit Stephen Shute, who was a merchant in that city. There he met and married Georgina Shute, Stephen's daughter, on 24

September 1857. They lived for a time in Formby, just north of Liverpool. However the family seemed to have moved back to Cornwall, for the 1861 census has a record for the parish of Egloshayle in Cornwall for Arthur and Georgina Norway and their two sons Nevill Edmund and Arthur Hamilton Norway aged 2 and 1 respectively. Some years later the family moved back to Formby and Arthur Hamilton, who was educated at the Liverpool Institute, entered the Civil Service in 1880, aged 21, by way of a competitive examination. At first he was assigned to the Inland Revenue in Liverpool, but in 1883 was transferred to the Post Office dealing with foreign postal services. Later he moved to the Staff Branch, which entailed a move to London.

Arthur was, by all accounts, a classical scholar and wrote a number of rather erudite books. He was fluent in Italian, and loved Italy, writing a history of *Naples, Past and Present* and a book on Dante's *Divine Comedy*. He contributed two books to the *Highways and Byways* series, one published in 1897 about Devon and Cornwall, his native county, and a second about Yorkshire, which was published in 1899, the year Shute was born. The writing of these must have entailed a considerable amount of travelling, judging by the maps of his journeys, and they were written in the slightly flowery language of travel books of the time.

The following extract from *Highways and Byways of Yorkshire*, describing York Minster gives an idea of his style:[3]

It is long past noon, and with relief I seek the shadow and the cool aisles of the Cathedral, concerning whose great beauty I can never speak without a throbbing of the heart. For, indeed, York Minster is to me a place of dreams too exquisite and too impalpable to be set down in words. Let other and more phlegmatic men attempt in cold blood to analyse a building which is beautiful enough to be the gate of Heaven. I turn my memory back on all the hours I spent there, and can recall nothing but the flushes on the stone-work as the warm sun streamed red and golden through the ancient glass, or, falling down in one long, lofty beam from the topmost region of the clerestory, cast green flickering reflections on the worn stone pavement.

He wrote one novel called *Parson Peter, A Tale of the Dart*, a book about Cornish life in the smuggling period. He also contributed to another—

The Government Official which he wrote with Charlotte Riddell. Being in the postal service and in a position to write its history, he published a *History of the Post Office Packet Service* between the years 1793–1815. This was about postal enterprise in the period of the American and Napoleonic wars.

Georgina Norway moved to the London area after the death of her husband in 1886 and at this time began writing books. These were books for children of which the first was *The Adventures of Johnnie Pascoe* published in 1889. This was followed by some 20 more with titles such as *A Dangerous Conspirator*, *The Loss of John Humble*, *Ralph Denham's Adventures in Burma* and *A True Cornish Maid*. These would have been on the bookshelves in the Norway household when Fred and Nevil were growing up and no doubt formed part of their boyhood reading. With both his grandmother and father being authors, the process of writing and publishing books was very familiar to Shute. Yet he showed no inclination to write books himself until he was in his early twenties.

His mother, Mary Louisa, was the daughter of a career Army Officer. Frederick Gadsden was born in 1830 and entered the army as a 2nd Lieutenant in 1850. He rose to become a Captain in 1864 and Lieutenant Colonel in 1876. He was on the Madras Staff Corps of the Indian Army and spent a number of years in India. Mary was born in Berhampore whilst the Gadsdens were stationed there. Her brother Edward joined the Indian Police and rose to become Inspector General of Prisons in India. By 1891, the family had returned to England. Frederick Gadsden had retired from the Army with the rank of Major General and the family was living in Ealing. It was here that Mary met and married Arthur in 1892 in the church of St John, Ealing. At the same church both Fred and Nevil were baptised by the Rev. Julius Summerhayes.

The household in Somerset Road was typical of that of a middle ranking civil servant of the time. The family employed three young domestic servants, Jane, Lillian and Daisy. Also living with the family was Anne Norway, Arthur's unmarried aunt. The two boys grew up in this safe, comfortable, middle class environment—Fred, good looking, scholarly and perhaps the apple of his parents' eye and Nevil, practical, good with his hands and less interested in scholastic pursuits. It was Nevil who made the models and was mad keen on anything to do with flying. One of his early memories was of watching a hot air balloon slowly descending in the fields near his home, but being much too young to go and investigate it on his own. Aviation was the new thing then and certainly featured in the penny comics he bought with his pocket money. He wrote later that "The new art of flying was my chief boyhood interest; Hamel, Grahame-White, and Farman were famous, well known names to me before I reached my teens."[4] He made models of wood, glue and paper, using rubber bands for motors, trying them out to see how well they would fly. He learned a lot from those models about longitudinal stability and negative tail incidence. He also recalled a model aeroplane made of sheets of metal soldered together, an indication that he was good with his hands and learning to use tools. In this practical way, and reading articles about aeroplanes in the encyclopaedia, he learned a lot about them. Perhaps, though, he felt a lack of confidence or self esteem when compared with his older brother, so much better than he as a scholar and with an ability in subjects such as Latin and Greek that their father valued highly. He was naturally left-handed but, as with many children at that time, was made to write with his right hand. This has been put forward as a contributory factor in causing stammering. For whatever reason, Shute began to stammer very badly from the age of five or six and continued to do so on occasions all his life. He claimed that it ceased to worry him in later life, but it was a significant impediment that was to blight some of his school days and his prospects when he left school to join the army. At that time he reluctantly agreed to undergo treatment when trying for a Commission. This was to no avail and he came to believe that stammering was incapable of a cure except by increasing self-confidence which came with age and maturity.

In 1907 his father was promoted to Head of the Staff Branch of the Post Office and the family moved to a larger house at 26 Corfton Road, still in Ealing. By this time Fred was away at Rugby School and no doubt Shute felt lonely at home during term time without the companionship of the older brother whom he adored. At this time Shute was attending a preparatory school in Hammersmith where he found life difficult for a boy with a stammer. Not only was he tormented by the boys there, but also by some of the masters, although he later singled out Mr Cox as one of the better ones. He travelled to school on the train from Ealing to Hammersmith and one day he rebelled, avoiding going to school by travelling to and fro on the train all day, getting out at stations on the way and sitting on the platform. He returned home at the usual time with only a small lie to explain why he had no homework. A day or two later he played truant again and found that by paying an extra penny he could travel on to South Kensington. There he discovered the delights of the Science Museum and spent some days wandering round the models of locomotives and engines and examining the aeroplanes on show. He was fascinated by them and in particular by the Blériot XI monoplane which had just flown the English Channel. That flight was in the summer of 1909 which suggests that Shute was about ten or eleven years old when he played truant.

For several days, he was able to forget his troubles during the day at the Museum but stored up mounting guilt and lies at home. The blow fell when the Headmaster of the school wrote to ask what had become of him. His parents acted wisely and did not send him back to the same school as they might well have done. They sought to give him a fresh start and sent him to Lynam's school in Oxford, where he lived with the Sturt family. The Sturts had lived in Cornwall, in fact in Egloshayle where Arthur Norway had been born, and the Norways had met them on holiday. Mr Sturt was a Don at an Oxford college and also an author of some note, and wrote books on politics and philosophy. The Sturts lived at 55 Park Town in a house just behind the school in North Oxford.[5] They had three children, were not particularly affluent, and were probably quite glad to have a paying guest. So Shute settled into a new life, going to school with the Sturt's son Oliver, who was a little younger than himself. So began a long association with Oxford that was to be both a happy one and a formative influence on his life.

Lynam's School was founded in 1877 as the Oxford Preparatory School. The school was started by a committee of Oxford dons with the remit of providing a high standard of academic grounding and pastoral care to the children of professors of the University of Oxford. Indeed, many early teachers were, or had been, dons themselves. When Shute was there, the Headmaster was C.C. Lynam known to everyone as the "Skipper" who ran it with his brother A.E. Lynam known as "Hum". The School, now known as the Dragon School, has been described as one of the most idiosyncratic of preparatory schools. Its alumni and its faithful staff, many of whom devoted their lives to the school, reflected a unique atmosphere, a paradoxical world of informality, nicknames, radicalism and scholarship. Here Shute settled in well, enjoying the life and carefree days during the summer holidays. He learned to fish and handle punts or canoes on the River Cherwell which runs alongside the school, or rowing boats or sailing dinghies on the Upper Thames. He paid the school the compliment that his stammer hardly mattered there. He seems to have flourished at the school. John Betjeman, the poet, was a pupil shortly after Shute and wrote that the Dragon School "was one of the happiest places in the world, and made all subsequent education seem repulsive."[6] Shute maintained his links with the school for many years after he left, submitting articles for the school magazine and leaving some of his own possessions for the museum.

In July 1911, the *Daily Mail* newspaper ran a Round Britain Air Race and Shute kept a diary on this during the summer holidays. The race started and finished at Brooklands, and competitors covered over 1000 miles with 11 compulsory stops on the route, which passed directly over Shute's home at Corfton Road. For him this was a highlight, for he knew all about, and could recognise, the aeroplanes which took part.

In August 1912 it was announced that Shute's father, who by then was Assistant Secretary to the Post Office in London, would succeed Sir Reginald Egerton as Secretary to the General Post Office in Ireland. This meant a move to Dublin and finding a new home. Shute later wrote that it was not a promotion, for his father was on the same salary, but that his father was glad to take the posting, for his mother's health was causing some anxiety and it was felt that a move away from London would be beneficial. There was another aspect to the appointment. The Secretaryship had traditionally been filled by one of the higher officials from London, which Arthur Norway certainly was. He was regarded as a safe pair of hands and also sympathetic to the case for Irish Home Rule. In view of his increasing deafness he may well have regarded the appointment as a short term one with the possibility of early retirement before handing over to an Irishman when Home Rule came into being. It was a move to be in complete control of a considerable enterprise, though in a smaller sphere; he would become, as Shute later put it, "a large frog in smaller puddle."[7] The provincial life was something that, he thought, suited his father, as it was to suit him later.

The new job held considerable prestige and required a home appropriate to the position. Arthur therefore rented a house called South Hill in Blackrock about 12 miles south of Dublin, at a rent of about £250 a year. The house was a large one, set in thirteen acres of grounds with a walled garden, stables and greenhouses, a far cry from the modern villa in Corfton Road that had served them in London.

There they had employed two servants but at South Hill the staff comprised three servants, a gardener and gardener's boy. Shute later wrote that his father could afford this without overspending his salary, despite the fact that both he and Fred were reaching the most expensive stages of their education. However wages in Ireland would have been significantly lower than in London. Here, his parents blossomed into the country life that went with their status and both parents were fully able to hold their own. His father, a classical scholar and author, was a good host with a keen sense of humour and his mother, daughter of a Major-General, was fully acquainted with the customs of polite society.

For the two boys South Hill was a delight—for Shute during the holidays but for Fred during term time as well. When the family moved to Ireland Fred, aged 16, left Rugby School where he had not got on well. At Rugby he had had two abdominal operations and had spent more time in the sanatorium than out of it. So after the move, his father sent him to Trinity College, Dublin. Trinity College was, and still is, the premier academic institution in Ireland; a University with a long history and high reputation, well suited to a young man of Fred's academic ability, although at 16 he was a young entrant.

Shute loved the holidays at South Hill with its country pleasures, for up to that time, apart from expeditions around the Dragon school, he had lived almost exclusively in suburbia. Now there was a pony to be ridden or harnessed to a trap, hay to be made in the summer and the greenhouses to be walked through and the produce wondered at. It was at South Hill that he learned to ride a horse, though he rode for pleasure for only one brief period of his life, preferring to ride or pilot something with rather more horsepower. Fred acquired a small revolver and he and Shute took pot shots at the weather vane.

Fred travelled to College each day and his room soon filled with books. Writing of this time, Shute mentions poetry and literature, noting in particular John Masefield, Swinburne, Algernon Blackwood and writers such as William Morris. It was probably at this time that he developed a lifelong love of poetry; he was to try his hand at writing his own and used poems in many of his novels, particularly the later ones. At this period, as a young adolescent, he seems to have been developing a sense of the romance of literature and poetry. Romance of another kind surfaced when his Cornish cousins, Patty and Margaretta, came to visit.

They were the daughters of Arthur's older brother, Edmund, a doctor in Newquay. Patty was the same age as Fred and evidently introduced him to a Geraldine Fitzgerald. Shute recalled Fred aged seventeen shyly proposing to Geraldine, a dark-haired Irish beauty, on the top of a Dublin tram. She gently refused him whilst nervously tearing up her ticket. However, this Geraldine was not the same Geraldine Fitzgerald who had a film career, as Shute wondered in *Slide Rule*. Geraldine the film star was born in 1913.

Shute was glad that his parents had the opportunity to lead this kind of life whilst they could. For his service to the Post Office, Arthur was later made a Companion of the Order of the Bath or CB, an honour given to distinguished civil servants, the CB being awarded to those who had served in Ireland. He would have attended a ceremony at Buckingham Palace to receive the award from King George V.

Shute was also happy both in the holidays in Ireland and also at the Dragon School, where he progressed well and took a great interest in the masters' tinkering with their motorbikes and cars. C.C. Lynam, the "Skipper", was an inspirational headmaster, greatly respected by staff and pupils alike and Shute wrote that "whilst The Skipper had good material to work with in his pupils, but I think the main credit for the happiness of the school must go entirely to the headmaster himself."[8] He acquired the nickname of Skipper because he was a keen yachtsman. In the holidays he would cruise in his yacht *Blue Dragon* round the north of Scotland, the Hebrides, the Orkneys and the Shetlands. Later he took a term off and sailed his boat across to Norway and up the coast to the North Cape. Hearing of these voyages may well have planted the seeds of Shute's interest in sailing, a recreation that he later took up and subsequently enjoyed for the rest of his life and which became so much of a feature in many of his books.

Shute summed up his carefree days of peace before the First World War with the poem *Romance* by E.F.A. Geach. Yet all was not peaceful in Ireland. The question of Irish Home Rule had been on the agenda in Parliament for decades and a third Home Rule Bill had been introduced in the House of Commons in 1912 but was fiercely opposed by Unionists, who formed the Ulster Volunteers to resist any actions by those in the South. The South countered by forming the Irish Volunteers to restrain Ulster. The seeds were sown for the Easter Rising in 1916 which Shute would experience at first hand.

The academic year 1912–13 was Shute's last at the Dragon School. He had swum for the school and taken part in a diving competition, achieving third equal in the under 14 group. During his final year he took part in the school production of *The Taming of the Shrew*. A photograph of the cast shows him as a rather serious-looking boy, playing the part of a servant. It was time for him to go to public school. Since Fred had not done well at Rugby, Shute's father did not send him there as might have been expected, the younger brother following in the footsteps of older brother as was generally the case. Instead he chose to send him to Shrewsbury School where he arrived in May 1913.

2
Born to One End

When Shute arrived at Shrewsbury in May, he went into Oldham's house, which he described as one of the newest and the best. Like other new boys he started in the Fourth Form and in a study which he shared with four other boys. The study monitor was H.S. Neville, and the other boys were A.L. Davies and D.K. Wolfe-Murray. There would inevitably been the period of adjustment and of home-sickness whilst he got used to his new surroundings and the regime at the school.

Shrewsbury was a fine school, not quite an Eton or Harrow, but was on the up-grade under a vigorous and imaginative young Headmaster, Cyril Alington. Alington had taught at Eton and moved to take up the Headship of Shrewsbury in 1908. He was "endowed with almost every gift to ensure a successful career. Extraordinarily handsome, especially in later years when robed and in the pulpit, he impressed the great majority of boys at Shrewsbury."[1] The school itself had a long history and could boast many distinguished alumni of whom probably the most famous was Charles Darwin, who had been at the school nearly a hundred years earlier.

The weekday routine was that the boys rose at 7:15 and took a "cold swill" (a shower). Chapel followed at 7:45 always with the same liturgy of a psalm, a lesson, a hymn and prayers. Breakfast followed chapel and then three periods of lessons and a break before lunch, known as "after twelve". Lunch was at 1:45 followed by at least an hour for games and then two more periods of lessons. Tea was followed by prep from 7:30 to 9, referred to as "Top Schools". The day finished with house prayers and announcements known as "Dix". The boys then went to bed in stages according to age with lights out for all, in theory, by 10:15. On Sundays there was full chapel in the morning, a divinity period in the afternoon and then Evensong.

Basil Oldham, Shute's Housemaster, was in his early thirties when Shute arrived, one of a number of younger masters that Alington had recruited. Oldham had taken it upon himself in 1911 to build a new boarding house. For this project he had obtained a bank loan, engaged an architect and had built No. 8 The Schools (renamed Oldham House) which opened its doors in 1912.[2] At that time School fees were paid to the Housemaster, with about a third being passed onto the school itself.

Oldham was a confirmed bachelor who devoted his life to the education and well-being of "his boys". The first of Oldham's characteristics that boys discovered was that, by keeping his mouth almost shut, he managed to mangle his words, which made him difficult to understand. This was accentuated by his pipe, which projected downwards at an angle of 45 degrees. His flow of words was sometimes as unintelligible as it was voluble and earned him the nickname of "The Gush". Nonetheless he sought to get to know his boys, to make friends with them even to the extent of having them down in his study after lights out to have free and easy informal talks without inhibition. Some boys took advantage of this initiative whereas others found it embarrassing. Oldham could be described as a homosexual, though never in the physical sense, just as one who preferred male company and a life in an all-male environment. True, the boys had mothers who were treated with courtesy and good manners, but when Old Boys brought along girlfriends or fiancées, Oldham tended to shun them.

Shute was one of many who became a lifelong friend to Oldham, and took to this eccentric schoolmaster and came, during his formative years, to absorb many of his values and beliefs. Oldham's was a version of Dr Arnold's "muscular Christianity" which valued manliness, honesty, integrity, loyalty, self-improvement and sexual restraint. Amongst his contemporaries Shute made other lifelong friends of whom one was Graham Heath, who became a solicitor, secretary of the Old Salopian Club and a Chapter Clerk of St Paul's Cathedral.

Shute swam for his house in his first year and joined the Officers' Training Corps. The OTC was a feature of most English public schools of that era, designed to give the boys a taste of life in the Army. The OTC would meet regularly during term time with masters acting as officers (of whom Oldham was one) and the boys in uniforms organised into squads and platoons and practising marching and drill with occasional visits from regular Army officers to inspect the corps. During the summer holidays there would be a camp where OTCs from various schools combined and the boys would live under canvas and carry out manoeuvres on a considerable scale with exercises and more drill, and these camps would be run by units from the regular Army. Interestingly, Shute remained a private throughout his time in the school OTC. Whilst it was not uncommon for boys to remain privates, many of his contemporaries would have risen to lance corporal, corporal or even sergeant. This may have reflected a lack of self confidence at this time, or may have been because of his stammer.

In the Michaelmas Term 1913 Shute moved up to the Shell form and the following year he was Confirmed as a member of the Anglican church. For this, as well as the school Chaplain, Oldham, himself a devout Anglican, took a hand in the preparation of his boys for Confirmation. This tended to take the form of serious talks which, though ranging far and wide, had a considerable content of what would now be called sex education so that Confirmation and sex education were, unfortunately, mixed together.

At the end of the summer term 1914 Shute was at the OTC annual training camp at Rugeley in Staffordshire and it was here that they heard, on the 4 August, that war with Germany had been declared. The Army was mobilised and the regular Army officers and other personnel left the camp almost immediately to resume their normal duties. The camp was disbanded and the boys and masters sent home, still in their khaki uniforms, the boys all very excited at the prospect of war. For there was, at the beginning, overwhelming national support for the war when it was felt that Britain and her Empire must resist and counter German aggression in their invasion of Belgium and thrust towards France. The British Expeditionary Force was immediately sent across the Channel to join their French counterparts in halting the German advance from Belgium into France. There was a patriotic fervour and a rush to enlist in the army. Public schools such as Shrewsbury were seen as the natural providers of officers for the Army. There was a feeling, on both sides, that the war would be won quickly and that "it would all be over by Christmas."

By the time Shute got home to Ireland that summer, he found that Fred, aged 19, had already applied for a commission in the Army. He had, however, failed the medical and had to have another minor abdominal operation. This gave his father a chance to consider Fred's options and he decided that Fred would be better off applying for a commission in the regular Army, which would give him the chance of a career in the Army if the war went on for some years. With the impatience of youth and given the feeling that the war would be over quickly, Fred was annoyed. He wanted to enlist straight away to join the fight. He felt that the war might well be over by the time he was commissioned as a regular officer. However his father was adamant about the commission, and Fred was admitted to Sandhurst in October 1914.

Fred thought that every officer should know something about motors, a rather surprising view given that he seems never to have shown any interest in mechanical things before. Perhaps it was just a ruse to persuade his father to buy him a motorcycle, knowing that his younger brother would be just as keen on the idea. His mother took the view that a motorcycle would help ease the loneliness that Shute would feel in the holidays when Fred was away at Sandhurst. So the parents bought a Rudge Multi motorbike, to be shared between them, at the great cost of £60. Fred was in hospital having his operation when the machine was ready for collection in September, so Shute went to collect it from the depot at St Stephens Green in Dublin. At 15 years old he had a comprehensive "theoretical" knowledge of motorbikes, in part gleaned from watching masters at the Dragon school working on their motorbikes. But he had absolutely no experience of actually riding one, let alone the Rudge which was a powerful 500 cc machine with, to complicate matters, a belt drive with variable groove pulleys giving 21 forward gear ratios. In those days there was no requirement for a licence to drive. St Stephen's Green was right in the centre of Dublin and Shute recalled the Rudge mechanic giving him a shove off and he being out of control in amongst the trams and traffic until he got the feel of the powerful machine. After a couple of circuits of the Green, he mastered the gear change. Then he rode it home to Blackrock in triumph. It was, he said, one of the truly ecstatic moments of his life.

No doubt he took every opportunity to ride the Rudge during what remained of the summer holidays. He was back at school in September and Fred had the Rudge at Sandhurst during the winter. In just a few weeks Fred passed through Sandhurst, so that by Easter 1915 he was a newly commissioned Second Lieutenant in the 2nd Battalion of the Duke of Cornwall's Light Infantry and stationed in Falmouth. He had elected to join the regiment which reflected his family's home county, Cornwall. There his Battalion was awaiting the draft to France.

In the Easter holidays Shute and his parents stayed in Falmouth for two weeks to see something of Fred before he left for France. He recalled Fred looking very smart in his new uniform, his Sam Browne belt newly polished, his sword impressive and a large new revolver, clean and smelling fragrant with gun oil, very different from the pistol they had used to fire pot shots at the weather vane at South Hill. When the visit was over, Shute rode the Rudge from Falmouth to Holyhead to catch the ferry back to Dublin. The journey of about 400 miles took him nearly four days; forty years later he attributed the time taken to poor roads, bad springing and recalled fatigue and aching wrists. He did nothing but ride and thought that 100 miles a day was good going. That he successfully completed this trip, the first long distance journey on his own, gave his self confidence a boost. He would have had to find places to stay along the way and buy petrol for the bike, which at that time cost two shillings (10p) a gallon. Very soon after he got back home to Ireland he would have had to pack again to go back to Shrewsbury for the summer term.

When Fred's Battalion arrived in France they were sent to the front line at Armetières to hold positions after the battle of Neuve Chappelle in March. By then the German advance had been halted and the front line was becoming increasingly static. In June he was badly wounded at l'Épinette. His section of trench was mined by the Germans and the explosive charge blew up the trench. He survived the blast, and under shell fire, led a party of men to dig out his sergeant who had been buried by the blast. It was then that Fred was wounded by a shell.

Fred was evacuated to the base hospital and recovered well for several days before gangrene set in and became uncontrollable. His parents went to France to be with him and he died on 4 July with his mother at his bedside, three weeks after being wounded. He was buried at the war cemetery at Wimereux, south of Calais.

Shute's shock on hearing the news, either by letter or telegram, of his brother's wounding followed by the news that he had died of his wounds can only be imagined. He had lost his only brother whom he adored and who had such a great future ahead of him. He later wrote "If Fred had lived we might have had some real books one day, not the sort of stuff that I turn out, for he had more literature in his little finger than I have in my whole body. He was only nineteen when he died, and after nearly forty years it still seems strange to me that I should be older than Fred."[3]

For Shute, as for millions of others, the attitude to the War changed as the casualties increased. It was no longer a romantic adventure. His thoughts were no longer of a career on leaving school. As he later wrote he was "born to one end" to go into the army and do his best before he too was killed. For him the services in Chapel played a significant part. The school casualties mounted almost daily with the names of older boys, whom he had known, being read out in chapel, and realising that younger boys might one day kneel in remembrance of him. The hymn, written by Alington at that time, which Shute probably sang, captures the mood.[4]

> For all our friends who, near or far.
> Heard and obeyed the call of war.
> For deeds determined, dared, and done,
> We praise Thee, Father, Spirit, Son.
>
> On earth, in air, by sea or land,
> Their times are in their Father's hand ;
> Teach them to know that Thou art nigh,
> And unto Thee they live or die.
>
> O Thou, strong Spirit, cheer and bless
> Their hours of fear or loneliness,
> And give us grace our worth to find,
> And serve Thee with a quiet mind.
>
> And grant that, through the grave's dark door,
> Our friends and we may meet once more,
> Through Christ our Lord, Himself Who gave
> In life to serve, In death to save.

As at Shrewsbury, so at the Dragon school, the names of casualties were read out. John Betjeman, who was a pupil at the Dragon School during that time, expressed it beautifully in his autobiographical poem[5] "Summoned by Bells":

> Before the hymn the Skipper would announce
> The latest names of those who'd lost their lives

For King and Country and the Dragon School.
Sometimes his gruff old voice was full of tears
When a particular favourite had been killed.
Then we would hear the nickname of the boy,
'Pongo' or 'Podge', and how he'd played 3Q
For Oxford and, if only he had lived,
He might have played for England—which he did,
But in a grimmer game against the Hun.

It was at this time too that Shute began writing poetry, all of it, he said, very bad. Yet life at school continued and brought its own rhythm of chapel, lessons, games and prep. At the end of the summer term, Shute rowed for Oldham's in the Bumping Races on the River Severn. Boats from each house were lined up one behind the other a set distance apart, and the objective was to catch or "bump" the boat ahead. The order of the boats was determined by their position in the previous year's race or round, with the winners at the front. If one boat 'bumped' the boat in front, both boats pulled to the side of the river and dropped out of the race. The boat in front dropped down a place at the next round, swapping places with the boat that bumped it. These races were greatly enjoyed by competitors and spectators alike and no doubt provided some light relief at the time.

The summer holidays of 1915 in Ireland must have been sad and lonely for Shute in a house that held, both for him and his parents, so many memories of Fred. His father took advantage of a break clause in the lease on South Hill to move out. They took up residence in the Royal Hibernian Hotel in the centre of Dublin which was very convenient for the Post Office, then housed in a magnificent new building on Sackville Street. Their furniture went into storage and valuables were locked up in a safe in the Post Office building.

In the Christmas holidays 1915 Shute and his parents travelled to Rome and Naples, a perfectly reasonable thing to do even in that time of war. The Western Front was static and it was quite feasible to take the train to Paris and then on to Italy. No doubt Arthur felt that a break well away from Ireland was required and where better than Italy and Naples in particular, a city he was familiar with, having written a book on its history. So as well as providing a much needed holiday, he would have been able to renew his acquaintance with it. Arthur took his full six weeks of leave for this holiday and Shute later wrote that he felt able to do this despite the pressures of war. This meant that, when the time came for Shute to go back to school, he did so on his own, travelling by train back through Italy and France to England. It was quite courageous of his parents to push him off on this journey alone, being now their only son. Despite speaking no Italian and only schoolboy French, his journey was uneventful, although he had to change trains unexpectedly two or three times. He arrived back at school with his self confidence boosted and to find that very few of the other boys had ever made a journey of that length.

Back at school Shute, now in the fifth form, was part of the Oldham's team in the Rope Drill competition, a gymnastic event requiring a good deal of physical strength and agility.

For the Easter holidays in 1916 Shute went to Dublin and stayed with his parents at the Royal Hibernian Hotel. Quite unknown to him at the beginning of the holiday, he was to be involved in the Easter Rising, the attempt by the more revolutionary Nationalist elements to establish an Irish Republican state. For some time, elements had broken away from the main Nationalist Party and formed the Irish Volunteers and they had been acquiring arms and ammunition. They had held parades and demonstrations. Shute, now aware of the tensions that were building up, took Fred's army revolver from his father's safe. He cleaned it, loaded it and gave it to his father, saying that he would feel better if his father were armed.[6]

Easter Sunday passed off peacefully enough. On Easter Monday Shute went on a motorbike ride in the country. His father said he had a lot of letters to write and would go to his Club to write them. He found he needed some letters from his office and went to the Post Office Headquarters to get them. There he got a phone call from Dublin Castle, the seat of British administration, to go there urgently, which he did. Just ten minutes after he left the building an armed detachment of Sinn Fein rebels, led by James Connolly, entered the building and took it over. There were guards on duty to protect the building, something that Arthur had arranged, but they had not been issued with ammunition for their guns. If Arthur Norway had been there when the rebels arrived, he would have been held hostage or perhaps even killed. The summons to the Castle gave him a very lucky escape. Once the rebels had occupied the building they issued the Proclamation of the formation of the Irish

Republic and declared the General Post Office to be the headquarters of the Army of the Irish Republic.

In other parts of the city armed detachments of rebels were active. A force of about 200 occupied St Stephen's Green and began digging themselves in. Later they were joined by Constance Markiewicz (Countess Markiewicz) the only woman leader of the rebels. Another attacked the Castle but did not pursue the attack. The shots alerted the Under Secretary, Sir Matthew Nathan, who was in conference with Colonel Price of Military Intelligence and Arthur Norway. When the attack was not pressed home they helped to close the Castle gates. The occupants of the Castle were thus trapped and unable to escape until help arrived.

Unaware of what was going on, Shute got back to the hotel from his motorbike ride at about 12:30, and with his mother, decided to walk up to the Club to collect his father for lunch. As they approached O'Connell bridge over the river, they met a crowd rushing down towards the bridge who were shouting "Go back, go back, the Sinn Feiners are firing." Shute said, "You'd better go back Mother, there's going to be a row. I'll go on to the Club and find Dad." His mother turned round and fled back to the hotel. As he walked up the street Shute witnessed a troop of Lancers, part of the 6th Cavalry Reserve Regiment, which was escorting an ammunition convoy, come under fire from the rebels firing from the Post Office windows. Four of the Lancers fell from their saddles, killed instantly and one or two horses went down. The crowd scattered in alarm, Shute with them, but within two or three minutes they were back again. These were the first men that he had seen killed.[7]

Shute, thoroughly alerted to the danger, and knowing that the rebels held the Post Office, returned to the hotel and told his mother what had taken place and that he had no news of his father. In the afternoon however they did get a telephone call from his father saying that he was at the Castle but couldn't leave, which relieved their anxiety. In the afternoon Shute went out again to see what was happening. All seemed to be quiet for the moment, so he persuaded his mother to come and look at the Post Office building. A large green republican flag had been hoisted and a notice posted announcing that it was now the Headquarters of the Provisional Government of the Irish Republic. As they were looking at this, two shots rang out and they fled once again back to the hotel.

The authorities acted swiftly and troops began to arrive from the Curragh, the closest army camp to the city, and over the coming days reinforcements and artillery arrived from elsewhere in Ireland and also from England in order to crush the rebellion, but it would be some days before the rebels finally surrendered. In the meantime Shute felt in his element; it was his cup of tea so to speak. He was mentally prepared for combat although just a youth caught up by accident in an armed struggle.

After tea that Monday he set out alone to see what was going on at St Stephen's Green, just a short distance from the hotel. He found that the rebels had dug pits all round the periphery, each with two or three armed men. There had been a lot of firing and several people killed, and the street opposite the Shelburne hotel was barricaded. That evening he went out again to see if he could get near the Castle to contact his father, but he couldn't. There was fighting and shooting as troops stormed the City Hall, which commanded the main gate of the Castle. He could go no further and as it was altogether too "hot", he went back to the hotel. City Hall was re-taken after some fierce fighting. Later on, Arthur and some other civilians in the Castle were able to creep out and make their way home. He arrived back at the hotel shortly after 11:30, much to the relief of his wife and son.

Beside handling the mail, the GPO Headquarters also housed the main telephone switch room for Dublin. Fearing that the rebels might intercept or cut the telephone lines, one of Arthur Norway's engineers went round Dublin in a car re-routing lines to the Royal Hibernian Hotel. By this means a temporary exchange was set up to maintain telephone communication with England. Mary Norway helped to man this exchange throughout the rebellion.

There was gunfire throughout that first night, both rifle and machine gun, as British forces took up positions around St Stephen's Green and elsewhere. By morning they had machine guns mounted on the roof of the Shelburne hotel and raked the rebels in St Stephen's Green Shute went out after breakfast to see again what was going on and reported a big fire in the shops on Sackville Street opposite the Post Office building. Later he and his father talked to an Army surgeon who told them that he had about 500 casualties, two thirds of them civilians shot in the streets. Again he went to see the effect of the firing by British troops on the Green. He saw a group of men clustered around a gate into the Green and went up to see what they were looking at. The rebels had stacked benches against the inside of the gate to barricade it. Lying on one of these was a civilian with his lower jaw blown away and he was bleeding profusely. Shute climbed over the railings, saw that the man was still alive, then turned and berated the spectators, asking if there was anyone willing to help him rescue the injured man. Three men climbed over and helped him remove the barricade and open the gate. Then they carried the man on the bench to the nearest hospital, but he died about five minutes after they got him there.

On Thursday the Red Cross asked for volunteers to help them as stretcher bearers and for next few days he helped convey the wounded from both sides. This was not without risk, as several times they ran up against barricades or came under fire. He was, he said, a callow youth acting as a labourer and a runner for more experienced people, but he undoubtedly helped to save lives. To quote from his mother's account of the rebellion:

This week has been a wonderful week for Nevil. Never before has a boy of just seventeen had such an experience. Yesterday he was at the Automobile Club filling cans of petrol for the Red Cross ambulance. In the afternoon he went round with the Lord Mayor in an ambulance collecting food for forty starving refugees from a burnt out district . . . and after tea he went out for wounded and brought in an old man of seventy-eight shot through the body. He was quite cheery about it and asked Nevil if he thought he would recover. "Good Lord yes; why not?" said Nevil and bucked the old man up![8]

The rebellion came to an end the following Saturday when the rebels surrendered. The Post Office had been their Headquarters and was bombarded by artillery and set alight, the blaze reducing it to a burnt-out shell. Many of the Norways' possessions were lost in that fire including many of Fred's things, which was a sad loss to his mother.

Shute, with many of the other volunteers, was inspected and thanked by General Sir John Maxwell, Commander in Chief of the British Army in Ireland. Some months later he received, from the St John's Ambulance Society, a very noble parchment talking about gallant conduct in tending the wounded at great personal risk. On 5th May Shute left Dublin to return to Shrewsbury. He would, as his mother remarked, have much to tell his school-fellows when he returned. And when he got back to school he found, to his own wonder, that people were beginning to listen to what he said, or rather stammered. It had indeed been a remarkable adventure for a seventeen year old boy.

The following May there appeared an article in the school magazine, *The Salopian*, entitled "Easter Week in Dublin".[9] Although not signed, the article was written by Shute, describing the sights he witnessed during the week, with a clarity that was to mark his later work. Also that May, following a series of Courts Martial, those who had signed the Proclamation of the Republic were executed, and they included Padraig Pearse the leader, James Connolly and Joseph Plunkett. Many years later in his novel *Beyond the Black Stump* Shute drew on his experience of the Easter Rising and used it to extract a kind of literary revenge on the rebel leaders, including Countess Markiewicz.

Back at school that summer, Shute represented his House in the Junior Challenge Oars when Oldham's second boat was beaten in the final by Rigg's by 7 seconds. He took part again in the Rope drill competition and was also in the second boat for the Bumping races. Still in the OTC, he took, and passed, the Certificate A exam which contained both written and practical elements. This would have been supervised by a regular Army officer and was designed to test the candidate's knowledge of the theory and practice of soldiering.

Michaelmas term 1916 was to be Shute's last at Shrewsbury. He was now in the Sixth form, Army class, which meant he was destined for service in the Army. He was also Study Monitor, which meant he wrote the entries in the study book. He shared the study with three other boys, Cooper, Dyer and Woolf. So at Christmas 1916 he left Shrewsbury. He had made little impact during his time at the school, being neither a scholar nor representing the school in sports. This is reflected in his valedictory entry in the *Salopian*, which is considerably shorter than those of other leavers who had distinguished themselves either in academic study or on the playing field. In the study book for that term he signed off simply "N.S. Norway 1913–1916 *Vale!* (farewell!)."[10]

His father thought that, if with his stammer, he could get a commission in the regular army he should do so. He sat the exam for this and failed it, but there was still time to try again before he reached the age limit of 18½ years. To make sure of this his father sent Shute to a cramming establishment in London for six months. This was made easier by the fact that his parents had moved back to London.

His father's appointment as Secretary to the Post Office in Ireland had been a sore point when it was made. He, an Englishman and a Protestant, had been appointed ahead of another candidate, an Irishman. Although he had handled the job with great tact and diplomacy, it was politically expedient after the Easter Rising to transfer him back to London and appoint an Irishman in his place. On their return, his parents took a large furnished flat at 23 Oakwood Court in Holland Park and it was here that Shute lived. His parents furnished a bed sitting room for him, buying a roll-top desk that was to accompany him for the rest of his life and at which most of his books were written.

In the summer of 1917 he entered Woolwich, having managed to pass the medical without stammering. He joined the Royal Military Academy at Woolwich and elected to join the Royal Flying Corps, then still part of the Army. His officers soon found that he stammered but he stayed on, training as a Gunner at Woolwich for nine months which he found he enjoyed. He did well at Woolwich, being top of the progress report for his Company. On 1 April 1918, shortly before he was due to pass out as a commissioned officer, the Royal Flying Corps and Royal Naval Air Service were combined to form the Royal Air Force. This meant that no more Woolwich cadets were commissioned into the air arm. By that time he was stammering very badly from overwork and his housemaster at Shrewsbury had noted that his stammer became worse after his experiences during the Easter Rising. At his final medical examination before passing out from Woolwich, he failed due to the stammer and was thrown out to become a civilian again.

His parents were still anxious for him to get a commission and he reluctantly agreed to try again. His father sent him to a specialist, Mr Payer-Payne, for treatment for his stammer, although Shute privately believed that it would be much better to go into the ranks than waste time trying to get a commission. At this stage he was depressed and apathetic and he failed in his attempt to get into the RAF. In August 1918 his father accepted the inevitable and Shute enlisted in the infantry, and was posted to the First Reserve Battalion of the Suffolk Regiment at the Isle of Grain at the mouth of the Thames. He became Private N.S. Norway 65675. His father later described this as "a deplorable waste of keen ability."[11]

Although he did not realise it at the time, the eighteen month period he spent attempting and failing to get a commission saved him from being drafted into the ranks earlier than he was, and thus going to the Front where he might well have joined the ever increasing casualty list. For by that time, as he later noted, men who were quite unsuitable for front line service were swept up in the increasing conscription demand for manpower. In *Slide Rule* he cites the case of Philip Bainbrigge, a master at Shrewsbury whom Shute would have known. In fact Bainbrigge joined the staff at Shrewsbury in the same year as Shute, 1913. Just seven years older than Shute, Bainbrigge was a brilliant scholar from Trinity College Cambridge and a Sixth Form Classics master at Shrewsbury. In 1917 he left the school and was commissioned with the Lancashire Fusiliers and served in France from February 1918. Shute described him as a tall, delicate weedy man with thick glasses, with a great sense of humour and enormous academic ability who should never have gone to France at all. He was killed in action at Battle of Épehy on 18 September 1918. In *Slide Rule* Shute quoted Bainbrigge's one war poem, a darker parody of Rupert Brooke's "The Soldier" and which reflected the changed mood expressed by later war poets of whom the best remembered is Wilfred Owen whom Bainbrigge had met. Owen was also killed, just days before the Armistice in 1918.

Life as a private soldier required some getting used to. Shute had to make adjustments, sleeping on a straw palliasse, eating coarse and dirty food and living alongside men for whom a public schoolboy in the ranks would have been a novelty. The language of the men was no novelty to him; he could out-swear most of them but, in his immature state, he found their attitude to women shocking. He had been brought up to treat women with greater respect than that shown by his fellow soldiers. His time at Woolwich had hardened him physically and his training in the OTC at Shrewsbury would have come in useful: he knew far more about soldiering than the other men. After the first few weeks he had adjusted and said that he knew of no more restful life than that of the private soldier. He was not required to think for himself, was told what he had to do and when he had to do it. The strain of the past eighteen months, trying and failing to get a commission, quickly eased and he was a competent and cheerful young soldier when, to his wonder, the war ended on 11 November.

For Shute, as for the country as a whole, the war had been a costly and devastating experience. His beloved brother and many of his friends from school had been killed. Indeed some 320 Salopians were killed during the

First World War. Shute had mentally prepared himself for the same fate but had been spared; he was one of the reprieved. He had a future and began to realise that there was such a thing as fun to be got out of life. But the end of the war did not mean demobilisation for him for some months. For one thing, in the autumn and winter of 1918 there was a pandemic of influenza which was particularly prevalent in soldiers returning from France. Those with mild symptoms tended to stay in France; those with severe symptoms were shipped back to England, crowded together in clearing stations and in the trains home, so that infection spread rapidly. Such was the death toll in the Army, Shute formed part of a permanent funeral party and became practised at the grand sweeping gesture of "resting on your arms reversed". He later recalled that whenever he heard "The Dead March" it reminded him of that time of excursions through Kent as a member of that funeral party.

In December he was transferred to Shorncliffe Camp near Folke-stone to train as a clerk to man the demobilisation centre. Here he discovered some hangars left from when it had been an RAF station. In one of them he found an old Sopwith Camel and spent hours sitting in it, studying the instruments and controls, and making sure he understood how everything functioned. He supplemented his aeronautical studies by buying two books, one on the theory of aeroplane construction and the other a comprehensive book called *Practical Flying* He seems to have had a good deal of free time and the discipline was lax because they had a mutiny at Shorncliffe, seemingly a rather light-hearted one, mainly to do with a complaint about the food. In response the Army declared that their course was over and Shute was sent to nearby Dover. The camp was close to Dover Castle and to the spot where Blériot had landed after his flight across the Channel. He worked at the demobilisation centre for two days and then walked through it to demobilise himself.

His father wanted him to go to Oxford, and Shute was willing enough but stipulated that he wanted to read Engineering. His application to Balliol College had already been accepted and now that, at last, he was free of the army he could go and pursue his studies there.

The cast of *The Taming of the Shrew*—Dragon School 1912.
Nevil Shute is seated front row second left.
(Dragon School)

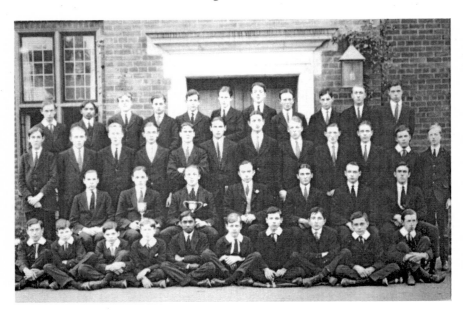

Oldhams House 1913.
Nevil Shute is in the front row extreme right.
(Shrewsbury School)

Shute as a member of Balliol College second rowing Eight 1919.
(Balliol College)

Shute in 1924 on gaining his Royal Aero Club Certificate.
(Royal Aero Club)

3
A Humdrum Undergraduate

Late in 1918, when it became clear that the War might soon be over, Shute discussed his future with his father. They agreed that Shute would go to Oxford, if he could gain admission, to study for an Engineering degree. Accordingly, on 23 October, Arthur Norway wrote to the Master of Balliol College asking whether his son could enter Balliol as soon as he was released from Military Service. He described his son's education at Lynam's and Shrewsbury schools, adding that he was sure that both Dr Alington and Mr Oldham "would report well of the boy." He wrote of his attempts to get a commission but that he "was disqualified on account of a stammer from which he has suffered since childhood" and also that "he did not exactly waste his time at Shrewsbury and certainly not at Woolwich, where he loved his work. I am not sure he has ever yet pulled his weight. He wants to pull it now and means to take life seriously. His definite objective is Engineering." He added that he had laid other suggestions before him but "the boy knows his own mind perfectly ... Oxford and Balliol are what he wants and as he has a strong and self-reliant character it seems to me likely that he will work better in surroundings chosen by himself than by any other." He went on to say that apart from the stammer "he has always been in perfect health, both making and keeping friends easily." He ended the letter by saying that "the boy has had hard luck & has faced it admirably. If you can help him to what he wants I think I can promise that he will do his best for his College."[1]

A few days later, A.L. Smith, the Master of Balliol, replied saying that in accordance with their rules they were writing to get a report on Shute from his Housemaster and Headmaster. They would require him to come for an interview which always preceded any admission of a candidate. They were not sure whether he would meet the College standard for admission without having to sit the College Matriculation exam, but they could determine this during an interview. The Master thought his war service might exempt him from the University First exam, so that he could start his Engineering Course at once, otherwise he might have to take a first course in physics and mathematics. That could also be looked into when he came for interview.

The report from Dr Alington, then Headmaster of Eton, was brief and to the point. "Norway was an excellent boy, with a badish stammer, which I now believe he has cured. He was at Lineham's [sic] School and from all I knew of him at Shrewsbury makes me think him quite a desirable fellow for you to accept."[2] Mr Oldham's report was that "Norway is quite a good person, quite sound and with a good deal of taste and ability. His great misfortune is a fearful stammer. I believe this is better now but it had got much worse as a result of his experiences in the Irish Rebellion . . . but I can altogether recommend him, as there is no reason why he should not do quite well."[3]

On 1 November A.L. Smith wrote that "as expected we have had very good reports from Dr Alington and Mr Oldham."[4] They would like Shute to come and talk over his plans and hoped this could be arranged before January. At that time Shute was stationed on the Isle of Grain and explained to his father what he needed to do to get leave so that he could go for the interview.[5]

Dear Dad

I asked the Corporal about my leave. He told me the best thing to do is to get a letter from the Master of Balliol asking me to come to Oxford for an interview. This I take up to the Office and probably get 2 or 4 days leave.

Can you get me this? It is a little awkward to ask you, I know. It would be better if he specified a date, but if he will write this letter I might be able to get leave this term all right. Otherwise my 6 days might come in vacation or might not come at all if the War ends.

If you don't feel you can ask this, write me as convincing a letter as you can yourself, saying that the Master wants to see me but you don't like to worry him and sign it C.B and all that. It won't be half so good for the purpose: get the Master's letter if you can.

much love,

Nevil.

On 8 November the College wrote to Shute as follows:[6]

It is essential that you should come up here to discuss the scheme
of your future work and to receive instructions from those who will
be your tutors and the sooner you can get leave from the Military
Authorities to do this the better. No doubt you will be allowed this
as it is important for your future, and it is also part of our regular
procedure.

This letter took some time to reach Shute, as he explained in his next
letter:

> Pte Norway
> Room 21 A. Coy
> 1st Res. Gan. Battn.
> Suffolk Regt.
> Milton Barracks
> Gravesend.

Dear Sir,

I am exceedingly sorry I have not acknowledged your letter
before. I can only blame the advent of Peace and an ensuing game
of General Post played by the units in this neighbourhood, during
which I have been moved three times.

As soon as things are a little more settled I shall certainly be
able to get leave on your letter. At the earliest opportunity I will
let you know the dates on this leave, when perhaps you will be able
to give me an appointment.

yours very sincerely
Nevil S. Norway

He did get leave and had his interview with A.L. Smith. In *Slide Rule*
he wrote that he could not remember what they talked about but that
at the end of half an hour he was accepted and told to come back when
he could get out of the Army. The interview actually took place on 23
November for there was a note from the Master to one of the tutors to the
effect that "he is quite good enough to come in without further examination and he would like advice as to what to read in the interval if he is to
come up for next term. He is here until Monday night and is available
at any time." Apparently a Mr Nagel gave advice to him the same day.

Now that he had been accepted for Balliol, he was impatient to get his release from the military but this was not straightforward, as he explained in a letter to the College:[8]

> Pte Norway 65675
> Hut 2 No. 2 Dispersal Centre
> St Martins Plain
> Shornecliffe Camp
> Nr Folkestone

Dear Sir,

I am sorry to say that I have changed my address, which is now the one above. I'm afraid this may cause you some little annoyance in applying for my release. It was a lightning move: I am now a clerk and my job is to demobilise other people.

I have been quite unable to get Form 215, and am writing to the Ministry of Labour to say so. I will mention my changes of address.

When one surveys the immaculate state of the Great Machinery of Demobilisation (as typified in this Camp) it seems incredible that anyone will ever get out of the Army at all!

yours sincerely
Nevil S. Norway

Early in the new year, 1919, Shute was on leave in London and was still uncertain as to when he would be demobilised. He wrote to the College:[9]

> 7.1.19   23 Oakwood Court
>   Holland Park
>   W.14
>   (On leave)

Dear Sir,

My father and I have been talking over the question of my coming up to Balliol for next term: we came to the conclusion that it was time to let you know something definite.

It is quite uncertain when I shall get my "ticket". So far as I can see, demobilisation is being purposely retarded. I came to this conclusion by studying the statistics of the dispersal camps (at one of which I work) and comparing them with the number of men per day that the French railways—the official source of delay—are said to be capable of carrying.

Under the circumstances, I think it would be best for you to assume that I am not coming up this term, but will probably be up for the summer term.

If in the course of the next few days I get my discharge I am prepared to take "pot luck", so to speak: that is, I could come up if you could fit me in at the eleventh hour, or else stay down till the Summer. I could usefully employ this time in rubbing up the hundred and one things that I should know but have forgotten.

Yours sincerely,

N.S. Norway

Shute was demobilised shortly after that and arrived in Oxford in February. Oxford was a place he knew well from his time at the Dragon School. He was allocated a room at Balliol and there joined other undergraduates, many of whom, like him, had had War service. Amongst them was Alexander Rodger who was to become a lifelong friend and later an original investor in Airspeed. Rodger had won an Exhibition to Balliol in 1913 but had enlisted at the outbreak of the war and had gone on to join the Royal Flying Corps, serving in it with distinction during 1917 and 1918.

The Engineering Department had just re-opened after the war and Charles Frewen Jenkin was Professor. It occupied a building on the corner of Banbury Road and Park Road, just a short walk up from Balliol. The subjects covered included mathematics, mechanics, structures, strength of materials, electricity, some chemistry and also surveying. At Oxford, then as now, engineering was treated as one; there were no divisions such as mechanical, electrical or civil engineering. Students had a thorough grounding in engineering science, all rather academic as might be expected. This was expected to, and did, fit them for a career in any of the branches of engineering. Shute later claimed that he could not pump up much enthusiasm for the theory of concrete dams or electrical machinery, and put this forward to explain why he only gained a Third Class Honours degree. Yet judging by the calculations he did later in connection with aeroplanes, he was clearly an able mathematician and well-versed in the theory of structures, knowledge that he could only have obtained from the lectures at Oxford. He was, however, no academic, interested in knowledge for its own sake, but had the ability to apply theory when it had a practical application, particularly in the design of aeroplanes.

Although he enjoyed Oxford life and made many friends, his work in the vacations for Airco and later de Havilland was where his great technical interest lay, and it is no accident that in *Slide Rule* he wrote much more about the time he spent at de Havilland than about his life in Oxford. For it was there that he learned how things take shape from the drawing board to reality. At de Havilland's he supplemented what Oxford taught him by learning the practicalities of engineering design. As an unpaid student during the vacations, he helped with wind tunnel tests. He would have learned about laminar and turbulent flow, lift and drag at Oxford, but in these tests he could see the results in practical applications and begin to realise how important they were in aircraft design. Results plotted on a graph now had real meaning for him.

Equally important for him was that, because of the scale of de Havilland's at the time, he could see what he produced on paper turned into a real component in the workshop. As an example, he designed propellers for a number of aircraft, working out the blade sections from the root to the tip and making sections in cardboard for the woodworkers to use. He could then see the design take shape on the woodworker's bench. The propellers would be fitted to the aircraft and tested in flight, and all within a short space of time.

Geoffrey de Havilland's recollection of Shute[10] at that time was that:

A very different young man came to us at Stag Lane in the early days. He was still at Oxford and applied to us to be allowed to work on aeronautics during the long vacation. We agreed and this quiet and studious student arrived at Stag Lane. He was clearly an able mathematician and possessed a good knowledge of aerodynamics, which was a surprising acquisition in those days. When Nevil Shute Norway came down we took him on permanently and he did a lot of good work for us.

Life at Oxford in term time was not all work. Having rowed at Shrewsbury, he rowed in the Second Eight for Balliol in 1919 and the following year. He had a wide circle of friends, and his motorbike was changed for a car, a Morgan 3-wheeler, which gave him mobility. Oliver Sturt, his friend from the Dragon School, had come up to Oxford after a short spell in the Navy and he answered an advert in the *Times* for two undergraduates to crew the *Aeolia*, a sailing yacht owned by a Southampton solicitor, Mr Hepherd. They got the job and embarked on *Aeolia* at Southampton on 19 July 1919, the day of the Official Peace Celebrations, which was to be marked with victory parades and bonfires. Shute recalled that it blew a gale that night and the yacht dragged its anchor in the soft mud of Southampton Water and ended up with the chain wrapped around Hamble Spit buoy. This was not a great introduction to the joys of sailing, but he did not have to dive in to free the chain; Oliver lost the toss and dived in. That voyage, through the long hot days of August, evidently made a great impression on Shute and laid the foundations for a recreation that he enjoyed throughout his life, and which featured in many of his novels.

Yachts in those days had heavy gear which required strength to handle, and it is not surprising that two able-bodied young men were required to crew her. The boat had no engine so that manoeuvring in confined channels such as the Hamble River was extremely difficult. Shute said he learned a lot on that first trip, which took them as far as the Scilly Isles and back. As well as handling ropes and gear and hoisting sails he would have learned how to steer a course, trim sails and much else.

By September he was back in Oxford and at this time he got engaged to a girl he had met during the war and who was a student at Lady Margaret Hall, the women's college. She was a brilliantly clever girl of a clever family. He confessed later that he argued her into the engagement and then worked hard to keep it going. Up to that time he had had very little contact with girls; his adolescence, through a time of war, had been spent in the all-male, almost monastic, environment of Shrewsbury, followed by his failed attempts to gain a commission and his months as a private soldier. He had lost his elder brother and had no sister in whom he might have confided his feelings. He certainly seems to have been much more at ease in male company and remained so throughout his life. The engagement seems to have been a rather one-sided affair because his fiancée was never quite sure of herself and he was, as he later admitted, looking for companionship rather than a passionate affair. They were engaged for two and a half years which, he said, was a very happy time, even though they couldn't marry because they hadn't any money.

So life at Oxford progressed through 1920, and in the summer vacation he went to work, unpaid, for the Aircraft Manufacturing Company

Ltd, or Airco for short. This job, which began his association with de Havilland mentioned above, came about through a contact of Professor Jenkin. Shute had written to Mr Walker at the company offering his services but had received no reply. Courageously, he went to the works in Hendon and found Mr Walker charming and very glad to have him a very junior unpaid assistant. Airco, which had been very busy in the War, had run down to almost nothing, and de Havilland and Walker were already planning to set up a new company. Although in a rather dilapidated state, there were still aircraft going through the shops and attention was being focused on the design of a new passenger aeroplane the DH.18. Passenger transport was seen as the future and indeed it was a converted DH.4 aeroplane that had flown the world's first scheduled international passenger flight, between Hounslow and Le Bourget in 1919. Shute found it very exciting to be in at the start of commercial aviation, where developments were rapid, although the industry was, financially, in a parlous state.

In 1920, his second year at Oxford, Shute won the Roger Hall Prize, awarded annually to students of history or science, in rotation—it was the turn of science that year. He spent the prize money of £5 on a set of drawing instruments and a copy of William Morris' *The Earthly Paradise*. The drawing instruments would be useful for his work at de Havilland. Morris' epic work, in a multi-volume set, reflected his interest in poetry and something he could never have afforded without the prize money.

By Christmas 1920 Shute's father, at the age of sixty, was approaching retirement and had decided to take his six week's leave at Bordighera on the Italian Riviera, along the coast from Monaco. Shute joined his parents there for the duration of his Christmas vacation. His parents, like many other older people, could escape the chill of an English winter, sitting in the sun and taking walks inland and other gentle pursuits.

The following Easter Shute went to work for de Havilland, again unpaid, and this time at Stag Lane aerodrome, Edgware, where the new company was starting up. Now he had the chance to learn about many of the aspects of the company, working as a junior assistant to a Mr King on stress and performance calculations. He also benefited from the discussions between Geoffrey de Havilland and his staff on the designs of new aircraft. He was in at the start of the new company and saw it as a golden opportunity to learn as much as he could. Everything was under one roof and, as well as designing and building new machines, the company had also started an aircraft hire business. One of his jobs as a student was to write up the reports on test flights from the information provided by the observer. Mostly this entailed tabulating data such as time, speed and height and plotting graphs but in this way he learned about the performance of aircraft under a wide range of conditions. This work also brought him into contact with the pilots some of whom, such as Hatchett, had flown in the war. Hatchett was also a skilled woodworker and worked on the bench when he was not flying. Another employee who flew on these test flights as an observer was A.H. Tiltman, and Shute wrote the reports for a number of his test flights, some of them with Captain de Havilland as pilot. Hessell Tiltman had joined Airco in 1916 and at the end of the war was involved in testing the record breaking DH.9R. When the de Havilland company was formed in 1921, Tiltman was invited to join and became an assistant designer.

It was with Hatchett that Shute made his first flight, a routine test flight of a DH.9 aircraft. Here at last was what he had wanted—to fly in an aircraft. Although it was only a short flight of about 20 minutes, it was his turn to be the observer, to record the readings and, on landing, to write the test report. He had written up the reports for others but now he could write "Observer: Norway". He attempted to capture his excitement at this first flight by writing a poem which he included in *Slide Rule* right after mentioning this first flight.

In the summer of 1921 Shute's fiancée graduated from Oxford and got a job as an agent for a Liberal constituency in the Midlands. There she met another man, older than she and below her socially. He was her landlady's son. Just five days after she met him she broke off her engagement with Shute. Shute, hoping perhaps that her new romance would not last, made her promise to wait six months. Oxford without her would not have been the same. It had been a one-sided affair, with him working hard to keep it going. But now she was gone, and five days after the six months were up, she married the other man and Shute never heard from her again. He thought it might have worked for them if they could have married but when she broke it off he was, financially, in no position to marry, being still an undergraduate and his vacation work at de Havilland's was unpaid.

The breaking of the engagement came at about the time Shute was preparing for his Finals in 1922 and he took it badly. He sat his Finals that summer and achieved only a Third Class Honours degree. He made light of this in *Slide Rule,* saying that his work at de Havilland's seemed much more important to him and that he could not raise enthusiasm for the subjects on his degree course. But his feelings over the broken engagement would not have helped. To make matters worse, other friends who sat their Finals at the same time did much better, notably Alexander Rodger who gained a First Class Honours in History and went on to be elected a Fellow of Balliol the following year.

That summer he went sailing again with friends in the Channel. De Havilland had agreed to take him on full time after he graduated, but in the autumn, they had to put him off until the new year because the company was in difficulties and having to economise. So he found himself without employment and without his fiancée and feeling at a low ebb. By that time his father had retired from the Post Office and intended to spend the winter in Bordighera again. He joined his parents there and spent several months that autumn learning a little Italian, exploring the countryside and writing. He had bought a typewriter and learned to use it. It is likely that at this time he wrote a short story called *Piuro,* which is set in Italy and in the town of Piuro which was buried in an earthquake in 1618. This story is one of several which he wrote during his lifetime which were never published. During this holiday he may also have begun writing *Stephen Morris* or at least planning it. This was to be his first full length novel and remarkably autobiographical in content. The eponymous *Stephen Morris* graduates in Mathematics from Oxford. He breaks off his engagement to a fellow student, Helen Riley. After a stint as a pilot in a joyriding enterprise, he obtains a job in an aircraft manufacturing firm doing calculations and produces a paper on the stressing of plywood structures and does tests on model aircraft in a water channel to visualise the flow around them. The following year Shute wrote a paper for the Royal Aeronautical Society about the use of a water channel for flow visualisation.[11]

In January 1923 Shute began work full time at de Havilland at the wage of £5 a week. The company was growing and had an order for eleven DH.34 passenger aircraft for the London to Paris route. He had achieved another ambition to have a job in the aircraft industry. To be close to his work, he had lodgings at 29 Stag Lane, just a short walk from the factory. There he settled down to work and in the next 18 months worked on very many of the aircraft designs. He never designed a complete aircraft himself; that was the province of men such as Tiltman, R.E. Bishop and de Havilland himself. As a technician he did calculations on such items as fuselage structures, propellers and wings. He would fill sheets with the analysis of, for example, the distribution of forces on structural members from which the size of individual members were determined, the stresses calculated for given factors of safety. His neat, precise, pencil calculations went to the draughtsmen who produced the working drawings for construction. The early empirical days of aeroplane design were over, replaced with methodical detail design and analysis of every component, work which Shute was very suited to do.

At that time Shute also flew as an observer on many of the test flights, more than when he was there as a student. One of the pilots he flew with was Alan Cobham who had joined the company in 1921. Before that, Cobham had formed the Berkshire Aviation Company, touring the country giving pleasure flights, one of many such enterprises started by demobilised pilots after the war. Most of them failed for various reasons, but Cobham's lasted for two years until receipts began to dwindle. He arrived at Stag Lane in 1921, bringing with him an aircraft, and negotiated himself a job as a pilot on the de Havilland air taxi service.

By day Shute was very much an integral part of the team of about a hundred or so employees, taking the opportunity to learn as much as he could about the whole business of producing aircraft and being schooled in the hard economics of this emerging industry. Only by producing the aircraft that the market wanted, and could operate economically, could success and growth be achieved. He came to realise that this required the meticulous approach with great attention to detail. Without it, the failure to take all aspects into consideration could, and did, cost lives.

In the evenings he wrote, usually two or three evenings a week, and by the end of April 1923 *Stephen Morris* was finished. He considered it worthy of publication and joined the Society of Authors, paying the annual fee of one pound ten shillings (£1.50), a significant proportion of his weekly wage. In the letter to the Society enclosing his payment, he says[12] that he has written *Stephen Morris*, a novel of a hundred and five thousand words which "deals with the experiences of a demobilised pilot of aeroplanes, first of all in Oxford after the war and later in the surroundings of Civil Aviation." He went on to say that aviation had been the butt of novelists for a very long time but had never before been treated in novel form by one who knew it intimately from the inside. "Whatever the shortcomings of my novel—and they are very numerous—I think I have succeeded in giving a picture of this bankrupt little industry that is of interest to the general public. The style is light, slightly introspective, and cheerful. One hopes that the book is witty and occasionally tragic. The technicalities are accurate: the general endeavour has been to minimise the sensational aspects of aviation and to present a true study of the types and characters that engage in this pursuit." When portraying the pilots in the book Shute certainly drew on the characters of the pilots such as Broad, Barnard and Cobham that he got to know at de Havilland.

Shute asked if the Society could give him the names of publishers who might be interested in the book. Was it usual to expect royalties on a first book and if so might he expect 10 or 15% of the published price? Rather optimistically he asked what sort of price he might expect if he got an offer to buy the book outright. The Society wrote back[13] saying they thought 105,000 words rather long for a first novel, but by no means too long. They suggested several publishers who might be interested, among them Cassell & Co., Chatto and Windus, and Hodder & Stoughton: he should certainly have a royalty agreement. For a first novel he could hardly expect a 15% royalty but should not settle for less than 10%, rising with sales of the book. The Society would be glad to look over any offer he received. In the event the book was rejected by three publishers and Shute was content to put it back on the shelf and try something else and, equally important, to pursue other activities.

Even as he was finishing the book that spring, he was learning to fly in the flying school that was another part of the company's operations at Stag Lane. He learned to fly on the standard training aircraft of the time, the Avro 548 biplane. This was fitted with dual controls in a tandem cockpit arrangement, the pupil in the front and the instructor behind with communication by a speaking tube. The 548 he learned on had a Renault engine which replaced the outdated rotary engines. He would have been taught using the so called Gosport system, a curriculum based on a balanced combination of academic classroom training and dual flight instruction. This system was based, not on avoiding potentially dangerous manoeuvres as had been the case before, but on exposing the student to them in a controlled manner so that he could learn to recover from them, thereby gaining confidence and skill.

The cost of flying instruction was £5 10 shillings (£5.50) an hour, just over a week's wages. As an employee of the company he tried to argue for a reduction but this was refused. This meant that his time was strictly limited by his finances, but his parents did help him out with the cost. He used to do flights of about 10 minutes, in which time he could fit in a couple of practice landings. He did about 9 hours of dual instruction before going solo, which was about average. These were the days before the private pilot's licence, but a pilot was recognised by the issuing of a Certificate by the Royal Aero Club. Their test required the pilot to ascend to 6000 feet, fly several figure of eights and land without damage. Shute took this test at Stag Lane, passed it, and was issued with Certificate No. 7954 on 4 March 1924. Probably due to shortage of money, it took him the best part of twelve months from his first training flight to obtaining his certificate. After that he handled the controls of a number of aircraft in the course of test flights, for in 1924 he flew fairly frequently as a test observer. One interesting example is a flight he reported on a DH.37 "Australian Machine". On 9 April 1924 he flew as observer with Hubert Broad (then Chief test pilot) on a flight to test the climb and speed at all -up weight. In a flight of some 30 minutes they reached an altitude of over 12,000 feet at which the indicated speed was 87 knots and the air temperature was -20° C. Weather conditions are recorded as "low cloud, light westerly breeze. Very cold." One has to imagine Shute in the front seat of an open cockpit plane recording time, height, airspeed, engine revs and temperature whilst bombarded with an icy blast.

In the spring of 1923, his parents returned from Italy and rented a house called Heathfield in Liss, Hampshire, and Shute would motor down to visit his parents at the weekend. Close to Liss is the town of Petersfield, and he soon discovered No. 1 The Square, an old half-timbered house run as a bookshop and art gallery. This was run by three women, Hester Wagstaff, Maria Brahms and Flora Twort. Hester was an artist, made jewellery, and acted as secretary to Dr Harry Roberts who had a farm at Oakshott a few miles outside the town, which became a focal point for artists and literary folk. Flora too was an artist who had grown up in London and showed an artistic flair from a very early age. On leaving school she trained at the Royal Drawing Society and established herself as a portraitist, setting up a studio in Chelsea. After the war she met Harry Roberts and his circle at Oakshott and soon moved out of London to live in Petersfield, which she loved. By the time Shute discovered it, No. 1 had acquired the reputation of being one of the finest bookshops in the south of England.

Shute always remembered his first meeting with Flora. He was upstairs in the history section and she asked if he knew where everything was. He said he did and she went downstairs and he heard her gossiping with the others. On other visits he and Flora would chat while he browsed and he would stay for tea. In no time they were firm friends. Flora found him very entertaining and great fun. She viewed it strictly as friendship but Shute soon realised that he had fallen in love with her, although he never expressed it in words. As well as being physically attractive, she was his intellectual equal and they talked about books and paintings and the things they were both keen on. She was an accomplished artist, painting many scenes of life in and around Petersfield, and she had a latent talent as a writer. She wrote articles for *The New Statesman*, and also a few short stories, but these were never published.

On his weekend visits they would take a boat out for a sail in the Solent, and once they went to watch the Naval Review off Spithead. It was a hot day and Flora wanted to jump overboard for a swim but he told her not to—the King might be insulted if she joined in the display![14] She would drive him in a pony and trap from Oakshott, where he was staying, to Petersfield. He found it very droll that the journey of four miles would take them two hours. He became interested in the history of No. 1 The Square Petersfield, for he did some research into its history and wrote an article on it. The article is not dated and was never published, but was probably written at this time.[15]

His friendship, and growing love of Flora dispelled the last of the hurt he had felt after his broken engagement. But he had a feeling that having had one failed engagement he was, so far as marriage was concerned, "damaged goods". He found it somehow humiliating that he could love as well a second time as the first, but he came to accept the fact that, with Flora, it was so. One of his fears had been that he might end up as a bachelor for the rest of his life, living entirely for himself with no-one giving a damn whether he lived or died.

It was in this frame of mind that he began writing a second novel early in 1924. In *Pilotage,* Peter Dennison takes to sailing in the Solent alone after his proposal of marriage is rejected and ends up taking part as a passenger and navigator in a risky flying experiment. Dennison shares rooms with Lanard, a crusty, sharp-tongued bachelor, perhaps a character Shute thought he himself might become if he did not marry. In this book, as in *Stephen Morris*, he wrote the happy ending where man and girl are reunited in the end. In the summer of 1924 he sent the manuscript for publication but again received a number of rejections. So like *Stephen Morris*, he put it back on the shelf. Both books were published in 1961, in one volume, after his death.

In *Pilotage* Dennison applied for a job with much better pay than his present one, to improve his prospects for marriage, and that may also have been a consideration in Shute's mind through 1924. He was happy at de Havilland doing work he enjoyed and feeling he was making a contribution. He flew when he could afford to, and his weekend visits to see Flora came to mean a great deal to him. But his colleagues at the company more senior to him, and more experienced, were only slightly older than him. So he began to feel that advancement, with an increase in salary, would of necessity be slow. If he was to be in a position to marry, and marriage to Flora was certainly in his mind, he would have to find another opening where the prospects were better. On looking around, he discovered that a Mr Barnes Wallis was getting together a team of calculators to work on the design of a new airship. The airship would be built by a new company, the Airship Guarantee Company, a subsidiary of Vickers Ltd. He knew nothing of airships and had never seen one, but the work would involve the sort of mathematical calculations that he had been doing at de Havilland, so on that score he probably felt he was qualified for the job. He applied for the job and was taken on, no doubt leaving de Havilland with some regrets. It was a gamble on his part, a leap, if not quite into the unknown, certainly into the unfamiliar. At least it offered an increase in pay and the possibility of more rapid promotion. And it would mean being in at the start of an aviation project of national importance.

4
Airship Venture

The Airship Guarantee Company that Shute joined in October 1924 owed its origin to the enthusiasm and persistence of one man, Charles Dennistoun Burney.

Burney was born in 1888, the son of Admiral Sir Cecil Burney. Sir Cecil was second in command of the British Fleet at the Battle of Jutland in 1916. Dennis was educated at Marlborough School and at Ranelagh and, like his father, joined the Navy. In the First World War he commanded various ships, but his main interest was in finding ways to protect vessels from mines. He invented a device called the paravane, an underwater hydrovane designed to cut the cables of mines. A number of naval vessels were fitted with this device, which proved to be successful in dealing with underwater mines without danger to the vessel. Later on, a variation called an otter was developed for merchant vessels.

Such was the success of the paravane that the Admiralty set up a shore-based establishment for the development and fitting of paravanes to Naval vessels. Burney received no financial reward from the Navy for his invention, but he was allowed to patent it and received royalties. It is recorded that the royalties he received totalled £350,000, a considerable sum for the time, and thus made him a fairly wealthy man.

After long discussions with the Board of Vickers Ltd., Burney set up the Airship Guarantee Company in December 1923 to promote his Airship Scheme. He was appointed Managing Director, with Sir Trevor Dawson, a member of the main Vickers Board, chairman. So keen was Burney to promote the cause of airships that he became a Member of Parliament in 1922 for the Uxbridge constituency and he retained the seat until the General Election of 1929 when he stepped down. He became an MP, not merely to represent the people of Uxbridge, but so that he could exert political pressure in the cause of airships.

At that time airships were regarded as the only practicable means of maintaining rapid communications within the British Empire, for they had what aeroplanes of that time lacked—range. The possibility of transatlantic flights had been shown by the journey in 1919 of the *R.34* airship to the United States and back. Because of the expense of airship operations, no private company would entertain their operation without some form of government subsidy. Burney's scheme required the construction of six new airships of five million cubic feet gas capacity, the taking over of the Government airship stations and the construction of new facilities for airships in Egypt and India. He convinced Vickers and the Shell company to back the scheme and it was all set to be adopted by the Conservative Government of the day when a General Election was called in December 1923 and the first Labour Government came to power, albeit with Liberal support.

The Labour Government appointed Christopher Birdwood Thomson as Air Minister. Thomson had failed to be elected to Parliament so was created a Lord and took as his title Lord Thomson of Cardington. In May 1924 the Burney scheme was cancelled and a Committee was set up to look into the future of airships. They decided that two airships would be built. One would be built by the Government at the Royal Airship Works at Cardington in Bedfordshire. Vickers Ltd was given first refusal for a contract to build the second ship to an identical specification.

Thus there were to be two organisations each to build an airship of five million cubic feet with a speed of 70 miles per hour, a fixed weight of 90 tons. The ships had to be capable of accommodating up to 100 passengers and of ascending and descending at a rate of 2000 feet per minute. Also they were required to withstand winds of 60 miles per hour when moored at the mast. Finally an endurance flight of not less than 48 hours had to be carried out before acceptance, to be followed by a demonstration flight to India with a stop in Egypt. This required a range of 2,880 miles.

Burney's original idea was that the design of the ship would be done by a committee, and he approached G.H. Scott, R.B.B. Colmore and V.C. Richmond to join his committee. Scott was an experienced airship captain who had commanded the *R.34* on its round trip to America. Colmore had served in the Royal Naval Air Service during the war. Colonel Richmond was an expert on the dope used on aircraft and airship fabrics and lectured on airship design at Imperial College, London. Originally Burney asked Barnes Wallis to be the committee's secretary. Wallis had worked on airships since the middle of the war and had designed the successful *R.80*. He had developed a growing belief that he alone knew how airships should be designed and refused Burney's offer to be Secretary. He was firmly against the design by committee approach, believing that one man should take ultimate responsibility for the design. In the end Burney agreed and Wallis was appointed Chief Designer. Richmond became Chief Designer of the *R.101* at Cardington and Colmore rose to become Director of Airship Development. Scott was to be in charge of flying operations for both ships.

On 24 October 1924, the Airship Guarantee Company (AGC) was awarded the contract to design and build the *R.100*. Three days later Shute was taken on as a calculator at a wage of six pounds ten shillings a week (£6.50), an increase from his five pounds a week at de Havilland's.[1] Both Wallis and Burney were to have significant influence on Shute over the coming years and he came to respect and admire both men, who were so very different from each other in character and attitude.

To increase his knowledge, Shute read many reports on what had been done on the stressing of airships. New rules had been introduced by an Airship Airworthiness Panel chaired by Professor Leonard Bairstow, an expert on aerodynamics, with Professor Pippard, an expert on aircraft stresses. Importantly this panel would oversee these aspects of both airships, acting as an independent arbiter of their airworthiness.

The panel had been formed following the *R.38* disaster, when, in 1921, this airship, while carrying out turning manoeuvres, broke in two and crashed in the River Humber near Hull, with the loss of 44 lives. The report of the Committee of Enquiry into the disaster concluded that no allowance had been made for aerodynamic stresses in the design. Also, while no loads had been placed on the structure during testing that would not have been met in normal use, the effects of the manoeuvres made had weakened the hull. No blame was attached to anyone; this was not part of the committee's remit.

When Shute read this report, he was shocked that no calculations on the aerodynamic forces had been done for the *R.38*; after all, this was exactly the kind of calculation he had done at de Havilland's. He went to one of his chiefs, presumably Wallis, to ask if it could possibly be true. He was told that not only was it true, but that no one had been censured for this omission. Moreover, he was told, the same men, all but one, were to design the *R.101*. Thus were sown in Shute's mind the seeds of distrust of government enterprise. Yet, it was not the case that the same men were to design the *R.101*. The design team at Cardington included men of ability such as Harold Roxbee-Cox, Shute's opposite number, Alfred Pugsley, Professor Southwell, Tom Cave-Browne-Cave and Michael Rope. Richmond made it clear in a lecture that "after the *R.38* disaster they (the Cardington team) were obliged to make a fresh start with new men." Roxbee-Cox, Pugsley, Southwell, Cave-Browne-Cave and Rope were these new men.[2]

Barnes Wallis was undoubtedly an inventive genius who was to achieve great fame later on with the design of the Wellington bomber, the dam busting bomb, the Tallboy and Grand Slam bombs. With the design of the *R.100*, he could at last be his own boss and design the ship according to the requirements of the contract and the rules of the Airworthiness Panel. What Shute would have admired in him was his thoroughness and meticulous attention to detail. By the time Shute joined the company, Wallis had set out the basic outline of the design, some of the details of construction and the programme of experimental and theoretical work that would be needed before the detail design and construction could begin.

At that time the Chief Calculator was J.E. Temple, who had worked with both Wallis and Burney before, and it was with Temple that Shute began on the preliminary work, at the same time gathering together a team of calculators. There was a great deal to do, since the ship would be much larger than anything built before. There was a whole mass of new theory to be worked out and checked. The forces acting on the ship under all conditions had to be taken into account and the size of components determined, new designs of girder to be evolved as well as the gasbags and the means of transmitting the lift from the bags to the structure. It was, as Shute said later, a time of urgent preparation, strenuous and stressful. Whilst the work was fascinating for him, it perhaps reminded him of his Engineering course at Oxford: pure theoretical work without the glimpse of real components being made and seeing the end product taking shape in the workshops that he had so enjoyed at Stag Lane.

His working environment too at this time was depressing. The preliminary work was done at the Vickers offices at Crayford in Kent. During the War the Crayford works had been a bustling hive of industry employing over 14,000 people producing, amongst other things, the Vickers Vimy bomber. In one of these Alcock and Brown made their historic flight in 1919 across the Atlantic from West to East. Now after the War the Vickers works were almost derelict.

Shute lived in digs in Hatherley Road in nearby Sidcup. As at Stag Lane, he wrote in the evenings as a relaxation from work and here he wrote another novel, determined this time to learn from his previously unpublished books and spare no effort to get *Marazan* published. He rewrote the book twice from start to finish and some parts of it three times before he sent it off to Cassell in February 1926. At that time he built a five-valve wireless set for his parents, no doubt buying all the necessary components or a kit and following a set of instructions carefully. It would have been quite an intricate project requiring delicate soldering of wires to connections and careful handling of valves. He would have derived great satisfaction when tuning it in to pick up various radio stations.

During 1925, whilst doing the airship work by day and writing in the evenings, he spent many weekends visiting both his parents in Liss and also Flora in Petersfield. He was certainly in love with her, though never openly affectionate. In September he asked her to marry him. She was so taken aback that she fell off her chair and then burst into tears, for she had no idea that he felt like that; he had never even kissed her.[3] Though she valued him as a friend, she did not love him but she did not want to hurt his feelings. A couple of days later he wrote to her, not to apologise for his proposal, but to tell her things about himself that, probably from shyness, he had not told her face to face. He told her about his engagement to a girl at Oxford, how she had broken it off and the bad time he had had after that, until he met her. He told her that he had come to realise that he could love just as well a second time, that he loved her and wanted to see her happy, and didn't think she would ever be really happy unless she married. He ended that letter by saying that he was not sorry he asked her to marry him—it had cleared the air.[4]

Two days later he wrote to her again in reply to a letter from her. He said his excuse for asking her to marry him, even though he knew she didn't love him, was that he thought she would be happier married than single. He went on to ask what she thought was best for them. He had been a friend to her for two years and he could carry on like that. The difference would be that she would know that he loved her and that he was satisfied that she couldn't marry him.[5]

For the moment he left it at that, but he not given up on the idea that one day she might marry him, or that he might argue her into marrying him as he seems to have done with his Oxford fiancée. Whilst he was working at Crayford, he could still see her at weekends, but once the initial phase of the airship work was over he would be moving up to Yorkshire.

It was agreed that *R.100* was to be built at the old Royal Naval Air Station at Howden in Yorkshire and the *R.101* at the Royal Airship Works at Cardington. Howden Airship Station had been established during the war as a base for airship patrols over the North Sea, and a considerable complement of men was stationed there at that time. In 1918 a new shed to house larger airships had been built by the Cleveland Bridge and Engineering Company. This shed was a colossal structure, with two adjacent bays each 750 feet long, 140 feet wide and 140 feet high with a floor area of over five acres. The station was scaled down after the Armistice in 1918 but continued to service R class airships. The ill fated *R.38* was bound for Howden when it crashed in 1921. After that the station was closed and sold to Douglas Hollis (Howden) Ltd., who proceeded to sell off as much as they could. The Airship Guarantee Company negotiated with Hollis to buy the site and, although they had been granted £50,000 to buy it, in the end the purchase price was £47,000. There was much correspondence between AGC and Hollis as to what was included in the sale, and negotiations were not helped when Hollis went bankrupt just as the sale was being concluded.

In 1925, AGC sent a small team up to Howden to begin getting things into shape for the manufacture of *R.100*. What they found there must have depressed them considerably. Most of the fixtures and fittings had been sold off. Heaps of debris littered the site and the large shed was in a neglected condition. But they set to and worked hard to bring order out of chaos. The bungalows were restored, water and sewage systems got working and a sizeable electricity plant installed. Much of the debris was cleared and the airship shed, with its offices and workshops, made as suitable as possible for the work of building the airship. Although the site had produced hydrogen by the water gas process and had large tanks for storing the hydrogen, a new plant was later installed to produce purer, drier hydrogen by the Silicol process.

In Crayford, Shute gathered together his team of calculators. His assistant was V.M. Harvey with W.T. Sandford and L.A. Lansdown as junior calculators. Their job was to take Wallis' preliminary design and to work out the forces, stresses and deflections of the structural members under a variety of conditions, taking into account the safety factors laid down by the Airworthiness Panel. The *R.100* frame was to be built from Duralumin, an alloy of aluminium with 4% copper. The structure comprised a series of 16-sided polygon rings with diameters ranging up to 133 feet and arranged to give the "tear drop" streamlined shape to the airship, which would give lower drag than the more cylindrical "cigar" shape used in earlier ships. Each of the rings, braced by radial wires, was connected by longitudinal girders at each of the 16 corners. The space between adjacent rings formed a cell, each of which would house a gas bag filled with hydrogen.

In *Slide Rule* Shute gives an insight into the type of calculation that was done for the 16-sided transverse rings. For these they had to solve a series of simultaneous equations and, being what is known as "statically indeterminate," they had to make initial guesses on the forces and deflections in the structure and bracing wires to solve these equations. The junior calculators would then work through these equations, finding in many cases that the initial guesses were incorrect and having to begin again with new assumptions. The computations were done by hand, using Fuller slide rules which, having spiral scales, could be read to greater accuracy than conventional slide rules. The calculators worked in pairs, jotting down figures and comparing each others' results from time to time as a check on accuracy.

Shute describes the elated feeling when the true solution was arrived at and all the forces and deflections were in balance. He described his feelings in *Slide Rule:* "The truth stood revealed, real, and perfect, and unquestionable; the very truth. It did one good; one was the better for the experience."[6]

Then they would have to begin all over again for the next section and move on to the analysis of another part of the structure. When the calculations for each section were completed and checked, with charts of forces and deflections produced, they were pigeon-holed with labels such as "Transverse section 3—final" and so on. The records show that dozens of such calculations were produced during the design of the ship.

By February 1926, Shute had finished *Marazan* and sent it off to Cassell, who said that they would like to publish the book and offered a £30 advance and royalties of 10% initially, rising with sales. They said they would publish the book in the autumn with a price of 7/6d (37.5 pence).

However they thought the title was not a good one from the selling point of view, but doubtless he would be willing to submit some alternatives. Shute sent a copy of Cassell's letter to the Society of Authors asking their advice on various clauses in the agreement, notably a libel clause and royalties from overseas sales. The Society replied with comments and suggestions on the clauses and Shute sent a letter to Cassell setting out his objections in detail to various clauses in the agreement. The result was that Cassell returned the manuscript to him in early March. On March 17, Shute wrote to the Society telling them that the manuscript had been returned and saying that he had approached A.P. Watt & Co. who had been agents for his father many years ago. He had approached Watt to handle the book because he was so busy with his work that he couldn't spare the time to go on "breaking lances" with the publishers and also 'I shall shortly be removing to a remote part of Yorkshire." He added that Watt was taking a considerable time to reply, from which he assumed they were debating whether it was worthwhile to handle the work of an author "who is completely unknown."[7]

In April Shute moved up to Howden, that "remote part of Yorkshire", and he took lodgings at 78 Hailgate in the centre of the town. The airship station was some three miles north of Howden and he would regularly walk there and back in company with other AGC staff and their dogs. At that time Shute had a black Labrador called Nero. One day one of the riggers found Nero lying in a ditch, shot by a local farmer, probably for chasing livestock. When the dog died of its wounds Shute broke down and sobbed.[8]

Although they would often walk to work, Shute soon bought a Morris Cowley. This served him well for a number of years and was very much more suitable than the Morgan three-wheeler he had driven until then. The arrival of the airship staff, and the employment of local labour, did something to revive the fortunes of the town, which had declined following the closure of the airship station in 1921. The airship people attempted to inject some night life but found it an uphill struggle because the residents of Howden were not night-life minded. Shute became a member of the St Leonard's Club in York and would go there with his colleagues for relaxation and shopping. Leeds was not far away by car for dining and dancing at the Palais, where dancing partners could be hired for the evening, something that would feature in his later novels.

The advance party had done its work at the airship station itself. Offices and workshops were ready and the large floor area of the shed cleared and ready to begin the manufacture of the airship. There was little that could be done, though, with the acres of corrugated iron roof which was none too secure in places. It threatened to blow off in gales and leaked in heavy rain. Here Shute and his team continued their work on the stressing of the airship whilst a large number of draughtsmen were assembled to produce the drawings for the ship. Barnes Wallis with his wife Molly had also taken up residence in a white bungalow on the station itself.

In 1926, following the resignation of J.E. Temple, Shute was promoted to Chief Calculator. Although Temple left the company, he was retained as a consultant. Newly promoted and with the work on the airship stretching ahead of him, Shute wrote to Flora once more about the question of marriage. He said it wouldn't work unless they both really wanted to marry. He said that Howden was not a bad little town in its own way, quite pretty and he thought she would like it. But he had been thinking about what she would do whilst he was away and it seemed obvious that it wouldn't work for them unless they had something more than they had now—she would need something to make up for what she would leave behind in Petersfield. He thought that "companionship marriages" worked well. They were the second stage of a happy marriage—he thought the passionate stage never lasted very long. For them such a marriage would be a jump in the dark, a gamble which he thought would work out for them. He knew that she didn't love him but still thought they could be happy together. He came down to London on business and called in to see her at Petersfield. The answer was still 'no' for, as she later said, she valued his friendship but: "You can't marry without love, can you?"[9] Shute accepted this and they remained great friends for the rest of their lives.

That spring, *Marazan* was published by Cassell. A.P. Watt had taken him on and had negotiated a contract under standard terms. No doubt he was pleased to have a book published at last, but was so busy with his airship work that he treated the matter lightly. He claimed not to have taken its publication seriously. However as Chief Calculator, and his position with AGC firmly established, he chose to publish the book under his Christian names, Nevil Shute. Mr Norway could then pursue his career as an aeronautical engineer and build up a sound reputation.

With *Marazan*, he abandoned the autobiographical elements of his two previous attempts. He wrote a police and spy novel with elements of flying and sailing and with a central character, Phillip Stenning, modelled on Alan Cobham. In this book, one literary influence can clearly be traced, that of John Buchan and of *The Thirty Nine Steps*. There are many similarities in plot theme.

Shute's writing was all secondary to his main preoccupation at the time, the detail design and construction of *R.100*. Now at last, the initial phase was over. Everything was under one roof, his team of calculators, the drawing office, the production equipment and the arrival of materials to begin making the parts. On 21st April, he wrote to Temple to arrange a meeting with him in London and said that "everything is going smoothly here—at last!" They were not yet quite ready to begin the detail design and there was still theorizing to be done, as is evident from a letter discussing details of transverse frame thicknesses and the effect on the calculations compared with what Professor Pippard's model had predicted. Temple guided him through the appropriate calculation methods for the transverse rings and how they should be carried out. In May and June there was further correspondence between Shute and Temple about the rudders and also about the gas valves. On the latter Temple wrote: "the Zeppelin system is a long way ahead of all the others for simplicity and every possible practical consideration." Zeppelin gas valves were proven technology and were used in *R.100*.[10]

Overseeing everything was Wallis who later claimed that he designed every part of the *R.100*. There is a good deal of truth in this, for not only had he laid out the conceptual design, but the means for its construction. For example drawn Duralumin tubes for the longitudinal members could not be produced to the required length, so he designed a machine to form the Duralumin tubes by rolling sheets in a helix which were riveted together at the seams. By the middle of 1926, this machine was in operation, producing the required tubes. Wallis had a flair, too, for production engineering. The *R.100* was built using a relatively small number of different parts, many produced in thousands as standardised parts that could be riveted together by unskilled labour into sub-assemblies. Wallis felt compelled to be involved in the minutiae of design, leaving nothing to chance. This had the benefit of ensuring that everything met his exacting standards, with the disadvantage that it held up progress.

Now that he would be settled in Yorkshire, Shute sought the opportunity to fly, something he had not been able to do whilst working at Crayford. He very quickly discovered the Yorkshire Aeroplane Club, based on the aerodrome at Sherburn-In-Elmet about 20 miles from Howden. This Club was one of the first flying clubs to receive an annual grant of £1,000 from the Air Council, which helped to make it financially viable, together with two DH Moth aircraft. It is quite possible that he went to the Yorkshire Air Pageant at Sherburn on 24 July 1926. This attracted a crowd of over 5000 people but the show was spoiled by heavy rain showers. If Shute was there he would have seen the demonstration flight by his old colleague Hubert Broad from de Havilland, the Inter Club relay race and also "a fine show of stunting and crazy flying by Bert Hinkler."[11] Being a pilot and an aeronautical engineer, he quickly gained acceptance at the Club.

In September he was in the Club's team of four taking part in the Inter Club Team Relay race at the Lancashire Aero Club at Woodford near Manchester. The race was run as a relay for D.H. Moths, in heats, two competing aircraft being placed on a line with the pilot behind a line 50 yards away. The pilots ran to their machines, took off, and flew a prescribed circuit and had to land and stop precisely on the line, leap out and run to tag the next pilot in the team. If the pilot overshot, then he and his partner had to wheel the machine back to the line, taxiing on the ground was not allowed. The Yorkshire team comprised R.W. Kenworthy, H.S. Carter, E.B. Fielden and Shute. In the first race the Yorkshire team easily beat the team from the London Aero Club. Next, the Newcastle team won against the Lancashire team. In the final the Newcastle team easily beat the Sherburn team, who lost time in landing and changing pilots. Each member of the winning team received an engraved silver tankard.[12] Despite finishing runners-up it would have been a good day out flying their two Moths over the Pennines from Sherburn and back again.

Back at work, Shute and his team were busy doing the stress calculations for the remaining parts of the *R.100* structure and in the shed the members for the transverse rings were being made and assembled. At this time, another job for Shute was to attend tests at Birmingham University on the longitudinal members and other structural components. This was an important test to check that strength and stiffness in a test on a real component were in accord with the calculations. In some cases they were in agreement and the tests were successful. In other cases they were not and components had to be strengthened. This was the case with the "spider" or "Y-V" joint that Wallis designed to connect the corners of the transverse frames to the longitudinal members. The design was altered and the joint passed a subsequent test.

At Howden, whilst Shute and his team were working on the stress calculations of the remainder of the structure, assemblies were being made and laid out on the floor of the shed. In late 1926, the first of the transverse frames had been assembled and was ready for hoisting into position. The ship was to be built hanging from runways in the roof of the shed. Rope slings were attached to the corners of the transverse frame ring and lifted up in the horizontal position until one side could be lowered gently so that it hung vertically, suspended by two slings at the 10 and 2 o'clock position. The riggers employed on this work had to have a good head for heights, for they were lifted up with the ring, often to a height of over 100 feet and secured by a rope around their waists tied to the structure—when they remembered to tie it on! Once the ring was vertical it was slid along the roof runway to the required position. Another frame was then assembled on the floor, hoisted and positioned ready to be connected together by the longitudinal members. When all 16 longitudinals were connected, one section of the ship was complete, ready to take a gasbag. Shute watched these operations going on, the riggers clinging on to the structure members as they were manoeuvred into position. He later recalled his apprehension as he climbed the gangways high in the shed, holding on tight and sick with fear. Yet, with time, he too was climbing on the frame having lost his fear of heights.

So the work on the ship progressed, slower than planned, the manufacture and assembly following hard on the heels of the design. When the contract was awarded in 1924, the completion date was expected to be mid-July 1927 and this included the shed and acceptance flight trials. Throughout the project the Aeronautical Inspection Department (AID) reported regularly on progress and these reports provide an objective account of progress. At this stage AGC were predicting shed trials in September 1927 but the AID Inspectors thought that 1928 was more likely and they did not think much of the efficiency of production.

By this time, Shute was regularly attending design meetings. One of the considerations was the type of engine to be used on the airship. To begin with, it was considered desirable to develop an engine using kerosene and hydrogen from the gasbags. The idea being that as fuel was consumed, and the ship grew lighter, the consumption of hydrogen would compensate by reducing the lift. Peter Brotherhood Ltd of Peterborough did a certain amount of development work on this type of engine, with consultancy provided by Harry Ricardo, a renowned expert on internal combustion engines. However it became apparent that it would not be developed in time to be used. Next, diesel engines of the type to be used on the *R.101* were considered. Although heavier, for the same power, than petrol engines they were rather more economical. This scheme too was abandoned and the choice was Rolls Royce Condor petrol engines of a type currently in aircraft service. So at the end of 1926, six of these engines were ordered. Two would be fitted in each of the three power cars each engine driving a 17 foot diameter propeller in a tractor-pusher configuration.

The choice of engine typifies the approach of AGC to use existing, established technology. They did not have the time, nor more importantly the funds, to indulge in experimental designs. Other examples of this approach include the use of Zeppelin gas valves and the decision to buy a complete set of gasbags from BG Textilwerke in Berlin, who were the established makers of gasbags for the Zeppelin company. The order for these was placed in August 1926, and in this context the name of Phillip Teed must be mentioned, for he was a key member of the AGC team. Teed originally trained as a barrister but became an expert chemist and published a book on the chemistry and manufacture of hydrogen in 1919.[13] He also experimented with new fabrics for gasbags and, being fluent in German, liaised with BG Textilwerke on the manufacture of the gasbags and translated all their documentation into English. With respect to the fabrics, gasbags and hydrogen, AGC could not have been served by a better or more versatile man.

At Cardington, the *R.101* team under Richmond produced their own design, quite independently of AGC. The manufacture of the components for the airship was contracted to the firm of Bolton and Paul in Norwich whilst the assembly was done in large sheds on the Cardington site. In *Slide Rule*, Shute claimed that there was no interchange between the two organisations. It is true that Cardington were kept informed of progress at Howden through the reports of the AID inspectors. The exchange of ideas between Howden and Cardington seems to have been thwarted mainly by the attitude of Barnes Wallis. As an example, he was sent details of the new type of gas valve that Cardington were developing for the *R.101*. He commented rather icily on its novelty but claimed that he had nowhere at Howden to keep confidential papers of this type and

promptly sent it back.[14] Ironically, in a debate in the House of Commons
in May 1927, Mr Wells, the M.P. for Bedford, asked if there was close
co-operation between the airship company and the Government in the
designing of these two airships. Sir Samuel Hoare, the Secretary of State
for Air replied that, so far as he knew, there was close co-operation.[15]

So through 1926 and into 1927 the framework of *R.100* was constructed, and by the middle of 1927 frames 3 to 12 were erected and in
position. Away from work, Shute's main relaxation was the Yorkshire Aero
Club, and in March 1927 he was elected as a Director of the Club, replac-
ing Captain J.R. Patterson who had resigned. He was elected because he
was both a pilot and an aeronautical engineer and therefore a useful man
to have as a Director of the Club. A fellow Club Director was David Little
of Leeds who was later to become a shareholder and Company Secretary
of Airspeed. The Club secretary was Jack Barnes.[16] In December 1927,
Shute was a delegate at a meeting of the Royal Aero Club in London
which, ironically, was chaired by Lord Thomson of Cardington who
happened to be Chairman of the Royal Aero Club. There had been a lot
of Inter Club meetings that year which many clubs had found difficult
to support, and it was decided that the number of club meetings would
be reduced by allocating one meeting to specific geographical areas. The
Yorkshire, Newcastle and Lancashire Aero Clubs became the northern
group, each hosting an event in turn.[17]

Early on at Sherburn, Shute distinguished himself by clipping the
boundary fence when landing a Moth and depositing it inverted on the
airfield, being lucky to escape without injury from that accident. A far
more serious accident occurred in September 1927, when a privately
owned Moth crashed just outside the airfield. The pilot, Captain Mil-
burn, with his passenger Miss Dorothy Ellison, had been attempting a
low speed manoeuvre when the aircraft stalled and spun into the ground
from a height of about 300 feet. The passenger, in the front cockpit, was
killed and the pilot, in the rear, was very seriously injured. As a Club
official, Shute would have been informed of the accident, if indeed he
was not there when it happened. Because of the fatality, there was an official accident investigation which said the accident was due to errors of
judgment by the pilot.[18] This accident would have cast a shadow over the
Club which attracted many of the young men and women of Yorkshire.
They came not only to fly and enjoy the pageants and Club meetings,
but also the social functions such as the regular supper dances held at

nearby Tadcaster. At that time, the club had over 200 members of whom about 100 were flying members, some owning their own machines. Shute was at the club regularly, often twice a week, to sort out the problems that arose, discussing the maintenance of the aircraft with the Ground Engineer, Reginald Morris, and ensuring that things ran smoothly. He wrote that he gained a lot of management experience at the Club which was to serve him well later on.

He had a good deal to do with the pilot instructors and formed his own opinions of the qualities required of a good instructor. Through 1927 and 1928 the instructor was Captain Geoffrey Beck, whom Shute described as a hard-headed bachelor and quite a merry customer. He was efficient and taught a number of members, both men and women, to fly and averaged around 10 to 15 hours flying instruction a week, depending on the weather. However because of his association with a married woman who was seeking a divorce, he became unpopular with the female club members. At the end of 1928 he resigned from the club and took a job in Canada. His replacement was Captain Harry Worrall, whom Shute described as the best of the lot. Worrall, then in his early forties, was happily married with a family and a stable life. He had been a pilot in the Royal Flying Corps in the war and a co-pilot with Cobham on some of his long distance flights. A contemporary description[19] of Worrall was that "he is of course an ideal pilot-manager for such a Club, and his geniality and rubicund countenance are well known amongst all those who fly." Shute knew that the pupils were in safe hands with Harry Worrall.

Once settled at Howden at his digs on Hailgate, Shute began writing again in the evenings as a relaxation from his daytime airship work. Following *Marazan*, he used an aviation theme but with an espionage plot. In June 1927 he wrote to Flora asking her to select a book from the shop as a birthday present and to send him the bill. In the letter he told her of the book he was writing:[20]

> . . . then for the last 10 days of July, I'm going to take my little car and drive down to North Devon alone and go and spend a week on Lundy Island all by myself. There's a farm there where you can stay, and it's nice and isolated and marine. I shall be just about finishing the first draft of my book by then, and I think that'll probably be as good a place as any to do it. And then in the autumn it will all have to be re-written from start to finish, but that's just hack work.

It's not a bad book in its way, and it's different to Marazan, which is the main thing. It's different, although I've used all the same ingredients. It is told in the first person, and it's all about aeroplanes, but it's turned out a tragedy. My, that's a new departure, isn't it? You'd hardly have believed it possible. But there it is, and it's going to be quite a good one, too.

It's about a young man, a pilot, who was down and out in England, and went to Russia to train the Red Army in aerial fighting, and eventually he comes over to take photographs from the air of a very secret bit of Portsmouth, for the Russians. And finally gets himself killed in a brawl. There's a bit of blood and thunder for you, but it's come out quite well. I'd like to call it "Renegade" but to my intense irritation I see that the House of Cassell published a book called Renegade only a month or two ago. And I can't think of anything else to call it. The fun of the book lies in working out how perfectly ordinary people behave when they are brought into contact with a renegade spy, and what a very ordinary young man a renegade spy can be. Quite a good book—and not having touched wood when writing that, it probably won't find a publisher.

A notable feature of this book, which was published in 1928 with the title *So Disdained*, is that it contains many musical references. The main character, Peter Moran, plays the piano and is writing a musical play. He entertains Lord Arner and his family by playing for them after dinner. Up till that point Shute had shown no interest in music, nor did he ever learn to play an instrument, and subsequent novels contain far fewer references to music. The inference from this is that, at this time, he met and got to know Frances Heaton whom he was later to marry. In *Slide Rule* he mentions that he met her at the Yorkshire Aeroplane Club and she was one of the merry crowd of young Yorkshire people who enjoyed the social life at the Club. Frances was a doctor, then working at York District Hospital. She was the second daughter of Bernard and Lillian Heaton. Lillian was a pianist of concert standard and Frances was herself an accomplished pianist and maintained an interest in music all her life. Shute's daughter, Shirley, thought later that she wasn't really cut out to be a doctor but that, being a second child and perhaps not expected to shine, had pursued medicine to prove a point. She did her medical training at University College London Medical School, achieving her

Bachelor of Medicine and Bachelor of Surgery in 1926 at the age of 24. Shute became attracted to Frances, fair-haired and blue-eyed, a doctor at a time when women doctors were something of a rarity, and his social equal. She was an ideal companion for him for the Club's supper dances and parties. She had, too, a love of adventure, which is what may have attracted her to the flying club in the first place. It is not known if Shute took her flying as a passenger but it would be surprising if he did not.

At Howden the airship took shape, the progress being limited by the pace of the design and it was this factor amongst others that caused the growing rift between Wallis and Burney. Burney became increasingly impatient at the slow progress of construction and with Wallis's insistence that he must oversee every detail of the design. The original Contract completion date of September 1927 had been missed. By then even the structure was only partially complete, although all of the frames were erected and the construction of the fins and rudders was under way. By the end of that year four of the six Condor engines were installed in the power cars and the mesh wiring for containing the gas bags had been started. This mesh wiring system was an innovation by Wallis and the first part of the ship to which the term *geodetic* could be truly applied. The Airworthiness Panel had stipulated that no lateral forces should be applied to the longitudinal girders on the structure, something that was felt to have contributed to the *R.38* disaster. Wallis developed a system of mesh wiring; each wire followed a *geodetic* curve on the gasbag it contained. The mesh pitch was closer at the top where the gas pressure was highest and more open at the bottom. No doubt Shute and his assistants did many calculations on the tensions in the wiring to achieve uniformity and to ensure that the lifting forces from the mesh transferred correctly to the transverse girders to which they were attached. A patent was obtained for this system and the method of attachment to the transverse girders. This was but one of many patents granted for the *R.100*, but is the only one to bear the name of Shute as well as that of Burney and Wallis, clearly a recognition, not only of his contribution to this particular innovation, but also his increasing importance in the company. A significant factor in this was his willingness, as construction progressed, to go down onto the shop floor and provide solutions to practical problems as they arose, for example, joints that would not close or wires that fouled.

Conditions on the shop floor were none too good at times. The airship station was on low lying ground where even in summer there was water not far below the surface. It was quite impossible to heat the cavernous shed and in winter it could be filled with a damp mist. Damp caused mould on the fabrics and corrosion of the aluminium, so much so that Wallis had the entire structure re-varnished, which took six months. On frosty winter mornings the structure might be coated with ice, making climbing on the structure dangerous and stopping construction work.

There were labour problems too. Shortly after Shute arrived in 1926 the site was affected by the General Strike in May, which brought activity to a halt and there were several further strikes as the ship was being built. Local lads and girls were employed. The lads were what Shute expected, many of them coming straight from local farms, but he was shocked at the uncouth, foul-mouthed and, in some cases, promiscuous behaviour of some of the local girls. Later, he was criticised locally for expressing his views on them in *Slide Rule*. However Shute admired the riggers for the work they did, climbing the frame with apparent nonchalance. Molly Wallis also found the riggers delightful, writing to a friend that[21] "This place is full of the darlingest men you can possibly imagine—all ready and willing to do anything on earth for you." The men probably found Mrs Wallis perfectly charming, pretty, innocent, the picture of sweet young wife-and-motherhood.

Despite the difficulties and delays, there were lighter moments. Shute recalled that one man, coming in search of work, was asked if he could climb. He said he could and was asked to climb an extending fireman's ladder used to reach the structure. He did so, but only after three attempts and two pints of beer! An inspector lost his footing whilst climbing the structure but managed to grab hold to prevent his fall. Unfortunately, he lost his false teeth in the process and they fell 50 feet onto the floor below, breaking into two pieces.

Another time, the Director of Airship Development flew his own Lynx Avro plane up to Howden to view progress on the airship. He parked his aeroplane some way from the shed and after his visit Wallis and Shute walked out with him to see him off. It became apparent that the Director, who had been a senior Air Force Officer, was not entirely familiar with how to start his plane. After half an hour swinging on the propeller, they managed to get the engine running, but only on five of its six cylinders. Having made a bonfire of his oiled up spark plugs, Wallis and Shute got him on his way, with the engine running sweet and true. After that incident, Shute thought that they should send a challenge to

Cardington for the Chief Engineer and Chief Mathematician of each airship staff to compete in starting up a Lynx Avro at the next Royal Air Force pageant, armed only with T squares and slide rules. This was a turn which, Shute felt, would send up the gate receipts quite considerably.[22]

By the end of 1927 the main framework of the ship was complete. The gas bags had been made but were being stored by BG Textilwerke in Berlin until they could be installed in the airship. However, gasbag No. 1, for the bow of the ship, was sent to Howden for a trial fit which was satisfactory. In April 1928 the first engine runs were being done. The full-scale engine tests were to come later. By the end of 1928 the design side of *R.100* was essentially finished but to keep the team together Burney obtained a contract for the design of a much larger ship of 7.5 or even 9 million cubic feet, known as the Atlantic ship, much larger than the *R.100* whose size had been set by the original specification and dictated to a large extent by the size of the Howden shed. When the doors were open to walk the ship out, the clearance was only a few feet.

As Shute had turned to writing as a relaxation, so Wallis, as the *R.100* design work tailed off, turned his thoughts to the construction of all metal aircraft. He visited the Blackburn aircraft works at nearby Brough, and as an exercise did a design for an aircraft wing which he discussed with them. Given the feud with Burney and the considerable effort he had expended on *R.100*, he longed for a change, to escape from Howden and move on to new pastures. Late in 1928, he was summoned to Weybridge by Sir Robert MacLean, chairman of Vickers Aircraft, and offered the post of Chief Designer to work alongside R.K. Pierson at Weybridge. There was a proviso that he must be available to see *R.100* through to completion. Sir Robert merely informed Burney of Wallis' new role in a memo and Burney apparently accepted it with surprisingly good grace. This may well have been because Burney had faith in Shute as a good right hand man at Howden and more receptive to Burney's way of thinking. They were working together on the Atlantic ship and what was called the elliptical ship, a concept Burney had in mind for an airship that could land safely on water. Also Burney was writing a book on airships and aircraft and wanted Shute to write a chapter on heavier-than-air craft.

To cater for Wallis' absences, two changes were made to the Howden team. Shute was promoted to Deputy Chief Engineer and he became, as he later said, a big frog in a little puddle. Hessell Tiltman, Shute's former colleague from de Havilland, joined the *R.100* team as Chief Designer.

The promotion was a significant personal achievement for Shute who, at the age of 30, assumed day to day responsibility for a major national aviation project. He would now have the task, with Wallis attending as necessary, to complete the building of *R.100*, hand her over to the Air Ministry and see her safely through her acceptance trial flights. He developed a close working relationship with Burney, as the correspondence between them from that time reveals.[23] There were letters and memos on everything from the design of the Atlantic ship to answering the numerous queries from Professors Bairstow and Pippard in relation to the airworthiness of the *R.100*. Shute now felt quite confident in his abilities to undertake assessment of the design of the larger ship, extending the concepts laid down by Wallis. He had evidently learned a lot from Wallis's tutelage, as he had before from Geoffrey de Havilland.

In addition to the day to day overseeing of work on the ship and the office and shop floor staff of well over 100, there was by then a constant stream of visitors to be shown round. Burney was extremely anxious to obtain more orders for airships and, having both an American wife and business connections in the United States, he spent much time in that country attempting to secure future contracts. Consequently Burney would arrange for parties of visitors from many countries to go up to Howden to see the ship for themselves. These parties included Naval officers from America and also potential clients from Japan. On July 5 1928, a party of MPs was given a conducted tour of the ship as well as tea on board, served by girls from the fabric shop acting as waitresses. At weekends, as the ship neared completion, long queues formed, as the public waited to be shown over the ship, paying a shilling for the privilege. The building of both the *R.100* and *R.101* were covered equally by the aeronautical press. Airships were making news headlines, with the flight of the Graf Zeppelin from Friedrichshafen in Germany to Lakehurst New Jersey in 1928. This was followed the next year by its round the world flight.

Although *R.100* was considerably behind the original schedule, so too was *R.101* upon which considerably more money had been spent. Eventually it was to cost nearly one million pounds, more than twice that of *R.100*. Shute later commented that Cardington regarded their ship as of great national importance and that if public money had been spent on something for the ship, into the ship it had to go, regardless of practicality. He claimed that Howden only learned about *R.101* through

Parliamentary reports in Hansard, patent specifications and the technical press. They learned that servo motors were to be used for moving the fins and rudders on *R.101,* whereas his calculations had shown that they could be operated on *R.100* by manpower alone. Whilst the servo motors were indeed originally fitted, they were later taken out to save weight, for weight was a major problem for the Cardington ship. The original specification had called for a disposable lift (for crew, passengers, freight and ballast) of 60 tons; *R.101* had a disposable lift, as originally built, of just 35 tons. Shute was correct in saying that one of the six engines in *R.101* was just to be used for a few minutes for going astern when coming up to the mooring mast. But this was only because there was a problem with the reversing gear, which would have been corrected given more time. The designers had not originally intended that this engine would be used only in reverse. Reversible engines were finally fitted to *R.101* in September 1930.

Building of *R.101* had started after *R.100,* but the efficient organisation in the Cardington shed under Works Manager Arthur Gerrish and Richmond's undoubted flair for organisation, meant that she was completed before *R.100.* A comment by the AID inspectors at the time was that James Watson at Howden was one of the world's worst works managers and that the Howden labour force were tending to prolong the job knowing that once *R.100* was finished, they would be unemployed.

However, during 1929 *R.100* was finally completed, two very important stages being overseen by Wallis himself. The first was the inflation of the gasbags with hydrogen. This operation was too important to be left to shop floor personnel. Shute took charge of one team of riggers and, Bill Horrocks, Chief Draughtsman, a second team. Climbing along the girders of the structure, their job was to ensure that the bags inflated smoothly and correctly and did not snag or tear anywhere as they filled with hydrogen. The whole operation was controlled by Wallis using a megaphone to give directions from the floor of the shed. In the production of the hydrogen, Philip Teed's ingenuity and cool head proved invaluable. He was in control of the Silicol hydrogen plant. Once the hot caustic soda was introduced to the ferro-silicon, the hydrogen production was continuous until the charge was used up. The gas was piped directly as it was produced to each bag, with no intermediate storage or means of turning off production once it had begun. However Teed found a way of controlling the rate of hydrogen production in the reaction vessel, a development for which he was granted a patent. Thus, to some extent, he could adjust the flow. Shute later wrote that "gas plants of this sort had once or twice exploded in the past with loss of life and two or three times during the inflation of R.100, a cool head was needed in the gas house to avoid disaster. We were all a little afraid of that gas plant; the member of our staff who ran it held a great responsibility."[24]

The gasbags were expensive, as was the cost of producing the gas. However the whole inflation was completed successfully after a period of what Shute described as "sweat and toil", with only one small tear. It would have been physically demanding work, moving about the frames, guiding the delicate bags into position, and keeping watch for any problems. The conduct of this operation certainly impressed Herr Strohbl, a visitor from the Zeppelin Works, who was present at the time. The workers on the shop floor, though, dubbed him "Here's trouble".

The engine trials were also something that Wallis felt he could not delegate, and he made elaborate preparations for them, designing an attachment for the nose of the airship to the portal of the shed doors and a system of guy wires and restraints to prevent the ship moving about too much in the slipstream from the propellers, for the distance from the tip of the 17 foot propeller blades to the shed floor was only 15 inches in the wing power cars. Shute thought that *R.100* was never in greater danger than during those engine tests, but much to Shute's relief, they were completed without incident.

The race to be the first airship to fly was won by *R.101*, for on 14 October 1929 she flew for the first time around Bedford and on to London, although she had only a provisional airworthiness certificate. Four days later, with Lord Thomson on board, she made a longer flight of over 9 hours over the Midlands and Yorkshire. As if to rub their noses in it, she flew over Howden. However when they got back to Cardington the weather forecast was poor and the *R.101* was put back into her shed, it being too risky to leave her at the mast.

Burney's book *The World, The Air, and the Future* was published by Alfred Knopf in October 1929.[25] Chapter 6 of this book, entitled "Heavier than Air Craft", was written by Shute at Burney's invitation. That Burney had asked him to write this chapter was surely a mark of his regard for Shute and his technical and writing capabilities. What Burney wanted, and what Shute wrote, was an assessment of the present state of development of aircraft and their future prospects. Shute divided the chapter into sections on the land aeroplane and the flying boat. In both cases, he examined the present state of development of passenger-carrying aircraft and came to the conclusion that, although the range might be extended in future to 1000 or possibly 2000 miles, this would be at the expense of payload. More than 2000 miles range would, he believed, be achieved only by carrying no useful payload at all—he quoted Lindbergh's transatlantic flight as an extreme example. If 50 percent of the weight was fuel and the remainder payload, a machine of the future would have a range of just over 1000 miles. For flying boats, the picture was similar with perhaps a somewhat greater range being achieved. His estimate of the timescale for the development of long range commercial aircraft was as follows:

> Finally, in what period of time is the aeroplane of the future, as indicated in this chapter, likely to be achieved? Here the answer must be pure guesswork, but the indications at present are that a period of fifty years for the attainment of the type would be a moderate estimate. Much, of course, depends upon the commercial demand for more efficient and for larger aeroplanes, and in regard to size it is still doubtful whether operators will require the maximum size of aeroplane that can be developed. Where speed is the object of a service, that object is better met by a service of aeroplanes each carrying ten passengers, and starting once an hour, than by a service of machines each carrying a hundred passengers, and starting once a day. Needless to say, however, the latter is the cheaper service of the two.[25]

Burney, in a footnote to the chapter, said that he did not agree with Mr Norway's figure of fifty years. He thought progress would be much quicker in view of the unlimited capital available. History was to prove Burney right: long distance commercial flights, for example across the Atlantic, were in service in less than twenty years from when Shute wrote that chapter. Writing the chapter gave Shute the opportunity to sit back and take stock of likely developments in aircraft and form a view of these developments that would shape his career over the coming decade.

On a personal level, once he had been promoted to Deputy Chief Engineer, he was now earning an excellent salary of over £800 a year. In this situation, living in lodgings in Hailgate might well have seemed inappropriate to him. His hopes of marrying Flora had ended. Had that still been a possibility he might well have thought of buying a house but instead moved to York, taking up permanent residence at the St Leonard's Club in the centre of the city. As a bachelor, club life suited him, with its congenial masculine atmosphere, meals provided and chores such as laundry done for him. It had the advantage also that it brought him closer to where Frances worked, York Hospital being but a short walk from the Club. He drove the 20 miles to work each day, and Sherburn in Elmet was a similar distance away. One time, however, when he had to make a visit to Cardington he flew a Moth from Sherburn. Leaving the Club at 7 a.m. he was at Cardington by 10 a.m. After his meeting there he flew back the same day, arriving back at the Club in time for dinner. The cost was little more than the rail fare.

Once the gasbags had been inflated, the completion of the outer cover took some time and there were numerous final details to be sorted out, not the least of which was the submission of documents to the Airworthiness Panel so that *R.100* could be granted a permit to fly. The final job was to carry out the lift and trim trials. The ship, with its gasbags inflated, floated in the shed but was held down by crates of weights attached along the length of the ship. To measure the total disposable lift, some of the weights were removed whilst the ship was held by a team of men holding onto the control and power cars. On the blast of a whistle, they all let go. If the ship did not rise, more weights were removed and this procedure was repeated until she floated motionless for several minutes. The total weight supported in this condition gave the net disposable lift. Like *R.101* this was less than the contract requirement, being 54 tons and not the stipulated 60 tons. This was, however, considerably better than *R.101's* 35 tons. The solution to *R.101's* poor lifting capability was firstly drastically to reduce the weight by taking out many of her fixtures and fittings, including the servo motors, and secondly letting out the harnesses to allow the gasbags to be filled with more hydrogen. These palliative measures were not enough and the decision was taken to fit an extra bay in the ship. She was to be cut in half and an extra bay with a gasbag inserted, which Shute described as a desperate measure.

For *R.100* also, the insertion of an extra bay to give more lift was something that was actively being worked on even before her final lift and trim trials. Both ships were short of disposable lift, *R.101* badly so and, although AGC argued that some of the shortfall in lift for *R.100* was due to water soaked up in the outer cover from rain leaking from the roof, this could only account, at most, for about 1 ton. The situation was, as Burney had pointed out in his book, that both ships were really experimental and simply not large enough to be commercially viable. Hence the work that Shute was doing on the larger Atlantic ship. The expectation was that if *R.100* proved successful, AGC would be awarded the contract to design and build the larger ship.

On 8 November 1929, Burney notified the Air Ministry that *R.100* was complete and on the 21st the permit to fly was issued. It seemed almost incredible to Shute and his colleagues that the ship was finally completed, albeit more than two years after the original completion date. Now the first flight of the ship depended on the weather and the availability of the mooring mast at Cardington. Although proposals for a mast at Howden had been drawn up, it was never built. Previously smaller ships at Howden had been moored to large concrete blocks, but this was quite impractical for a ship the size of *R.100* which, moreover, had been built to embark passengers through the nose of the ship when moored to a mast. In November 1929 *R.101* was occupying the mast, and weather conditions remained adverse, for a period of dead calm was needed to walk the ship out of the shed. Finally the forecast for December 16 looked promising and so it proved. The ship was walked out early in the morning, cleared the shed with only a few feet of clearance and emerged accompanied by a great cheer from the assembled crowd.

The start of that first flight was an anxious time for Shute. Would the ship perform as predicted from his calculations so painstakingly done? Would it be possible to steer the ship with its large rudders operated by man power alone or were Cardington in fact right that servo motors were needed to assist in rudder operation? He need not have worried, because from the outset the ship performed well; the rudders could be operated from the 4-foot wheel, application of rudder being increased as the ship took up the turn. They cruised around Howden, then over York and, satisfied that the ship was performing well, they set course for Cardington. Shute went for a breakfast of bacon and eggs, no doubt a relieved man. They flew again the following day and then *R.100* went into the shed at Cardington. Over that Christmas period Shute went skiing at Murren in Switzerland, greatly enjoying a well earned holiday and coming to it in the knowledge that the ship, for which he had sole day-to-day responsibility, had flown successfully and was about to be formally handed over to the Air Ministry, even if they were competitors.

The formal handover took place on the 10th January 1930, the document being signed by Colmore on behalf of the Air Ministry.

The *R.100* officers were all experienced airship men on the Cardington payroll. They got to know the ship before she finished building and had been at Howden when the gasbags were inflated and the engine tests carried out. The Captain, Squadron Leader Ralph Booth, was originally from the Royal Naval Air Service but had been transferred to the RAF in 1919. Booth distinguished himself during an incident when in command of the *R.33* airship in 1925. During a gale she had been swept out over the North Sea after being torn from her mast at Pulham in Norfolk. He nursed the damaged ship during the gale which carried them over to Holland. When it abated he was able to gain height and slowly make his way back to base and for this act was awarded the Air Force Cross. Captain George Meager was *R.100's* first officer who had been flying airships since 1915 and had experience of both rigid and non-rigid types. Although assigned to *R.100*, he flew on two test flights aboard *R.101*. On the second flight he became worried about the behaviour of that ship. She felt 'heavy' and tended to over correct on the elevators, that is to say that she would go into a sharp dive and then the elevators would bring the nose up and climb back to flying height. When the coxswain levelled out, the ship would begin to dive again. He was very relieved when they moored up back at base. Meager reported this behaviour to Booth and told him that, unless he was definitely ordered to do so, he would not fly in *R.101* again.

On Shute's return from his skiing holiday, he waited for *R.100* to be taken out of the shed at Cardington for further test flights. On his birthday, 17 January, he arranged a party in Leeds for friends from the Aero Club including Harry Worrall and Frances. In *Slide Rule* he recalled that he got the news that *R.100* would be taken out of the shed the following day, and that he had his party and drove through the night to Cardington, arriving late because of icy conditions on the road.

The final test for *R.100* was to be its flight to Canada. Although a flight to India had been in the original contract, Canada was substituted because of fear over the flammability of the petrol for the engines in tropical climates: *R.101* with her diesel engines would fly to India. No doubt Shute assumed that Burney and Wallis would be representing AGC on that trip. Of course Wallis wanted to go but this was vetoed by Sir Robert MacLean. Firmly and irrevocably he gave his instruction;

Wallis could kill himself if he so wished in one of the aircraft he was going to build, but not in the "airship contraption". Shute, sensing that it might be possible for him to go on the flight to Canada, wrote a memo to Burney on 16 May 1930:

> I see there is still a chance for me to get over to Canada in the ship. I should like very much to come of course but am a little concerned about the possibility of being landed in for heavier expenses than I could easily afford. In the normal course of events there should be no reason for very heavy expenses of course, but if for any reason I should get hung up over there or have to return by steamer I should like to feel that my expenses were covered in some way. In the present state of the Company I should not propose to put in for expenses below my ordinary standard of living; that is to say £35 per month. I should however like to feel that if through unforeseen circumstances this trip should run me into over £100, for example, that I should be covered in some way. I had hoped to be able to do this myself by means of journalism but that does not seem to be very easily possible now; moreover the uncertainty of whether I am going or not precludes any previous arrangements of that sort.[26]

A couple of days later Burney sent him a telegram to say that he was to go on the Canadian flight. Shute responded with enthusiasm:

> Many thanks for your telegram of Saturday informing me that I am to go on the Canadian flight. I am collecting everything that will be necessary for this trip and will come down for the trial flight ready to go off without returning to Howden.[27]

He was premature, because there were delays. During another test flight the tip of the tail of the ship collapsed. *R.100* went back into the shed and the tail was replaced, this time with a rounded end rather than the fine point she was built with—Shute thought it spoiled her looks.

The further flight trials around England proved that the ship flew well under a variety of weather conditions. Shute described these flights in detail in *Slide Rule*. By the end of July, she had flown for a total of over 100 hours and travelled over 4000 miles. One continuous flight of 53 hours had been accomplished, which was an original contract requirement.

Unlike *R.101*, AGC got paid only when these contract milestones were achieved. Whilst on board smoking was strictly forbidden, not surprisingly with 5 million cubic feet of hydrogen and 35 tons of petrol on board. At the end of this long flight many of the crew hurried to disembark so that they could have a smoke.

Now she was ready to make the proving flight to Canada. Just before he left Howden he sent the following telegram to Bamber, the Secretary of AGC:

DEPENDING ON YOU TO FIX MY EXPENSE ACCOUNT CREDIT IN CANADA STOP GOING CARDINGTON NOW NORWAY.

The evening before departure, Shute dined well at the Oxford and Cambridge Club in London and followed the meal with a cigar and brandy. He then went to Burney's fashionable house in Carlton House Terrace and drove with him to Cardington. (During the trip to Canada he kept a diary, which he only did during travels of this sort.) The ship left the mast early in the morning of 29 July and took a northerly course over Liverpool and Northern Ireland before shaping their course across the Atlantic. This enabled them to fly in favourable winds as much as possible. By the 31st they were running up the St Lawrence River after an uneventful crossing. Shute commented on the Navigating Officer, Squadron Leader Ernest Johnston, whom he described as a splendid navigator who worked like a horse. Much of the navigation was done in the traditional way by taking sights with a sextant and assessing drift by dropping flares onto the sea where the smoke gave an indication of wind direction and strength. Navigation by taking bearings from wireless stations was in its infancy, but served as a cross check of position.

It was whilst flying down the St Lawrence that they ran into trouble. They got into a wind from the north side of the river, which made the ship pitch and yaw and gave the worst motion the ship had so far encountered and gave rise to tears in the fabric of the fins, one, as Meager said, big enough to drive a bus through. They headed south out of this disturbed air and managed to do makeshift repairs to large rents in the fabric. At one stage there were 15 riggers attending to these repairs, with one of them, Clarence Flatters, outside the hull attached by a lifeline and poised 1000 feet above the river. After passing Quebec they received a warning by wireless of a storm ahead of them. Shute remembered seeing that storm right across their path with bronze-tinted clouds and rain underneath. Flying operations were directed by Major Scott who ordered Captain Booth to fly through it rather than go round. Against his better judgement Booth agreed. The ship hit a vertical gust and was carried up rapidly to 4000 feet in a matter of moments. The elevators were moved to hard down and the ship went 20 degrees nose down. A circuit breaker tripped out, plunging the ship into darkness, and a tin of red dope spilt its contents, looking like blood in the eerie emergency lighting. No one slept very much that night whilst they compared notes on what had happened and attended to further damage to the outer cover.

They landed at St Hubert, Montreal, to a tumultuous welcome from the Canadians, in the early dawn on 1 August. Thousands of people had waited hours or days for the arrival of *R.100*. Burney, Scott, Colmore and other senior members of the party emerged from the mooring tower to face newsreel cameras, press interviews, speeches and a welcome that lasted for hours. Burney was asked what he thought of the way the ship had behaved. His reply was: "I think the ship behaved very well. There is no doubt we shall have to pay more attention to our fabrics. But so far as the ship herself is concerned when in the air she is absolutely stable and controllable and, in my opinion, more comfortable than a liner."[28]

Shute kept a low profile during the twelve days they spent in Canada. He had work to do; with Canadian Vickers he saw to the preparation of patches for repairing the damage to the fabric. He stood down from the trip that *R.100* made to Toronto and Niagara Falls to allow the maximum number of Canadian passengers to be carried. When the ship returned to Montreal from this flight, the reduction gear of one engine failed. The failure meant an engine change and, although they had a spare engine and could have changed it at the mast, the slinging derricks to allow them to do this had not been shipped out. This was another black mark against the Cardington organisation so far as Shute was concerned.

It was not all airship work for Shute though, for he learned as much as he could about the aircraft the Canadians used and what conditions of service were required in that country. He gleaned what he could, from talking to the Vickers organisation whilst arranging the fabric repair, and from Bill Shaylor, a pilot who was flying reporters to and from the airship. He spent some hours talking about aircraft to Shaylor. This interest stemmed not only from the research he had done writing the chapter for Burney's book, but also from an aircraft scheme that he and Tiltman had been discussing back in England, a design for a three-seater biplane.

He caught up with an old friend from his Balliol days, Percy Corbett. He was a Canadian who had graduated in Jurisprudence at Balliol at the same time as Shute. Corbett was buying a farm at Lake Magog, some seventy miles from Montreal, and a visit there gave Shute a glimpse of the way of life in the Dominions, and the standard of life for English-speaking people living outside England. For Shute it was an eye opener. He liked the way these people went about things, their vitality and physical health. He wrote in his diary that "I have never been in a place [Canada] that has got hold of me as much as this has done."[29] When the time came to leave for England he was sorry to be going home. During the time they were there over half a million visitors came to see the airship, this wonderful new means of transport that the Mother country had built. The crew were feted like heroes and the Canadians even composed a song in her honour.

They left for England in the evening of 13 August. Only five of the six engines were working but they had no choice in the matter and it was a perfectly safe thing to do knowing that the prevailing winds would be in their favour on the return trip. Somewhere out over Anticosti Island at the mouth of the St Lawrence River, Shute was photographed in the little bow cockpit, the only surviving photograph of him from this trip. He has a big grin on his face and looks as though he is thoroughly pleased with the flight. Some 57 hours after leaving Montreal they were back at Cardington, very nearly a record time. The welcome they received was, as George Meager recalled, something of an anticlimax compared to their reception in Montreal. Shute wrote "we slink in unhonoured and unsung in the English way."[30] Nothing could have equalled their arrival in Canada, but several hundred people did flock to see *R.100* safely home and Lord Thomson himself was there to welcome them back, and the newsreels recorded her homecoming. In his welcome home speech Lord Thomson said "I welcome you home from Canada and congratulate you on having accomplished this first and successful step in the development of our new generation of British airships. This contribution to our Imperial communications will be of incalculable significance." He went on with a reference "to my friend Barnes Wallis who must be a proud man today; deservedly so. I wish to express my high appreciation of the work of all those who have been responsible for the design and construction of

R.100 and to pay a special tribute to the officers and staff of both flying crews and ground organisation."[31]

In a short space of time, all the passengers disembarked and dispersed, Shute to travel up to York, no doubt keen to see Frances and tell her all about the trip and to discuss with Tiltman what he had learned about aircraft in Canada. The *R.100* crew stood down and were relieved by *R.101* crew. Later on when the ship was being refuelled, the tanks were overfilled, one of the duralumin members gave way and the tanks were damaged. News of this damage filtered back to Howden and Shute got an account some days later of what had taken place, which he recorded in a memo to Burney:[32]

I have had a further and more highly coloured account of the Cardington affair from Cyril Watson who is up here on leave from R.100. Some allowance must be made for his exaggeration but I think the following account is substantially correct.

The alcohol which the R.101 crew got hold of was in Steff's cabin; he brought over 16 bottles of Canadian whiskey, presumably for his own use. As soon as the R.101 crew got on board they commenced to rifle the cabins, and discovered this amongst other souvenirs. They also rifled Johnston's cabin which produced a further incident later on.

Up till midnight Atherstone and Hunt were in charge of this crew and it was during this time that the drink was consumed and the tanks broken.

At 3 o'clock in the morning the handling party arrived from Henlow to put the ship into the shed. This process is normally carried out by Johnston and Steff one being in charge of the bow of the ship and one the stern. It was soon apparent that Steff had been celebrating the safe return of the ship to England, a circumstance which was indicated by the fact that he found it more suitable go about his duty on his hands and knees, and having attained this position was unable to assume the erect position without assistance. In this condition he was not very much use in helping the ship into the shed and finally retired from the field. He was subsequently reported to the Air Ministry by the Henlow officers.

I cannot find out whether there was any incident in getting the ship into the shed, but she seems to have gone in smoothly. As soon as she was safely berthed Johnston went on board and found that his cabin had been rifled and all his personal property and souvenirs stolen. He came out into the shed extremely angry and said exactly what he thought of the conduct of the R.101 crew to those members of the crew who were standing about. These men were still in a partially intoxicated condition and one of them started to take his coat off to Johnston, whereupon Johnston gave him a straight left and knocked him down, dislocating his jaw. I think you will agree that this incident is true to the tradition of the Merchant Service.

The Court of Enquiry is still sitting. Steff seems likely to get the most severe treatment as the charges against him are, first, smuggling alcohol into this country and secondly conduct unbefitting an officer and gentleman. The R.101 crew are likely to escape without much action against them as they are making great play with the fact that they were struck by an officer. The man who Johnston hit is still in bed.

The above seems like something from a cinema, but I believe it to be substantially correct.

Back in Yorkshire, Shute took a short break from work. With the successful trip to Canada completed and his position as Deputy Chief Engineer, with its excellent salary, he felt secure. On the strength of this, he proposed to Frances and she accepted. They announced their engagement officially on 7 September. For Shute, this was a high water mark in his career and personal life. In his 4 years in Yorkshire he had matured considerably from the rather inexperienced young man who had travelled north in 1926. His rise in AGC had been rapid and he had formed a good friendly relationship with Sir Dennis Burney. He had the prospect of marriage to look forward to and every hope that, with the success of R.100, AGC might be awarded further airship work. Although R.101 had been the first to fly, he would have felt that R.100 had stolen a march on the Cardington ship and issued the challenge that said "this is what we have done, now let's see what you can do." He had too, in embryo form, an insurance policy just in case AGC failed to secure further airship work, his light aircraft design project. If prospects at AGC took a turn for the worse, the design and marketing of this aircraft would be a fall back position.

On the negative side, *R.100* was now the plaything of Cardington, and they would decide what became of her, what her future would be. After being put back in the shed, a programme of work to modify and improve her was being prepared in consultation with Howden. To increase her lift, a new bay would have to be fitted and her outer cover, a weakness on both ships, would need to be changed. Through August and into September 1930, there was considerable discussion on the programme of work to be done on *R.100*, and in his dealings with Cardington he had an ally in Booth, who had great faith in *R.100*. On 28 August he wrote to Shute, hoping that he had recovered "from his dissipations in Montreal" to say that he was still sitting in the shed and would be for the next six months or so. He told him of the modifications that Cardington wanted to do. The fitting of a new outer cover was necessary he thought, (it had leaked quite badly in the rain on their homeward flight from Canada) but their idea of fitting reefing girders, as had been used on *R.101*, would achieve nothing and would add about 4 tons to the weight. He added that "I cannot find out why this is being done except to make a bastard R.101 out of R.100!" A few days later Shute sent a note to Burney on these proposals: "As you will see, Cardington want to fit R.100 with an inflated outer cover and reefing girders. This would add about five tons on to the weight of the ship, and would, I think, be a very great mistake. . . . I feel at the moment, however, that we must fight them as hard as we can, as I think that the cover of this nature must be regarded as highly experimental, is wrong in principle, and most extravagant in weight."[33] In the end, it was agreed that the new outer cover would be to Howden's specification and also that the design work for the modifications would be done by the AGC staff under the existing Design Contract. This contract, won for AGC by Burney, was to do continuing work on the larger airships. Although most of the shop floor staff had been laid off when *R.100* was finished, this contract had given the Design Office staff additional work.

On Saturday 5 October *R.101* departed on her flight to India with Lord Thomson and senior officials on board. As he was about to board the ship, Lord Thomson was handed a letter from Burney with good wishes for their journey. *R.101* left late that day in poor weather. Seven hours later it crashed into a hillside near Beauvais in France and immediately caught fire. Of the 54 on board only 8 escaped, two of them dying later from their injuries. It was a major disaster, British aviation's equivalent

of the *Titanic*. The reaction was of shock and horror, typified by a letter written the following day by Harold Roxbee-Cox, Shute's opposite
number at Cardington, to his mother. He had applied to go on the trip
to India, but his application had been refused—the passenger list was
full. On that Sunday he wrote:

> So you can see that it is as well that I didn't start for India in R.101. I
> haven't heard details yet—Monday's papers will have enough—but
> I 'phoned Cardington and it seems they are all dead—Richmond,
> Scott, Colmore, Brancker, Lord Thomson and many others I knew.
> I can scarcely realise it yet, it is so terrible: only seven of the crew
> appear to have survived. It was a great shock to me when I heard
> this morning. There will be a lot of 'I told you so's' these next few
> weeks, questions in the House and a long enquiry. It is, I am afraid,
> the end of airships in this country. It is all very sad.[34]

It was sad too for Shute and his colleagues at Howden. Many of
their friends and comrades on the flight to Montreal were dead—Ernest
Johnston, whose navigational work Shute had so admired, Maurice Steff,
smuggler of whiskey, but a fine second officer and many others. For the
victims of *R.101*, the machinery of State swung into action. Their bodies were brought back to England and lay in state at Westminster Hall,
where thousands paid their respects. There was a Memorial Service in St
Paul's Cathedral on 11 October amidst great national grief. Their bodies
were laid to rest in a communal grave in the churchyard of St Mary's
at Cardington. AGC applied for tickets to the Service in St Paul's, the
company to be represented by Sir Trevor Dawson, Chairman, Sir Dennis Burney, Mr and Mrs Wallis and Mr N.S. Norway and fiancée. For
whatever reason they were not present at the Service, but it is recorded
that Shute waited for hours in London to see the procession pass in order
to pay his respects.

A week later Shute went to Cardington, as they wanted him
on hand whilst they deflated gasbag No. 2. In a memo to Burney he
said that he had an informal design meeting and fixed a lot of detail
modifications to *R.100*, some of which they were to design at Howden
under the design contract, and some of which Cardington would do.
He ended the memo with what he had learned of the cause of the
R.101 crash:

The immediate cause of the loss of 101 is almost certainly a large rent in one of the forward gasbags, possibly aggravated by the fact that the ship was flying rather low at the time and had no room in which to recover. They had plenty of fuel and ballast on board to jettison to compensate for this loss of lift, but apparently had no time to do so before she hit the ground. What caused the gasbag to become torn is not at all certain that might be one of several minor accidents which have happened to that ship from time to time.[35]

The question on the minds of Shute and the staff at Howden was what would the effect of the *R.101* tragedy be on the future of airship work and their futures in particular. Would the present design contract be extended as hoped? The answer was not long in coming and it came in the form of a memo dated 20 October from Burney to Shute. At a meeting with the Air Ministry Burney had been told that the design contract would not be extended beyond 30 November. Burney wrote: "There is nothing therefore to do except to inform the whole of the staff that their operations will cease on the 30th of November and that members of the staff can be released as and when they are able to obtain employment elsewhere. In the meantime the company will, of course maintain all those who do not get prior employment up till the 30th of November."[36] Burney met Sir Robert MacLean, who thought the Vickers factories at Weymouth and Southampton could absorb quite a number of the Howden staff. He mentioned to Sir Robert that he thought Tiltman would be of considerable value in their design department.

Shute, knowing he had a good design team and not wanting to see them disbanded, drafted an advert to be placed in the North American aviation press:

The technical staff of the Airship Guarantee Company Ltd, builders of H.M. airship R.100 will shortly be free to accept other employment. The experience of this staff, which includes the Chief Engineer and Chief Designer, is unique in the design of light metal structures. Further, the senior members of the staff possess an intimate knowledge of present day aeroplane practice and are competent to undertake the design, construction, and operation of aircraft of all types.

It is the desire of the staff to secure financial support for the establishment of a company in Canada to produce aircraft to suit Canadian conditions.[37]

The Board of AGC refused permission to submit the advert as worded, particularly the final paragraph, on the grounds that Canadian Vickers alone held the rights to design and manufacture Vickers aircraft in Canada. The advert was re-drafted as follows:

Owing to the early completion of the contract of H.M. airship R.100 several members of the design staff may be free at an early date to accept other employment. Their experience in light metal construction is unique. Further, all of these engineers, having been recruited from the heavier-than-air aircraft industry, possess an intimate knowledge of present day aeroplane practice, and therefore are competent to undertake the design, construction and operation of airships of all types. The Airship Guarantee Company will be prepared to give references to those engineers on request.[38]

Nothing came of this because, as Shute later wrote, airship expertise was at a discount at that time. There was now nothing for it but to see as many of the design and calculating staff, numbering about thirty, into other jobs. Shute, being in charge at Howden, had the responsibility of carrying this out. In this he seems to have been successful, no doubt helped by other Vickers sites taking on some of the staff. Both he and Tiltman did everything they could to help the staff, writing letters of introduction and references for them. By the end of the year he could report to Burney that all but one of the staff had found other jobs.

He relayed the gloomy news to Frances that the rising star of the Airship Guarantee Company, its Deputy Chief Engineer, to whom she was engaged to be married, was now about to be out of a job. She apparently "took the loss of my job remarkably well, as she has taken all the succeeding crises in our lives."[38] Both he and Tiltman could have found themselves other jobs, or been absorbed into other Vickers teams, and at this time Shute did have a meeting with Sir Robert MacLean at which his future would, no doubt, have been discussed.

But Shute liked the idea of being his own boss. With Tiltman he decided to take the risk and set up their own company to produce aircraft to designs they had been working on since the summer. A less auspicious time to do it can hardly be imagined. The depression in America following the Wall Street crash of 1929 had been going on for over a year and the repercussions in England were being felt with unemployment mounting daily. However they had faith in their technical abilities, and Shute had the experience of man management at Howden. What they lacked was capital and knowledge of how to set about starting up a company.

From Wallis, Shute had learned that only through meticulous attention to detail, a methodical approach to design and construction, could true success in an engineering project such as designing an airship or aeroplane be achieved. From Burney, he learned entrepreneurial skills, that taking a broad view of an industry and likely developments was vital to staying ahead of the competition. From him he also learned that taking risks was permissible, and even necessary, in the interest of a common good or objective. These were, in a sense, two sides of the same coin and he was to apply what he had learned from both these men in starting and running his own company.

Construction of *R.100* framework in the Howden Shed, 1927.
(BAE Systems)

Completion of the outer cover; Howden, 1929.
(BAE Systems)

R.100 flying over Farnborough.
(BAE Systems)

Shute (right) in the bow cockpit on
the flight back from Montreal.
(Dragon School)

Crowds rush to see the arrival of *R.100* on her return from Montreal.
(Airship Heritage Trust)

5
Starters and Runners

The aeroplane scheme that Shute and Tiltman had been discussing, even before the *R.100's* voyage to Canada, was a light aircraft, a biplane with a pilot's cockpit and two side-by-side seats behind, built to the standard of a luxury motor car. It would, they thought, be popular with the private flying market and appeal to the private owner. It was this scheme that Shute had in mind in his discussions during his stay in Montreal. He had wanted to find out if this type of aircraft might appeal to the Canadian and American markets.

Tiltman produced a general arrangement drawing of the proposed aircraft and sketches that showed how the machine could be adapted for various uses. They would set up a company to produce the aircraft and estimated that they would need capital of around £40,000 to establish the company on a sound basis. Shute, then living at St Leonard's Club, approached A.E. Hewitt, who was a member of the Club and also a partner in the firm of Smithson, Teasdale & Hewitt, leading commercial solicitors in York. Much to Shute's surprise, Hewitt thought the scheme appeared to be sound and coached him in the necessary legal steps in setting up a company. On 22 October, just two days after Burney's memo saying that airship work would end on 30 November, Tiltman wrote to Sir Alan Cobham. Cobham knew both Shute and Tiltman from their days at de Havilland, and Tiltman told him about their proposed scheme. Tiltman said that he would be in London the following weekend and asked if they could meet to discuss the scheme. They met and Tiltman took with him the drawings and sketches. In a letter on his return to York, Tiltman told Cobham that "Norway and I have been pushing [the scheme] full throttle and with encouraging results."[1] They already had several influential people who were interested in subscribing to it in varying degrees.

Hewitt knew nothing about the aircraft business and, with a lawyer's caution, wanted an expert opinion of whether Shute and Tiltman's proposal was likely to succeed. It so happened that Hewitt's brother-in-law was Group Captain John Baldwin, then in charge of the Central Flying School at Wittering near Peterborough. So Shute went down to meet Baldwin and convinced him that what they proposed was technically sound and that they seemed capable of making a success of it. On the basis of the favourable report, Hewitt said he would take a seat on the Board and invest in the company on behalf of Baldwin. The latter was uncertain of his future in the RAF, and his Service commission prevented him from taking a commercial interest in the aviation industry. If however he left the RAF he would have this investment to fall back on.

In early December Cobham wrote to Tiltman assuring him that he would help in any way he could, and if he could arrange for them to meet possible interested parties, he would write to him immediately. But this was not what Shute and Tiltman needed. They wanted Cobham to come onto the Board, for his name was very well known both in aviation and to the general public. He had received his knighthood for his pioneering flight to Australia and back, as well as making a flight to Cape Town and back. Moreover he was advising councils up and down the country on the location of airports. Shute and Tiltman well knew that having Cobham on board would add credibility to the launch of the company. On 7 December Shute wrote to Sir Alan offering him not only a position on the Board, but also that, because of the value of his experience to the company, they would offer him a percentage of the profits. Shute added that, on the production of 150 machines a year, which is what they were aiming for, Sir Alan might expect around £250 a year. Shute mentioned in this letter that he had discussed this arrangement with both Hewitt and also Lord Grimthorpe, the Chairman.

Lord Grimthorpe was a local land owner, living at Easthorpe Hall near Malton. He was also a director of other companies and a well known and respected figure in Yorkshire society. He was Master of the local hounds, and was also learning to fly at the Yorkshire Aero Club, and it is probably there that Shute met him and asked him to be Chairman of the company. He agreed. In May the following year he was awarded his aviators certificate and also became President of the Club. With his enthusiasm for flying he was interested in the company, particularly the fact that it was a local enterprise and would give employment in the York area at that time of growing unemployment. He became the company's financial backer and saw it through its early struggles for survival.

The company had to have a name, and early on Shute and Tiltman decided against naming the company after themselves. Although Shute later claimed that he dreamt up the name Airspeed in his bedroom at the St Leonard's Club, another version is that he decided that the name should begin with A and Tiltman's wife, Miriam, thought up the name Airspeed.[2] Shute thought the name was euphonious and stated what the company intended to do.

At the end of the year, Cobham had still not decided if he would join the Board and both Shute and Tiltman travelled to London to meet him, and try to persuade him to join. It was only after a meeting with Hewitt that Cobham finally decided to become a director.

As 1931 dawned, Shute could look back on probably the most momentous year of his life. 1930 had begun, for him, with such high hopes, the successful completion of *R.100* and its first flight. The trial flights had gone well, culminating in the trip to Canada and back and his exciting taste of life in one of the Dominions. He had got engaged to Frances, acted as Chief Engineer to AGC and all had seemed set fair. Then suddenly everything had changed after the *R.101* disaster. Further airship work was cancelled; he had to wind down operations at Howden and help the staff find other jobs. He had chosen not to be absorbed into Vickers or another organisation, but to strike out on his own to start Airspeed in a time of increasing economic difficulty. He had just two published books and was by no means established as a writer. He would never have entertained the notion that Frances, as a doctor, might support him whilst he tried to gain a reputation as a novelist. For him it was the duty of the husband to support the wife financially and have the income to do so, a theme that occurs in a number of his novels, and which had been the case when they got engaged. However, it must have seemed to Shute, as he looked forward to his forthcoming marriage, that his personal financial position would be precarious. He had about a thousand pounds saved, some of which he could invest in Airspeed, but little prospect of any significant income until the company was producing and selling aircraft.

In the early months of 1931, his main preoccupations were to prepare the prospectus for Airspeed, to go flat out to raise the required capital to start the company and his forthcoming marriage. The prospectus[3] was drafted and re-drafted several times before it was finally issued to prospective subscribers. Shute, Tiltman, Cobham and Hewitt all had a hand in its drafting and wording. What emerged was an optimistic document, couched in terms to attract investors. It stated that flying for the private owner had come to stay and that "for the manufacture of aeroplanes there should be an almost unique opportunity for quick and unlimited expansion on similar lines to that enjoyed in recent years by the motorcar industry." It spoke of demand in the Dominions, where distances could be covered in an hour that would normally take a day, that a rancher could locate his herds with ease and have easy access to towns. Also that "In a very few years the aeroplane will be indispensable to those classes in the Empire."

Given that £40,000 of share capital was the target, the section on profits was as follows:

> On a rapidly expanding market of this nature, free from serious price competition, it is anticipated that the production of machines will rise rapidly to at least 150 per year. This production represents a turnover of about £112,000. It is estimated that such a production can be carried out on the capital now offered for subscriptions.
>
> On this production the net profits of the company are expected to exceed £10,000.
>
> It is confidently anticipated that this production will be reached by the end of the second year of the company's existence and thereupon substantial earnings should be available for dividends.

The prospectus also mentioned that the coming year should see a tremendous wave of motor-towed gliding sweep the country, as the sport provided flying for the million at a cost of only a few pence per flight. To cater for this market the company would manufacture a glider of a suitable type as its first product.

It was Cobham who first suggested the idea of a glider as something the company could produce quickly and cheaply; he felt there would be a big boom in towed gliding providing the means of flying on the cheap. In mid February Shute went to Sherburn to see a towed gliding demonstration and the same day obtained his gliding 'A' license with, as he put it,[4] "an epoch making flight of 34 seconds." He thought gliding was best done near the edge of a hill to stay soaring in the up current. However he agreed with Cobham that gliding had come to stay and their best bet would be to produce a high performance sailplane with air brakes to spoil its glide when desired. He and Tiltman studied all the information they could lay hands on and the latter began the design of the sailplane that was to become Airspeed's first product—the Tern.

With enthusiasm and optimism they set about raising capital. Tiltman reported early on that they were in touch with several influential people who had expressed an interest in subscribing. Shute had approached Victor Waddilove of Bradford, a man estimated to be worth two million pounds and reportedly interested in aviation. Shute had tried to interest him in Airspeed with a view to investment. Waddilove considered it seriously then turned it down. Shute wrote to Cobham asking him to write personally to Waddilove, hoping that Cobham's reputation might make him reconsider. Cobham did meet Waddilove but nothing came of it. Similarly an initial interest expressed by a Yorkshire industrial concern came to nothing. In February Shute was still optimistic, reporting that they had started negotiations with York Council to rent half of the bus garage on Piccadilly and that had triggered local interest, particularly from the Terry family, whose chocolate company was a significant employer in York. He also expected that "we shall pick up two or three thousand in Newcastle." He had been up there twice recently and would shortly be going again. He expected another two thousand from Wolverhampton and had "a whole heap of people sitting on the fence until the company is formed." Cobham had been in contact with a director of Napier's, who produced aero engines, trying to interest them in the company.

By late February the Prospectus was being printed, negotiations for the bus garage were in progress, but frustratingly slow. Shute and Tiltman rented a small office to make a start on the design work. The company was all set to be registered and had opened a bank account with Barclays Bank. Barclays now required the fee of 100 guineas (£105) for their name to be added as the company's bankers. It was, they said, their usual practice. The Directors were furious as they certainly had not got that sort of money to spare and objected to the request on principle. They immediately closed their account with Barclays and opened an account with the Midland Bank, which waived all such fees.

On Saturday 7 March Shute and Frances were married in the Parish church of St Peter and St Paul's at Bromley in Kent, Bromley being the town where Frances' parents were living. They left for their honeymoon in Switzerland, with Shute reportedly taking the calculations for the Tern glider with him. What his bride thought of that is not recorded.

It was while Shute was away on honeymoon that Airspeed Ltd was officially registered with the Registrar of Companies on 13th March. The final prospectus, with share application forms could then be distributed. Potential subscribers had until the 25 April to apply for shares.

At this time Cobham wrote to Sir Herbert Austin, chairman of the motor car company that bore his name, to try to interest him in Airspeed. He visited the Longbridge works on 9 March and after his visit thanked Sir Herbert for "the very happy interview you granted me." Tiltman said that he and Shute would prepare a special report for Austin.

On return from their honeymoon, Shute and Frances took a flat at 7 Clifton in York, close to York hospital, where Frances worked, and within walking distance of the office in Piccadilly Chambers. No. 7 was a large 4 storey town house divided into three flats. The other flats were occupied by Mr & Mrs Forrington and a Miss Davies. This was to be their home for the next two years.

Back at work Shute caught up with the latest situation and the prospects did not look good. Austin had decided against investing and the take up of shares was very slow. Writing to Cobham on 9 April Shute said that that they might just scrape the £7,000 that was the minimum subscription instead of getting double that, as was hoped, for a minimum. If they had to start on £7,000 then they must "go flat out for records with the glider." The present records were quite low and could easily be captured by an energetic company. Shute completed his calculations on the glider and Tiltman finalised its design. After frustrating negotiations with York Council they finally rented half the bus garage and could at last have some space to begin manufacture, although they had temporarily rented a local shop premises.

Airspeed's first Board meeting was arranged for the 28 April, and Shute and Cobham met before that at the St Leonard's Club, because Shute felt "we should deal with the technical stuff before and present an agreed conclusion at the meeting." Also he wanted Cobham to meet Tom Laing, "who is joining the company as a sort of assistant works and business manager and is putting some money in." In a P.S. he remarked that "money is terribly slow in coming in and time is getting very short. This is really the burning question now."[5]

At the Board meeting it was all too evident that the share issue had been a complete failure. A total of about five thousand pounds had been promised, mostly by the Directors themselves but included a thousand pounds by Tom Laing on condition that they took him on as an employee. With this level of capital they could not proceed with the programme set out in the prospectus, but rather than admit defeat they set out to see what they could do with five thousand pounds. They applied to the Registrar of Companies for permission to trade on the reduced capital and there was a further meeting to allot shares. They were also looking round to see what consultancy work there might be. One idea was to consult on the re-conditioning of *R.100* and Shute wrote to the Air Ministry about this and also sent a copy to Booth, who he knew would be in favour of the consultancy arrangement, and he knew that what Booth said would carry weight. Nothing came of this because the Government decided against re-conditioning *R.100* and it was broken up for scrap at the end of 1931.

Shute and Laing set up the work benches and equipment in the bus garage so that the woodworkers could get on with making the components for the Tern glider. They built and shared a small office in one corner. In the drawing office just up the street Tiltman was just able to keep ahead of construction. At this time Cobham came up with the proposal for Airspeed to design and build two 10-seater passenger aircraft, later to be christened the Ferry. He was about to launch his National Aviation Day Display company, a touring aviation display on a rather larger and better organised basis than other air circuses, a number of which had come and gone since the war. His mission was to make the country "air minded" and he wanted two machines capable of taking off and landing from fields for mass joyriding. He was prepared to order the machines from Airspeed at a price of £5,000 each, but he would need time to organize his finances. Cobham felt confident that more capital would be forthcoming once Airspeed had something to show for its endeavours. As Cobham was due to come up to Hull for an Air Pageant in early June, Shute wrote to invite him and Lady Cobham to supper on Sunday evening to give them a chance to discuss the new machine. He was sorry that he could not put them up for the night but would be glad to collect them from Sherburn. In the event Cobham had to return directly to London.

By early June, Airspeed had the specification for the Ferry firmed up, but if Cobham wanted it delivered by the following April, that only left just over nine months, which Shute thought almost impossibly short, as time for airworthiness tests had to be allowed for. He had costed the two machines at £8,375 for the pair or £4,187 each. But, so far, Cobham had not placed an order for them. Finally, the order was placed for the two Ferries in mid June for a contract value of £8,870, with a stipulation that they should be delivered for type testing a Martlesham by the following January. It was a very tight schedule and a keen price but at least it gave the prospect of designing and constructing a proper powered aeroplane.

Meantime the Tern glider was in construction in the workshop, with two more being made for future sale. The wings could be detached quickly and easily and wheel assemblies were provided so that it could be towed behind a car. The first Tern was towed to Sherburn in August and test flown with Shute himself at the controls. It flew well, was stable and delightful to fly and so the first Airspeed plane took to the skies.

During the last few months of 1930 and into 1931 Shute had been working under pressure, dealing with the winding down of AGC operations at Howden and starting Airspeed. Apart from his honeymoon in March he had not taken a holiday and even on honeymoon he seems to have been preoccupied with business matters, rather more perhaps than a bridegroom should be, for Airspeed was launched whilst he was in Switzerland. In August he found that, at short notice, he and Frances could get away for a short holiday. What they did was to hire a motor cruiser from Stamford Bridge and spend a week cruising down the Rivers Derwent, Ouse and Humber as far as Hull before retracing their steps back. The article he wrote about the trip[6] tells of a very different kind of boating from his previous sailing in his undergraduate days. Perhaps too it was a way of introducing Frances to the pleasures of boating in the gentler environment of rivers and estuaries, and it certainly enabled them to get right away from the pressures of work. He wrote that funds for the holiday were not too plentiful and that the whole trip cost fifteen pounds for the two of them.

Even before his marriage whilst living at the Club, he made the time to write in the evenings as a relaxation from daytime work. Now he wrote another novel, later published as *Lonely Road*. He was still preoccupied with police and spy themes but the first chapter was experimental, a dream sequence which set the scene, rather tortuously, for the novel, but which he later admitted defeated some readers. As before, he wrote it through twice from start to finish, but was rather more pleased with the character development, and the love story than the plot and this aspect pleased him most. He drew on his own experiences and wrote of a dancing partner, Molly Gordon, from a Palais in Leeds, the kind of place he had visited in his early bachelor days at Howden. The story describes in some detail a long car journey from Leeds across the Pennines and down through the Welsh borders to Bristol and Dartmouth. This is the sort of journey that he would have made to visit his parents at this time. Shortly after Shute moved up to Yorkshire, his parents had given up the house in Liss and taken to living in hotels in the West Country in the Torquay and Dartmouth region, areas which were well known to Arthur Norway. It is quite probable that Shute and Frances made this journey so that he could introduce his fiancée to his parents.

During that summer the Tern captured British gliding records, being flown by Carli Maggersuppe, a young but experienced German glider pilot. The resultant publicity attracted more local subscribers whose investment was welcome for, as quickly as they worked, debts piled up quicker. They sold the other two Terns but that finished their work on gliders because the sport of gliding did not take on as they had expected. The design of the Ferry was completed very quickly that autumn and although there was a need for haste, all the drawings for the Ferry were models of clarity and precision. Earlier that year it was quite evident that Tiltman alone could not cope with all the design work, and they took on A.E. Ellison in the office with another two draughtsmen. Ellison stayed with Airspeed for the rest of his working life.

Tom Laing had been the first to become a working shareholder, and later on David Little, Shute's co-director at the Yorkshire Aero Club, joined the company as its first Company Secretary at a salary of £400 a year. He came from a wealthy family of clothiers in Leeds and took up £3,000 of shares at a time when capital was much needed. Another original shareholder was Amy Johnson, a native of Hull, who took up £100. The previous year she had achieved international fame by being the first woman pilot to fly to Australia and back. Quite how she got to know about Airspeed is not clear. She may have met Shute at an air display at Sherburn or from his visits to Hull, whose development corporation was keen to attract Airspeed to their airport. It is more likely that Cobham, who had advised Amy on the flight to Australia, mentioned his interest in Airspeed and perhaps persuaded her to buy shares in the company.

By the end of 1931 the list of Shareholders in Airspeed included principally the Directors, with Hewitt acting as proxy for Baldwin, and working shareholders such as Tom Laing and David Little. Apart from local interest including Mr Terry of the chocolate firm, other shareholders were either family of friends. Shute's parents had £50 of shares and his parents-in-law, Mr & Mrs Heaton, £10 each. Shute and Tiltman had £100 of shares each. Other subscribers included Shute's aunt, Grace Gadsden, with £50 and his old friend from Balliol, Alexander Rodger, with £10. All shares were in the ordinary class because they had decided against issuing preference shares which entitled the holder to a first call on profits. On being allotted the shares, the holders were required to pay ten shillings (50 pence) and the balance when called upon. On taking up his job, David Little spent some time chasing up payment of share balances.

As 1932 began, the Ferrys were being built and the infant company established but operating on a financial tightrope. Shute, surveying activity in the bus garage at that time, well knew of his responsibility to the 50 workers on the shop floor, of having to pull some rabbit out the hat in order to pay the wages at the end of the week. At this time, he was paying his suppliers strictly on time to build up a sound reputation but there were some weeks when the men were told they could be paid only part of their week's wages, but were promised another payment the following week. The overdraft at the bank was over £1,000, guaranteed by the directors, chiefly Lord Grimthorpe.

If Airspeed was an infant company to be nurtured, Shute knew too that there would soon be another infant to be taken care of; Frances was pregnant, with the baby expected in May.

Even before the Ferrys were barely off the drawing board, Shute, Tiltman and Cobham were discussing what they should build next. They anticipated the need for a fast aeroplane for four or five passengers plus pilot, to be operated by small airlines. As they were drawing up the specification for a low wing monoplane powered by a single radial engine, an article in *The Aeroplane* magazine described the new Lockheed Orion, which had a retractable undercarriage. Shute knew as soon as he saw this, that the next Airspeed aircraft must also have this innovation. They must be a pioneering company; to follow current practice would spell failure, for the larger companies would always have the advantages of scale. Shute was very keen to learn what he could about the Lockheed undercarriage and asked Cobham if he might write to Lockheed, as an aircraft operator, to see what information they might release to him. In other words Shute was asking him to indulge in a little industrial espionage and Cobham agreed to find out what he could. The design for the Courier, as the new plane was to be called, took shape during 1932, Tiltman producing an attractive low wing monoplane capable of flying at over 150 mph, carrying four passengers. As a compromise the undercarriage did not retract fully into the wing, and the lower half protruded, which meant that the plane could be landed with the undercarriage up, the only damage being, generally, a bent propeller. Tiltman designed every part of the undercarriage system, including remarkably, the hydraulic actuator. A patent for the retractable undercarriage was applied for in 1932 and, although Shute was much involved in its inception, the patent carried just the names of Airspeed Ltd and Tiltman.[7] Shute's name did not appear on the patent. Some years later, Shute had an idea for an instrument for indicating to a pilot the relative density of the air. Air density was a significant factor for optimum petrol consumption, with engine mixture settings being adjusted accordingly. With increasing altitude the air density decreased but also air temperature played a part—colder air was denser than warmer air. All aircraft had an altimeter to show the height and some had an indicator for outside air temperature. Shute's idea was mechanically to combine the readings from these two instruments to give the pilot a visual indication of relative air density. He was granted a patent in 1938 for this invention[8] and it bore his name with that of Airspeed.

By early March 1932 the first Ferry was finished and ready to be test flown. The limitations of the bus garage had become all too apparent as it was being built. The wings were in sections, so that the fuselage would just fit through the door at the end of the building. When they did a trial fitting of the wings inside the garage, the fuselage had to be slewed round diagonally to accommodate the full wingspan. In its dismantled form the Ferry was towed late at night from the garage the twenty miles to Sherburn and this was not without incident. Firstly, the bolts holding the tail shoe onto the towing vehicle broke, and a local garage proprietor was roused to provide new bolts. At 2 a.m. they met a large truck with the rudder of the liner *Berengaria* going the other way and had to manhandle the machine into a side road to let the truck pass. Finally they got to Sherburn just as dawn was breaking. There had been much discussion as to the test pilot for the crucial first flight. Shute would have liked to pilot the Ferry himself, but decided that his flying experience was inadequate. After some discussion they engaged Harry Worrall of the Yorkshire Aero Club as the pilot, but they could afford only £30 for his services. On 12

April, when the machine had been assembled and checked, Worrall taxied around the aerodrome for a while to get the feel of the controls, turned into wind and took off after a short run. Worrall was delighted with the aircraft, and only minor adjustments were needed after the flight.

The Ferry was designed to carry ten passengers, and this in itself had raised a problem with the Air Ministry. Regulations required that all aircraft carrying ten passengers or more had to be fitted with wireless. Shute wrote to the Ministry, requesting that this regulation be waived for the Ferry, as it would be used only for joyriding purposes. Back came the reply that "after careful consideration" the Ministry was not prepared to grant an exemption that wireless be fitted. It took the combined pressure of letters from both Cobham and Shute before the Ministry finally agreed to exempt the fitting of wireless.[9] The irony was that, because of the bulk of wireless equipment in those days, two seats would have to be removed to fit it, thus making the aircraft an 8-seater and exempt from this regulation!

Now that the Ferry had flown, Cobham and Shute were anxious to get it through its airworthiness test without delay so that it could join the National Aviation Day Display fleet as quickly as possible. In those days the test flights were carried out at Martlesham Heath near Woodbridge in Suffolk. No doubt to everyone's relief, the Air Ministry and RAF gave this priority and it passed through Martlesham in just four days without any trouble and received its Certificate of Airworthiness. The first Ferry, named *Youth of Britain II*, was flying with Cobham's display by the third week of April. Over the coming years it flew many thousands of passengers in the displays, giving most of them their first experience of flying.

Airspeed had the second Ferry in production and planned to build two more for stock. Shute appreciated that marketing was as important to the company as producing a good product. He corresponded a good deal with Cobham on this aspect and followed up every potential sales lead for the Ferry that came up, one enquiry being for its use to provide a local air service between Bristol and Cardiff. He produced a brochure on the Ferry, which gave details, not only of its specification and performance, but also included the favourable comments on its handling by the Martlesham pilots.

The second Ferry was delivered to National Aviation Display shortly after the first, and the second two were sold to Midland and Scottish Air Ferries whose director, John Sword, made Airspeed take his 6.5

litre Bentley in part payment for the fourth aircraft. Shute drove this magnificent car from Ayr to London. It was a difficult car to sell in that time of depression and was eventually sold for about £400. The Ferry was built to suit Cobham's rather specialised requirements, but it did have the potential for providing economical air passenger transport. However the prospects for sales of more Ferries were killed off by the arrival, early in 1933, of the de Havilland Dragon, an aircraft that was faster than the Ferry and cheaper.

For Shute two events, one happy the other sad, happened within weeks of each other. On 31 May 1932 Frances gave birth to a daughter who was christened Heather Felicity. On 25 June his mother Mary died in Devon at the age of 71. The major general's daughter, who had born the loss of her first son in the Great War, had lived to see her second son achieve an important job in his chosen career of aviation, marry and produce a granddaughter. It was probably partly at Shute's urging that Mary Norway's book on the Sinn Fein rebellion had been published.

Two main problems beset Airspeed in its early years, the continual shortage of cash and the fact the bus garage was really quite unsuitable for the production of aircraft in any numbers. It was right in the heart of York, with difficult access and remote from any aerodrome. On the financial side, the bank overdraft rose continuously, so that by the end of 1932 it stood at around £6,000 guaranteed by its directors, principally Lord Grimthorpe. It came as a surprise to no one that the company recorded a loss at the end if its first full year of trading. During this period the combined salaries of Shute, Tiltman and Laing was £1,700 a year. The total wage bill for the workshop staff amounted to around £3,500. Woodworkers were paid 1/6d (7.5p) per hour, the foreman £4 10/- (£4.50) a week and the typist/secretary £2 10/- (£2.50) per week.[10] By the end of the first year invested capital had increased to around £11,000, but the Ferry aircraft had been built with slim margins and were being paid for in instalments from the profits of National Aviation Day.

What Airspeed needed was, ideally, a factory adjacent to an aerodrome. From the outset Hull Development Corporation had actively tried to interest Airspeed in moving to their airport. The Blackburn aircraft company was established there and the Corporation wanted to see more aviation companies in the same place. They wrote to Cobham, and Shute himself visited Hull to see what they had to offer, but in the end Hull could not offer sufficient incentives. However Shute would visit

National Aviation Day as it toured the length and breadth of the country to correct minor problems on the Ferrys. He would discuss new locations for Airspeed and try to secure an order from Cobham for the Courier. Shute loved to watch the flying displays with stunts and aerobatics, and Cobham's National Aviation Day featured, many years later, in his novel *Round the Bend*. Crashes and mishaps were not uncommon. In October Shute and Frances were present at one of Cobham's displays in nearby Harrogate where a pilot, with two passengers on board, failed to pull out of a spin and crashed in an adjacent field. Frances, being a doctor, rushed to give what assistance she could, but one passenger died and the pilot was badly injured.[11]

Gradually the choice of new location for Airspeed was narrowed down to Portsmouth. It was a hectic time for Shute, entailing a lot of travelling, days away from home whilst keeping an eye on the company and up to date on the evolution of the Courier design. By July 1932 negotiations were well advanced with Portsmouth, who offered Airspeed what Shute later called generous terms to make it attractive for them to move to a new factory on the airport there.

Portsmouth was the eighth largest municipal aerodrome in the country, and a very new one. Opened on 2 July 1932, by Sir Philip Sassoon, the Under-Secretary of State for Air, it had an area of 204 acres, with grass strips 4,500 feet (1372 m) and 2,400 feet (732 m) long. The opening was a gala event, with over 100 visiting aircraft and an air display watched by 50,000 people. The *Graf Zeppelin* marked the occasion by diverting to fly over the display, and, no doubt, have a look at the Naval Dockyard. The local flying club offered flying lessons, and a pilot's 'A' Licence cost £30. In August Sir Alan Cobham brought his National Aviation Display to Portsmouth and took members of the Corporation for trips in the Ferry. His comment was that it was the best aerodrome from which he had operated.

In April 1932, Cobham had placed an order for the Courier, which he wanted for carrying out further development work on in-flight re-fuelling. His idea was to put this on a better basis than merely lowering jerry cans from one aircraft to another as had been done previously. His method was that the aircraft to be refuelled would fly in formation just behind and below the tanker. The tanker aircraft would then trail a line which was picked up and pulled in, bringing a hose through which the refuelling was done. For his experiments he wanted a fast light aircraft and, for publicity, he announced that he would attempt a record-breaking non-stop flight from England to Australia using in-flight refuelling. The Courier was to be that aircraft, Lord Wakefield having agreed to sponsor the record attempt to the extent of £10,000, made up of £5,000 for the aircraft and £5,000 for incidental expenses.

By the middle of 1932 the design of the Courier was well advanced but the engine for it was a point of concern. For the Ferry, Airspeed had bought the Gipsy engines from de Havilland, in effect buying engines from a competing aircraft manufacturer, no matter that it was one that Shute and Tiltman knew well. Lord Grimthorpe was chairman of a company in London that had the agency for Wolseley cars and it was through this connection that Airspeed became interested in the aero engine that Wolseley were designing. Lord Grimthorpe went to visit the newly formed Wolseley Aero Engines Ltd to discuss their designs. It was early days, for Wolseley did not expect to be in production with their engine until 1933. So the choice for the Courier was the Armstrong Siddeley Cheetah engine. At least Armstrong Siddeley confined themselves to making cars and engines and not aircraft.

With prospects for further sales of the Ferry almost nil and a move to Portsmouth in the offing, the future of Airspeed depended upon making a success of the Courier. It is little wonder that Lord Grimthorpe, who had the greatest financial stake in Airspeed, questioned Shute on whether the Courier really needed so novel a feature as a retractable undercarriage. He had asked an eminent designer; who thought it would do well if Airspeed would forget about the retractable undercarriage; the designer had looked into it and it could not be made to work reliably. This subject was raised in a cafe whilst Shute and Lord Grimthorpe were waiting for their train after a meeting with Portsmouth Council about the move to the airport. Shute had to think hard and talk hard to convince his chairman that Airspeed had to be innovative and not merely follow what other companies were doing. That route, to Shute's mind, would spell failure, for the larger companies would inevitably win out. Their only hope was to lead the way. It says much for Lord Grimthorpe's faith in both Shute and Tiltman that he allowed them to go on with the retractable undercarriage.

The designer that Lord Grimthorpe had consulted was either Sydney Camm, who later designed the Hawker Hurricane or R.J. Mitchell, designer of the Spitfire. Shute later wrote that "wild horses" would not make him reveal which of these men Lord Grimthorpe had consulted. He merely noted that both these famous aircraft, of course, had retractable undercarriages.

Although hopes for the company were centred on the Courier, other avenues were explored, principally designs of small light aircraft for the private market. Both Shute and Cobham had looked into designs for this type of aircraft and had rejected many of them as unsuitable. However Airspeed were contacted by W.S. Shackleton and Lee Murray to produce a light aircraft of their design, known as the SM.1. Their design was for a tandem two-seat aircraft with a parasol wing and pusher engine arrangement. The parasol term meant that the wing was connected to the fuselage by struts. It was in fact almost a copy of the American Curtis Jenny. Airspeed built the SM.1 in the winter of 1932–33 when work on the Ferrys had tailed off and the prototype Courier was being built and it gave the workshop something else to build. Only one was ever built and its costs escalated to a point that gave little confidence in its future. The one that was built, registered G-ACBP, was powered by a German Hirth engine of 60 hp. Shute must have flown it, probably at Sherburn, for he described it as slow and underpowered but delightful to fly. The SM.1 was bought by A.A. Bathurst (Lord Apsley) & Miss D. Miles-Yate. It lasted until 1937 when its was broken up. The SM.1 was Airspeed's last excursion into light aircraft for the private flyer market and was the only time they built an aircraft that they had not designed themselves.

The contract with Portsmouth City Council for the new factory was signed and the move down south was being planned. Employees were notified that "In the present difficult circumstances, the Company can pay no removal or travelling expenses of any sort to any employee. This applies to all grades including Directors . . . If any employee wishes the Secretary to keep back a portion of his pay to provide for the unavoidable personal expenses which will have to be incurred, he should see Mr Little about it."[12]

On completion of the design work on the Courier, several draughtsmen had to be dismissed. To add to their troubles the centre engine and fuel tank on the Ferry for John Sword was a new design, and everything fouled due to unsatisfactory work on the part of one of the draughtsman. Delivery was set back, and this in turn affected work on the Courier.

The Royal Aircraft Establishment at Farnborough had been consulted over the stressing of the Courier wing. There was very little data on

cantilever wings and it was not easy to determine whether the deflection
of the wing due to flight loads imposed a similar deflection on both front
and rear spars. Also the influence of the retractable undercarriage on stress
levels was not clearly established. It was finally agreed that R.A.E. would
send a team to York with a lorry full of sand bags. The wing would then
be proof loaded and the deflections measured under simulated flight loads.

In March, 1933 the company moved in a convoy of lorries from York
to the new Portsmouth factory. Of the hundred or so men then working
at York only about 50 moved south. Later some of those who could not
find jobs and were doubtless influenced by the prospect of better weather
followed on, and did not return to the north. With the nucleus who did
move south, Airspeed built up a competent and stable labour force in a
short time. One working shareholder who moved with the company was
Lord Ronaldshay, a nephew of Lord Grimthorpe. He had been working
on the shop floor in York, unpaid, but had quite suddenly announced
that he would invest £1,000 in Airspeed. This may have left him short of
money to buy a house in Portsmouth, for an estate agent there was rather
surprised to find a titled gentleman looking for cheap housing in the area.

At last the whole of the Airspeed team was under one roof, with a
fine aerodrome outside the door. They had a working area three times
the size of the York premises and were optimistic that lower unit costs
could be achieved. Cobham's Courier was almost complete when the
move took place. It only required rectification of slight damage caused
in transit before it was ready for testing.

Shute and Frances, with baby Heather, moved from their flat at 7
Clifton and rented a house at 44 Craneswater Park in Southsea just a
mile or two from the new factory. For Shute it marked the end of his
seven remarkable years in Yorkshire, but he no doubt moved south full
of confidence that, with the new location, a vast improvement on the
old bus garage, Airspeed could now firmly establish itself as a significant
manufacturer of aircraft.

Since publishing *Lonely Road* he had written no more novels, but he
had not given up writing altogether. At Clifton he wrote a number of
articles and short stories. "Down the Humber in a Motor Cruiser",[13] the
article about his boating trip on the Yorkshire rivers, has 7 Clifton on
its front page as does "Knightly Vigil",[14] a story about a pilot the night
before he is due to undertake a long flight, and "Tudor Windows",[15] a
strange story about a haunted house.

At this time he also wrote a short story entitled "The Uttermost Parts of the Sea"[16] which is arguably one of the best of this genre. It tells the story of a naval captain of an aircraft carrier rescuing a downed female transatlantic flyer and the resulting loss of some of the rescue aircraft. The story was never published but contains elements that Shute adapted for later novels.

Cobham's proposed non-stop flight to Australia with refuelling along the way had prompted him to sit down one Sunday in May 1932 and write to Cobham,[17] setting out the details of a non-stop transatlantic flight in the Courier, with a single in-flight refuelling over Iceland. He had worked out the details, distances, flight times, fuel consumption and reminded Cobham that he knew what he was talking about—he had flown the Atlantic twice (in *R.100*) and had worked on so many of Burney's schemes for an Atlantic service that he was very familiar with the whole thing. He measured route distances on a large globe, to fly to Reykjavik, over Greenland and on over Labrador to Rimouski. He believed it could be the sort of "trail-blazing Empire flight that might appeal to Lord Wakefield after the organisation had been proved on the Australian flight." He thought it would be "a red hot stunt". The flight never took place, but the details he had worked out he would use again in the epic flight of Donald Ross in *An Old Captivity*.

Once the Courier was ready at Portsmouth, the choice of a test pilot was again a concern to Shute. The future of the company and all its staff depended upon the Courier, and any error or accident at this critical stage might well mean ruin. The move had played havoc with finances, so a large fee for one of the major civilian test pilots was not affordable. Shute contacted Flight Lieutenant George Stainforth, a serving officer in the RAF based at the Royal Aircraft Establishment. He held the World Speed Record in the Schneider Trophy Supermarine S6b and was one of the finest test pilots in the country. He was greatly interested in the Courier and had no difficulty in obtaining permission from his superiors to fly it. So, for a very meagre fee, Stainforth was engaged for this very responsible task. The retractable undercarriage had been thoroughly tested statically, but in flight the loading conditions were an unknown quantity.

The first flight was a surprise even to Tiltman, who had calculated a top speed at sea level of 155 mph. Farnborough had predicted 145 mph. The actual figure was 163 mph. The difference in speed with the undercarriage up and down was 37 mph, which was greater than envisaged and a testament to Shute's belief that the Courier must have this feature.

Stainforth was very impressed, for the Courier handled extremely well. He flew it for about five hours, and by masterly flying, saved it from disaster. He was taking off over Langstone Harbour and was at 300 feet climbing steeply with the wheels up, when suddenly the engine failed. Stainforth reacted instantly, the nose went down to maintain speed and the wheels went down as he turned gently down wind and landed smoothly on the aerodrome.

On another occasion an engine failure caused a rather rough landing just outside the aerodrome. Both radius rods collapsed, but by a miracle they jammed against the structure in a manner which prevented total undercarriage collapse and serious damage.

Stainforth completed the initial performance trials and there was great interest in the subsequent Airworthiness trials at Martlesham. Later in the year when Shute and Tiltman were flying with another pilot to Brooklands to demonstrate the aircraft, a hydraulic connection failed. Fortunately it was accessible in the air and Shute, in the second seat, was able to hold the two parts together whilst the undercarriage was pumped down and locked.

There were other occasions where Couriers landed with the wheels retracted, in some cases because the pilots forgot they had to lower the undercarriage before landing! The reliability of the Retractor undercarriage, as it was called, was attested by the Portsmouth, Southsea and Isle of Wight Aviation Company which operated Couriers from Portsmouth airport. They wrote that the undercarriage had been raised and lowered over 5000 times, a testimonial that featured in a Courier brochure.

The publicity for Airspeed aircraft, starting with the Courier, was done by twin brothers, Cavendish and Concord Morton. Both were trained artists and had set themselves up as C&C Morton, of Bembridge in the Isle of Wight, to do commercial work. Cavendish, or Cavvy as he was known, had a great interest in aircraft and knew George Stainforth and it was through him that they got an introduction to Airspeed. It was Concord, known as Conc, who designed the Airspeed logo with its art deco lettering. The brochures they produced, whilst giving all the necessary technical information, were well illustrated with an artistry that marked them out from the usual bland technical publications. Cavvy was a gifted painter of both land and seascapes; he and Shute became good friends and later sailed together in the Solent on more than one occasion.

The omens were initially favourable for the Courier. The Air Ministry became very interested in this new aircraft which was to have an impact on the design of military aircraft. Also Cobham's projected flight to Australia had been widely publicised in the national press, and the Courier had been the subject of very favourable comment in the aviation press, but orders were slow to materialise. The Aircraft Exchange and Mart Company were appointed selling agents for the Courier and on 4 September 1933 they took delivery of their demonstrator, G-ACJL; two other machines were being built. Cobham, with Squadron Leader Helmore, was developing flight refuelling techniques for the flight to Australia in G-ABXN. This Courier had a hatch in the roof just behind the pilot. Shute himself later recalled standing in the roof hatch attempting to catch the trailing weight lowered from the tanker aircraft and then hauling in the transfer hose.

An early test of this sort almost ended in disaster. The four-pound weight on the trail rope was near to the Courier with Helmore trying to catch it. Cobham banked slightly to bring it within reach, when he suddenly found the machine was in a violent sideslip with a jammed aileron control. The weight had entered the aileron gap and wedged itself solidly in position on the port side. Attempts to centralise the stick and stabilise the Courier only jammed the controls more tightly, height was being lost at an alarming rate and six turns of a spiral dive had been completed before it was realised what had happened. Cobham threw the stick violently to starboard and the weight dropped out, but by that time the aircraft was perilously close to the spire of Chichester cathedral. Both Cobham and Helmore were considerably shaken by the time they landed.[18] Then, one of the ground engineers produced a condom which, filled with water, could act as the trailing weight but burst if it got trapped. They tried this next day and it worked well. Larger versions of this were made by Dunlop but when writing of this episode years later, Shute used the term "child's toy balloon".

The move to Portsmouth and the consequent disruption of production had been expensive. The move alone had cost just over £1,000. The Board had decided to lay down a production line of six Couriers and the overdraft had risen to £10,000. Lord Grimthorpe took up another £1,000 of shares and gave a personal bank guarantee of another £5,000. This prompted a bold and generous gesture on the part of the group of working shareholders who were not members of the Board. They were so convinced that the company would prosper that they collectively, with-

out consulting either Shute or Tiltman, offered the Company a further
£12,000 in the form of debentures. Certainly faith in the future of the
company was needed, for the orders for Couriers came from impecunious airline operators who required hire purchase terms and paid initial
deposits of as little as £5.

During that period, finance was a recurrent nightmare, and to add
to their problems, an extension to the factory had been agreed with the
Portsmouth Corporation to cater for Courier production. One day Shute
said to Tiltman that they were in serious trouble. It was Thursday and
the following day, Friday, they must pay the wages. They were over their
overdraft limit with the bank. He had approached the other Directors
and no one could cough up another penny. Tiltman wondered what on
earth they could do. Shute sent for the man who collected the wages and
briefed him to take the wages cheque to the bank in the normal way,
whistle blithely as he handed it over, and say "Wages please." When he
had the money he was to leave the bank quickly. It worked. The money
was handed over without demur. Fortunately a Courier was sold during
the following week, and the financial problem was sorted out for the
time being.[19]

Three Couriers were ordered by Stanley Bell, of London, Scottish & Provincial Airways Limited. Two were delivered and based at
Sherburn in Elmet, where the Ferry had first flown. The route was from
Sherburn to Paris, via Nottingham and London, and the flight time,
including stops, was less than three hours. It was hoped to extend the
service to Glasgow.

The Couriers were supplied on hire purchase and the struggling
airline was always in financial trouble. Just before a take-off for Paris,
two bowler-hatted gentlemen appeared and told the pilot that they had
instructions to impound the aeroplane in settlement of a fuel bill for
£300. The pilot was somewhat nonplussed as he had three passengers in
the cabin, but he rose to the occasion and suggested to the bailiffs that
they should at least have a look at the machine they were to impound.
They took the bait and climbed inside. The pilot immediately slammed
the door and took off. On arrival at Paris the unwilling passengers were
promptly taken into custody for arriving without passports, whilst the
Courier went about its normal business. The oil company, to whom the
money was owed, was so amused by the incident that, apparently, they
gave the airline a further three months credit.[20]

By the end of 1933 with the cost of moving to Portsmouth, an expansion of the factory under way, but orders for Couriers few and far between,
Airspeed once again made a loss for the year. The Shareholders meeting,
at which the loss of £6,846 was announced, was held in Shute's office
at the works, attended by the Directors and working shareholders. This
produced no sense of crisis, since those who worked for the company knew
its precarious financial state. There were some hopeful signs though. The
Air Ministry had placed an order for a Courier, and the Society of British
Aircraft Constructors were to admit Airspeed as associate members. The
S.B.A.C. had reached an agreement that only Society members would
receive Government orders. Admission to their "circle" would mean that
Airspeed did not have to rely solely on civil orders. Another distinction
at that time was that Shute and Tiltman were both elected as Fellows of
the Royal Aeronautical Society. Both had been Associates of the Society,
a professional requirement for practising aeronautical engineers with a
degree. They were awarded the honour of Fellowship by virtue of their
work on the retractable undercarriage, but also, in Shute's case he thought
his work on the *R.100* was also a factor.[21]

At the start of 1934, although they had achieved technical success
and had been noticed by the Air Ministry, financially the company was
in dire straits. The monies owed to trade creditors were mounting, and
payment of monthly salaries was falling in arrears. New capital was
urgently needed or the company would surely go under. It was really too
early for a public issue of shares, for there were only two years of losses
to show for their efforts. Shute had always advocated a bold approach,
for example, persuading the Board to produce batches of Couriers. He
encouraged Tiltman to press ahead with the next design of aircraft, a
twin-engined passenger aircraft to suit the airline market, a design which
became the Airspeed Envoy. He therefore set about the search for new
capital investment and embarked on a path to obtain it that was to earn
him a reputation for recklessness.

At this time Swan Hunter and Wigham Richardson, the long
established shipbuilders on Tyneside, took an interest in Airspeed. Shipbuilding was in decline. The Airspeed factory was adjacent to Langstone
Harbour, which was expected to be the base for flying boat services.
Swan Hunter reasoned that Airspeed could build such flying boats with,
perhaps, the hulls being built in the empty slipways of Tyneside. After
months of discussion through the intermediary of the Federated Trust

and Finance Company an agreement was finally reached with Swan Hunter. The original Airspeed company would be liquidated and a new company formed in which Swan Hunter would have the controlling interest. There would be a public issue of shares in the new company which was to be known as Airspeed (1934) Ltd. The issue was to be for a mixture of ordinary and preference shares which, after costs, was expected to raise £78,000 of new capital. Swan Hunter would acquire all the existing plant, machinery, buildings, stock and work in progress. The question Shute had to decide was how to value the company's assets and in particular the stock and work in progress.

This valuation would be crucial to the success of the share issue. The stock and work in progress was, of course, the Courier aircraft, and their value depended on their saleability. Most of them were ordered by impecunious airlines on hire purchase terms. If the purchasers defaulted, then the aircraft would come back to the company, most likely to remain unsold. To the auditors of Airspeed this was a reason to write down or even write off their value. Shute argued that all the aircraft in production would be sold and at the market price. This was based on rumours of re-armament and a hunch that, if a war broke out, the Couriers would be snapped up. If he agreed with the auditors that the Couriers should be written off, then £20,000 would be taken off the value of Airspeed with the prospect that the new company would continue making a loss and therefore not be an attractive prospect for new shareholders. To give full value to the Couriers would indicate that the new company could move forward to making a profit and make it an attractive investment.

Having set his hand to creating Airspeed, Shute was determined that it should succeed at all costs. For himself and the other directors he was not so concerned. If the company folded they could all get other jobs and perhaps Frances could take up her career again as a doctor for a time, though that would be difficult with an infant child. Shute felt his responsibility to the workforce very keenly, for Airspeed now employed 400 on the shop floor. With the prospect of new capital Shute had increased the manpower and materials to the limit, having persuaded the Board to lay down production for batches of aircraft. If he did not do his utmost to ensure the success of the share issue then 400 workers would be out of a job in a time of high unemployment. No doubt his mind went back to laying off staff at Howden when airship work came to an end. Now he had responsibility for many more workers and their families. He took the risk, stood firm, and insisted that the stock should be valued at full market price, and in the end he won his battle with the company's auditors Messrs Peat, Marwick, Mitchell and Co.

So the complicated process of the public share issue began and complex it was. There was Montagu Vincent, the liquidator of Airspeed, the issuing firm of Federated Trust and Finance Corporation, the stockbrokers Messrs Vowler Paine, one law firm for the issue and another for the company. All these parties had to be involved. For Shute it was a steep learning curve and there was no-one to coach him as Hewitt had in the early days, and as before, there was a new prospectus to be drafted and issued. He had to cope almost single handed with all this. He spent a considerable time in the City of London dealing with the formation of the new company as well as overseeing the running of the existing one. At the same time he kept abreast of the progress of the new Envoy, then being built on the shop floor.

Finally on 24 July the new prospectus was issued[22] with invitations to subscribe. There, for all to see, were the assets of the old company that Airspeed (1934) had been formed to acquire. The stocks and work in progress "as certified by the Managing Director" were valued at £23,004. Also in the small print was a statement by the auditors that the loss for 1931–32 was £2,371 and for 1932–33, £3,437 but these losses were calculated before charging expenditure on experimental work, design, jigs and patents and the cost of moving to Portsmouth. This made the previous losses seem less than in fact they were. It was also stated that, on this same basis, the company was now running at a profit. Further, the prospectus said of the original Airspeed that "As is inevitable in establishing a production business, losses have been incurred which are in the nature of development expenditure. That stage has now been passed . . . and a net profit is now being earned."

Shute's desired objective, an attractive proposition for investors, had therefore been achieved. The prospectus also revealed that the new company had entered into a contract "appointing Mr Norway joint Managing Director for five years at a remuneration of £1,000 [per year] together with 5% of the net profits earned by the company in any year." Tiltman also had the same contract terms. Their jobs would thus be secure until 1939.

The share issue was a great success, with Swan Hunter taking up the majority shareholding. However all was not quite plain sailing with the issue. There were irregularities in the allotment letters to shareholders, sufficient to warrant investigation by the City of London police. Their initial enquiries with Federated Trust and Finance, the issuers, revealed that about 15,000 allotment letters were affected where names were wrongly spelt or addresses incorrect. This represented a sum of about £4,000 in share value, but that only about £1,200 of cash had been paid. Shute made a statement to the press[23] that "We first discovered the irregularities when letters were presented to a broker for sale. The clerk noticed that the names were wrongly spelt. When the broker's attention was drawn to the matter he consulted the share register and found that names did not correspond. We have no reason to think that fraudulent dealing in the shares has forced up their price." The irregularities were cleared up and there was no further action by the police. This investigation must have come as a shock to Shute that such, possibly fraudulent, activities could happen in City institutions.

The share issue was in fact over subscribed, probably helped by the fact that the new Airspeed Envoy aircraft appeared in public at that time. Tiltman had done a superb job, creating a good looking twin-engined machine capable of carrying up to 8 passengers. The aircraft used the new Wolseley Aires aero engine which Shute was enthusiastic about. The initial discussions by Lord Grimthorpe had evidently born fruit.

With the new capital, the future of Airspeed must have seemed assured. Yet another extension to the factory was put in hand to cater for production of Envoys. Also the company started the Airspeed Aeronautical College to provide training in all aspects of the aeronautical profession. The decision to set up the College may well have been inspired by the equivalent de Havilland Aeronautical Technical School which had been established some years earlier. Clearly Airspeed intended to be seen as a rival in this aspect as well as in aircraft design and manufacture. The Airspeed College offered a three year course at a fee of 250 guineas (£262.50). The course involved the students spending time in all the departments both on the shop floor and in the design and drawing offices with attendance at evening lectures from 5 to 7:15 p.m. The idea was to give students a good all-round training, both theoretical and practical. Indeed the College brochure[24] contains the following in its Introduction, which may well have been written by Shute: "The theoretical side of the student's training is most important, but theory alone will never enable him to earn his living in the aircraft industry. It is the practical application of theory that is of vital importance right from the commencement of his training and that is why a student at the Airspeed Aeronautical College attains a high standard of efficiency in practical aeronautical engineering during his three years' course of instruction."

Over the years the College produced a number of aeronautical engineers who went on to have distinguished careers in the industry.

In 1934 the MacRobertson Air Race from England to Melbourne was announced and this attracted pilots who approached Airspeed to build aircraft to take part. Not only that, some of the Airspeed Directors wanted the company to sponsor entrants, believing that it would provide excellent publicity, although Shute was not convinced of the value of such publicity. Airspeed were quite flattered with the number of pilots who approached them to design aircraft, amongst them Amy Johnson who wanted a fast twin-engined machine specially built for the race. Airspeed had no capacity to quote for such a machine. She and her husband, Jim Mollison, went to de Havilland and entered one of the three special DH88 Comet machines for the race. In the end, two Airspeed aircraft were entered for the race. One was a Courier flown by Squadron Leader Stoddard and his nephew. The second was a special version of the Envoy to be flown by Neville Stack and S.L. Turner. So many modifications to the Envoy were needed that the machine built for Stack was designated the Viceroy. Cheetah engines, supplied free of charge, were fitted together with long range fuel tanks. Stack had difficulty raising the required finance and contracted to buy the machine from Airspeed on hire purchase terms. Due to various delays the aircraft was not ready until the day before the race entry list closed. Stack and Turner arrived at Portsmouth to collect the Viceroy on Saturday 13 October. In order to be allowed to compete in the race they had to be at Mildenhall airfield in Suffolk the following day. Before flying the aircraft from Portsmouth they had to sign the hire purchase agreement and were given assurances that the aircraft had been flown by Airspeed's test pilot and was in good order. They started the race with all the other entrants on 20 October, were forced to land at Abbeville in France and finally retired from the race at Athens.

They then began a legal action against Airspeed for rescission of the hire purchase agreement and repayment of the £2,448 paid by them to Airspeed.[25] They alleged that Airspeed had been negligent in ensuring that the aircraft was airworthy. The case came before Mr Justice Finlay in the High Court in London on 10 December 1934, and Shute was present in Court throughout the case, which lasted 3 days. Giving evidence, Stack said that Airspeed had demanded he sign the hire purchase agreement before he was allowed to fly the plane from Portsmouth. During the week before the race he had found a number of faults on the aircraft despite Airspeed's assurance that the plane had been flown by their pilot and was satisfactory. During the race they found the compass in error, they smelled burning crossing the Channel and landed at Abbeville to investigate only to find that the electrics on the undercarriage had gone wrong. They found one of the brakes binding and stayed the night to cure the problem. The following day they found the fuel consumption much higher than it should have been and finally landed at Athens to retire from the race.

One by one the barrister for Airspeed questioned Stack's claims. He asked Stack if he remembered Mr Norway remarking on his tiredness before the race, asking him if he and Turner really wanted to take part. Stack did not remember that. Gradually under questioning Stack admitted that his claims about fuel consumption might have been exaggerated and the defects rather more trivial than he claimed. Certainly they had not made the machine unsafe to fly. On the third day Stack and Turner withdrew their action, agreed to return the plane to Airspeed together with a further £1,850 that was due to the company.

In conclusion Mr Justice Finlay said that both parties had taken a wise course. It was "certainly satisfactory that charges of fraud made against men of high standing in their profession [among them Shute] had been withdrawn." Airspeed's reputation was upheld and Shute had spent three days in court absorbing, with his writer's eye, its procedure and detail, which he was to use in future novels.

The Courier entered by the Stoddards put up a good performance in the race arriving at Melbourne in 9 days 18 hours to finish 6th overall on handicap. Amy and Jim Mollison in their DH 88 Comet led for much of the race until forced to retire in India with engine trouble. The winners on handicap were pilots from the Dutch airline KLM flying the new all-metal Douglas DC2 aircraft.

In September Cobham was at last ready to attempt his long-delayed non-stop flight to Australia with in-flight refuelling. On 22nd the Courier flown by Cobham with Helmore on board, took off from Portsmouth and was refuelled over the Channel. They flew on to Malta where a second tanker aircraft was stationed for the next refuelling. This was completed satisfactorily but the throttle on the Courier was no longer effective; the butterfly on the carburettor was spring loaded fully open and could not be closed. Cobham had no choice but to land at Malta and just managed to land with full tanks. The fault was trivial. A split pin on the throttle control had fallen out and the linkage had become detached and, as designed, the throttle sprang fully open. When he landed Cobham was told that the W10 tanker used in the first refuelling had crashed whilst returning to re-join National Aviation Day. All the crew had perished in the crash. He returned to England at once.

With the formation of Airspeed (1934) Ltd, Swan Hunter had appointed three new Directors to the Board. Charles Swan was Vice Chairman of Swan Hunter and Sir Philip Wigham Richardson one of its Directors. These rather elderly gentlemen could not understand the mentality of these, to their mind, frivolous aeronautical engineers. One of them reportedly asked why it took 35 draughtsmen to design the aeroplanes when Swan Hunter had designed the liner *Mauretania* with less. The third appointee was the younger George Wigham Richardson, son of Sir Philip, who was keen to learn all he could about Airspeed and became an enthusiast for it. With the formation of the new Board, Lord Grimthorpe stepped down as Chairman and George Richardson took his place. Lord Grimthorpe, living in Yorkshire, had found it increasingly difficult to devote the necessary time to Airspeed after its move to Portsmouth. He remained a Director of the company. Shute had good reason to be grateful to Lord Grimthorpe for his faith in the company and its two founders. Without his financial backing in the early days it would surely have gone bust.

Another Swan Hunter man who joined Airspeed was Alfred Townsley. As a senior production man at the shipyard, he was appointed to help sort out production problems at Portsmouth. His shipyard friends thought he was mad to make the move, but he went ahead and spent the remainder of his working life with Airspeed and made an immense contribution to its success. To begin with he worked alongside Tom Laing and Jimmy Watson the works foreman. Watson, who had worked on the *R.100* at Howden, and had been laid off when the Airship Guarantee Company closed down, joined Airspeed in the early days and moved south to Portsmouth.

1934 had been a remarkable and eventful year for Airspeed, with the formation of the new company, the share issue, Cobham's Courier flight and the MacRobertson race, not to mention the start up of the Aeronautical College and the production of the Envoy. Towards the end of the year Shute knew too that the following year he would become a father again. Frances was pregnant with the baby expected in March.

From the start all Airspeed aircraft had been built from wood, but the new technology of all-metal aircraft was emerging. The Douglas DC2 in the USA was leading the way and at that time Barnes Wallis was perfecting the geodetic design of metal construction for the Welles-ley and Wellington bombers. Anthony Fokker, the famous Dutch designer and manufacturer, then held the manufacturing rights to the DC2. The Swan Hunter members of the Board saw an association with Fokker as offering an independent view of the operations at Portsmouth. Tiltman and Shute too were initially impressed, as Fokker seemed to share their views on aerodynamic refinement and economic production. During the autumn and winter of 1934, Richardson and Shute conducted negotiations with Fokker, an elusive man who seemed to have no settled home. Meetings were held in places such as restaurants and at different times of day. On one occasion Colman, the Airspeed pilot, flew Tiltman and Shute from Portsmouth to Gravesend in Kent in a Courier for a meeting with Fokker who was flying in from Amsterdam. They very nearly met their doom, for the weather closed in badly and they had to make a forced landing in a ploughed field near Sevenoaks. As they landed, the Courier tipped on its nose as it came to rest. They were lucky, as the only damage was a bent propeller. When they eventually reached Gravesend by car they found that Fokker has flown the DC2 to Gatwick.[26]

Eventually an agreement was signed with Fokker who required a down payment of £20,000 for his services plus a further payment of £20,000 when turnover reached £100,000 and a 1% commission on turnover. It was, as Tiltman noted, a high price to pay for Fokker's services Tiltman himself visited Douglas in the USA to study the latest developments, but he privately doubted that Airspeed would ever build the DC2 under licence. In fact they never did and both the Envoy and the Oxford which evolved from it, were of wooden construction.

The agreement with Fokker produced no benefits at all for Airspeed despite the hopes of the Swan Hunter Directors that he would somehow magically transform the fortunes of the company and their dreams that flying boats would be built to operate from Langstone Harbour. In the spring of 1935 an enquiry was received from the Greek government for fighter aircraft. Though they favoured the Fokker D.17, for currency reasons, they could not buy from Holland. It seemed logical that Airspeed should build them under guidance from Fokker. Shute and a Fokker representative made arrangements to visit the Greek government to see if they could negotiate a contract.

Shortly before he went out to Greece, Frances gave birth on 6 March to their second daughter, Shirley Anne. Flora Twort, by then a friend of the family, was Shirley's godmother.

Shute and the Fokker representative spent three frustrating weeks in Athens attempting to obtain the contract to build the Fokker aircraft. The negotiations dragged on but got precisely nowhere. Shute came to the conclusion that the Greeks were impossible to deal with and flew home. He did acquire a store of experiences in that country that he would use in his next novel.

Back home, sales prospects for the company were improving, particularly for the Envoy. Orders were received from buyers of a better class than the cash-strapped operators who had bought Couriers on hire purchase terms. In particular the Envoy suited overseas airlines and Airspeed had active sales agents, notably Lord Ronaldshay and R.D. King, both ex-Airspeed employees, who had set up R.K. Dundas. However, despite better sales, profits still eluded Airspeed although an interim dividend was paid in January 1935 when orders in hand were sufficient to expect profitable working. At the end of the financial year in July 1935, the first anniversary of the new company, the new Chairman, George Wigham Richardson, had to announce a net loss of £4,353 due to sales falling short of expectations, particularly at home. Some of the smaller unsubsidised airlines for whom Airspeed's aircraft were suitable, had gone out of business. Looking ahead, the Chairman said that in the last half of the year "a considerable change for the better has taken place in the affairs of the Company, and I feel justified in pronouncing the prospects of the business to be very encouraging. In the last half year we have booked a considerable number of orders, which have resulted in sales to subsidised air lines operated under the control of various foreign governments. This type of business is most satisfactory, and I am confident that when we meet again I shall be able to report a further expansion of our business in this direction."[27] He indicated that the association with Fokker was yet to bear fruit but that work on the Douglas type of aircraft was being prosecuted energetically.

In fact this was not the case. Tiltman had his doubts about ever building the DC2 and both he and Shute were conscious of the fact that payments to Fokker were in reality draining cash from the company. In fact, Airspeed made another share issue in January 1935 to increase the capital by £130,000, in part to fund the payments to Fokker. Also Fokker, being a foreign national and privy to Airspeed's designs, was proving an impediment to obtaining orders from the Government, where constructors were required to sign the Official Secrets Act.

The growing difference between the outlook of the Swan Hunter directors, and Shute in particular, is perhaps exemplified by the response to an invitation from the Air Ministry at this time to tender for a high speed fighter. Shute had thought of the revolutionary concept of an aircraft with the pilot seated right aft and above the main airframe so that he could judge his landings with extreme accuracy. He discussed the idea with Tiltman and they produced the A.S 31, a Rolls Royce-engined aircraft with the pilot in a nacelle right in the tail of the aircraft. Wind tunnel tests on a model gave exceptionally good results but there was no support from the Ministry and it would, no doubt, have been an anathema to the conservative Directors on the Board.

There was another distasteful aspect to being Managing Director which began at this time. By early 1936 the company employed well over 500 people and those initial employees, such as David Little the company secretary, were just not able to cope with their jobs on this scale and had to be replaced. Another one was Tom Laing, who admitted he was out of his depth in dealing with trades unions, wages and rate fixing. In Laing's case he was happy to work under his replacement as Works Manager, H.W. Denny, and remained with Airspeed until his death in a road accident during the Second World War. Others however, such as Alfred Townsley, although from a shipbuilding background, proved his worth. He learned quickly about the aircraft industry with energy and enthusiasm and in July 1936 was appointed General Manager of the company and ultimately became a Director. George Errington had joined the company in September 1934 as an aircraft inspector. However his skill as a pilot was soon recognised by Colman, who chose him to be another Airspeed test pilot. Another who joined Airspeed at about this time was Sydney Hansel with whom Shute formed a lasting friendship.

With the outbreak of the Spanish Civil war, a number of the Couriers were sold and for prices above their market value. Shute had been right to value them as he did when the new company was formed and he may well have taken some satisfaction in proving the auditors wrong. The machines destined for Spain were stored in a hangar, but one morning two Airspeed employees broke in, started up a Courier, taxied it out and attempted a take off but crashed into a ditch at the edge of the airfield. Joseph Smith and Arthur Gargett were hoping to fly the machine to Spain, either to make their fortune or because they were Republican sympathisers. Neither had ever flown a plane before. In the crash Gargett died and Smith was badly injured. Shute gave evidence at Smith's subsequent trial. Smith was convicted and went to prison for four months.[28]

For the Envoy, the chosen engine was the Wolseley A.R.9 radial. This engine was modern in design, had a geared propeller, and Shute thought it was a considerable technical advance on other British aero engines in its power range of 250 hp. It also had the advantage that it saved Airspeed from buying engines from their competitors for it had been developed by the Nuffield motor car organisation. It suited Airspeed's aircraft well and at that time almost all of their production had been switched onto the Wolseley engine, which had been developed at a cost of £200,000. So it came as a real blow when Lord Nuffield announced in 1936 that they would cease making the engine. Nuffield's decision arose from the system adopted by the Air Ministry. The ordering procedure used I.T.P. (Instruction to Proceed) contract terms. These specified a maximum fixed price, which could, after investigation, be less. Lord Nuffield got the I.T.P. contract documents for the Wolseley radial aero engine and realised the implications. The terms would have required re-orientation of their offices with an army of accountants to keep track of production costs. He decided to deal only with the War Office and the Admiralty, who did not use the I.T.P. procedure. So the aero engine project was abandoned, much to Shute's dismay. He regarded it as a major disaster for Airspeed and decided that he must make an effort to see if Nuffield could be persuaded to change his mind. After a brief telephone call with Richardson he arranged a visit to Lord Nuffield in Oxford. What Shute hoped for was to persuade Nuffield to give Airspeed his engine business for nothing, for they hadn't anything like the £200,000 to pay for it. Another possibility in Shute's mind was to create another public company to take the aero engine business over.

Lord Nuffield received him courteously. This was the same William Morris whom Shute, as a schoolboy, had watched building his cars in

Longwall Street, Oxford. Recently ennobled, he was the head of a large motor car manufacturing business which included Wolseley. He listened carefully to what Shute had in mind and was sympathetic but reminded Shute that he had the Air Ministry to thank for his decision to stop manufacture of the aero engines. He was angry with the Ministry and told Shute that he had "sent that ITP thing back to them and told them they could put it where the monkey puts his nuts."[29] Although Shute tried to persuade the Airspeed Board to mount some means of acquiring the Wolseley engine production, they were not interested. Airspeed was still running at a loss and there were good prospects for orders from the Air Ministry for trainer aircraft based on the Envoy. The Wolseley episode left a sour taste in Shute's mouth. He was convinced that, had Airspeed acquired the Wolseley engine, it would have worked out in the end with the increasing armament programme. To his mind civil servants, with their restrictive practices and small minded attitude, had deprived the country of an excellent aero engine.

The Envoy had been produced as a "convertible" version so that a gun turret could be mounted. Ten man hours of work were needed to do the conversion and a batch of seven machines were produced for the South African Air Force. By 1936 the Envoy was in service with airlines all over the world and the Air Ministry were certainly taking notice of Airspeed. After some time, the Ministry issued an invitation to tender to a specification that was clearly based on the Envoy. For the first time the Ministry revealed that Airspeed was a serious contender for military orders, despite the fact that, officially, only members of the Society of British Aircraft Constructors (S.B.A.C) were permitted to tender. At this time Airspeed were admitted as full members of the S.B.A.C. Tiltman and his staff produced the specification for a version of the Envoy that became known as the Oxford and the Ministry issued an I.T.P. for a batch of 50. The Oxford was a great success and became a standard training aircraft for the RAF crews until the end of the Second World War, by which time over 8000 had been produced.

Now that the company had a good run of work ahead of it Shute felt that he need not devote all his attention to Airspeed. Up to that point the company had absorbed virtually all his time and energy to the detriment of family life and other pursuits. With two young daughters, the house at Craneswater Park became too small so in 1936 the family moved to a larger house at 14 Helena Road, just off the sea front at Southsea and a mile or two from the factory. After his move south and probably with the more secure financial position after the Swan Hunter takeover, Shute had bought *Skerdmore*, an old ten ton yacht. He and Frances, with the children, had sailed her at weekends in the Solent, as time from the demands of Airspeed allowed. *Skerdmore* had her own history, having been originally owned by Ahto Walter, a young Estonian yachtsman who had sailed her across the Atlantic and back in 1931. On returning to England Walter sold her for £200, though whether that was the price Shute paid for her is not known.

Frances too liked to travel and on one occasion, when Colman was to deliver an Envoy to Indo China, she went on the flight as far as India. Indeed she had spent part of her childhood in India and took the opportunity to re-visit the country and look up old friends.

Shute took up writing again. Although he had not written a novel since *Lonely Road* was published, he had not abandoned writing altogether. He wrote an account of the *R.100's* flight to Canada for the Royal Aeronautical Society,[30] and in 1933 an article entitled "The Airship Venture", an account of his work on the *R.100* project which was published in Blackwood's magazine in 1933.[31] He used extracts from this article when he wrote *Slide Rule* many years later, but the Blackwood article is notable for being a rather more straightforward account without the bitterness that is evident in *Slide Rule*. Now he wrote another piece, a short story with the title "Air Circus". This drew on his experience of observing National Aviation Day at the time when he was chasing it all over the country, fixing problems on the Ferry aircraft and trying to obtain an order for a Courier from Sir Alan Cobham.

The ideas for his next novel arose out of his experiences over the previous two years. From Townsley he learned about the shipbuilding industry and for several weeks quizzed him about the operations of a shipbuilding yard. He heard from the Swan Hunter directors about the effects of the depression on shipbuilding, the closing of yards in the North East and the effects it had on those who were laid off. He motored up to these areas and saw conditions for himself. In several journeys he covered more than 2000 miles around Tyneside and up as far as Blyth, gleaning information. In raising capital for Airspeed and the formation of Airspeed (1934) he had close dealings with bankers, issuing houses and stockbrokers in the City of London. Also there was his frustrating experience in Athens attempting to negotiate a contract for aircraft with the Greek government.

Now he wove together all these experiences into a story based on a merchant banker, Henry Warren, who buys a derelict shipyard in the North East, raises the first order for the yard by a dubious deal from a foreign government, and drafts a prospectus containing information that he knows to be inaccurate. Warren's deception is discovered. He is charged with fraud, found guilty and serves a prison sentence but the shipyard he rescues thrives, bringing much needed employment to a depressed town. This book marked a departure for Shute. His previous published novels, though based on his own experience, had a police and spy theme. *Ruined City* is the first novel where a single person achieves a remarkable outcome through hard work and determination. It has the "ordinary people achieving extraordinary things" motif that was to characterise many of his later novels. Shute began writing the book in 1936 and worked steadily on it over the next eighteen months.

In 1936 King George V died and was succeeded by the Prince of Wales. The new King was an enthusiastic supporter of aviation. Between 1929 and 1935, as Prince of Wales, he had purchased 13 aircraft. He had also inspected the aircraft at the start of the MacRobertson race. When the Prince ascended to the throne in 1936 as Edward VIII, the King's Flight was formed as the world's first aircraft unit for a head of state. To begin with, the Flight used the King's own de Havilland DH.89 Dragon Rapide. After his abdication in December 1936 it became necessary to find a replacement aircraft. In April 1937 Airspeed received an order for an Envoy as that replacement. It was the first aircraft bought specifically for the purpose and naturally a special effort was made over the furnishing and finish. Edward VIII had appointed E.H. Fielden as his personal pilot and made him Captain of the King's Flight when it was formed. Fielden discussed the specification of the Envoy. It had to accommodate four passengers, a wireless operator and a steward. Shute questioned the need for a steward but was told that this was essential to cater for the needs of royal personages after the fatigues of public visits. The Envoy was delivered in June 1937 and continued in service until the outbreak of war in 1939 when it was replaced by an armed Lockheed Hudson. Interestingly Fielden resumed his post as Captain of the King's Flight after the war and was confirmed in his post when the Queen's Flight was renamed on the accession of Queen Elizabeth II in 1952.

Shute later wrote that, with this order for the King's Flight, Airspeed achieved its peak. No matter what the profit and loss account might show, no company could receive a better endorsement of its products.

Another diversion for Shute resulted from the sale in 1936, of the film rights to *Lonely Road*. When writing the book, he had Clive Brook, a well known film actor, in mind for the main character, and had sent Brook a copy of the book. Now Shute had the interest of visiting Ealing studios to see the film being made and he also travelled down to Slapton Sands in Devon to see the filming of the opening sequence on location. Shute seems to have been content with the adaptation of his novel by the scriptwriters. He was probably just pleased to have a novel turned into a film. The film *Lonely Road* was released in Britain in August 1936 and in the USA with the title *Scotland Yard Commands* the following January.

By the time the King's Flight Envoy was delivered, Oxford trainer aircraft were beginning to roll off the production line. Ahead of Shute stretched a long period of producing these Oxfords which were being built under the Air Ministry's I.T.P. system, which amounted to a cost plus small profit for each one produced. The order may have pleased the conservative members of the Board, giving the long sought promise of continuity but it added to Shute's growing sense of disillusionment. He felt that the company had lost the sense of adventure and innovation which had marked its birth and early development. True, Airspeed was now firmly established as a major player in aircraft production. This fact was marked by a visit that June from the Air Minister himself, Sir Kingsley Wood, who brought with him the Chairman of the Society of British Aircraft Constructors. Sir Kingsley praised the staff and said that Airspeed was a progressive firm that was making a valuable contribution to aircraft production. He added that, since starting production for the Ministry, Airspeed had never let them down and that was the highest praise he could give to the firm. He praised "the real team spirit in the factory."[32]

And indeed there was a team spirit in the workforce, now approaching 1000 in number, both in work and outside working hours. There was a social club with its annual dinner and dance, a works choir which was well patronised in the Portsmouth area and the Aeronautical College now turning out well qualified people for the industry. The Company had all the trappings of a mature organisation. All this came at a cost. The growth in the number of employees, tooling up for the production of Oxfords and other factors resulted in a net loss for the year to July 1937 of £58,650 and a bank overdraft of £102,131. However, this was at the start of the production run of Oxfords and there was every sign that the company would soon be in profit as further batches were ordered and delivered. Shute foresaw that in the coming months, or even years, his main task would be to ensure that production ran efficiently with as little lost time as possible so the aircraft might cost the taxpayer less. That would be a job for a runner, not a starter of companies, and he classed himself as a starter and useless as a runner. Also the aircraft produced would be for military purposes, with fewer opportunities for the design and production of civilian aircraft. Above all, for Shute, the spirit of enterprise had gone from the company he had started. He became increasingly at odds with other Board Members, whose cautious policy he so disliked. The other Board members perhaps saw him as a maverick, something of a trouble-maker. In their view he had been reckless over the 1934 share issue, and in attempting to acquire the production of the Wolseley aero engine with its huge potential cost implications. He had unconventional ideas about the design of aircraft such as the AS 31 fighter with its rear-mounted cockpit. This might well have seemed a hare-brained idea to the Swan Hunter Board members.

Such friction at Board level was quite alien to Tiltman's temperament and early in 1938 he decided to resign and told Lord Grimthorpe of his decision. Lord Grimthorpe, although no longer Chairman, was still a substantial shareholder. He was appalled by Tiltman's decision. He wrote Tiltman a sharp and critical letter expressing his great disappointment and sense of shock that Tiltman, of all people, should throw his hand in when difficulties arose. He thought that from a sense of loyalty and good faith, Tiltman should stick it out and do his utmost to put things right. Lord Grimthorpe said he was profoundly upset and considered Tiltman was letting his backers down. He hoped it was not too late for Tiltman to reconsider his attitude and for the "managers of Airspeed to resume their former happy relationship."[33]

Tiltman was considerably shaken by this outburst, for loyalty and straight forwardness were two of his strongest characteristics. He had assumed that Shute held all the cards but believed that there was simply no longer room in the company for its two founders. When the proposition to get rid of either Shute or Tiltman, was put to the Board there was really no contest. The company could much more easily replace one Managing Director than find another aircraft designer of Tiltman's undoubted ability and flair.

Shute accepted the Board's decision that he must go. His five year contract had fifteen months to run until July 1939. In April 1938 he went on indefinite leave whilst his final settlement was decided upon. When he left the company it employed 1,035 people and had over a million pounds worth of orders in hand. In July the company accounts showed a profit for the first time: £21,155. Perhaps, Shute later wrote, it had all become too easy and he quoted Robert Louis Stevenson that "to travel hopefully is a better thing than to arrive, and the true success is to labour."[34]

A few months before he left he had completed *Ruined City* and sent it off to the publishers. His American publisher, Morrow, was very enthusiastic about the book and had taken an option to buy the film rights within three months. This was encouraging and maybe, cushioned by a good financial settlement, Shute thought he might have a future as a full-time writer.

Yorkshire Aero Club, Sherburn-in-Elmet, c. 1930.
L-R Lord Grimthorpe, Nevil Shute, Reg Morris, Harry Worrall, H.A. Love
(Richard Morris)

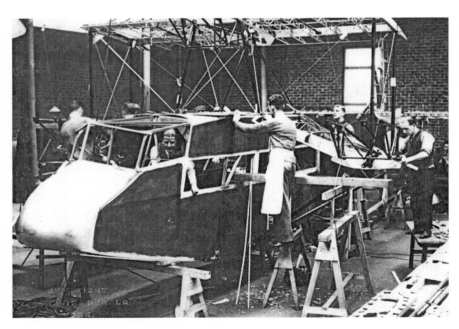

Ferry Aircraft being built in the Airspeed factory, York.
(BAE Systems)

A.L. Naish and B. Brady of Aircraft Exchange and Mart take delivery of their Courier from Nevil Shute, Hessell Tiltman and Lord Grimthorpe, Sept. 1933. (Flightglobal archive)

Airspeed Envoy G-AEXX built for the King's Flight 1937. (Airspeed Bulletin)

6
Overture

Shute left Airspeed in April 1938. Although he later wrote that the Directors were probably right to get rid of him, it was no doubt a blow to his pride to leave the company that he had helped bring into being some seven years earlier. When he left he went on what would now be called "gardening leave". His resignation from the Board is recorded officially as 9 November 1938. He was pleased with the financial settlement that had been agreed, being enough to keep him and his family for five years. Having not taken a holiday for a number of years, he and Frances stuck a pin in a map of France. It landed on St Claude in the Jura mountains. It could not, he said, have fallen on a better place. They left the children in the care of friends and motored through France and stayed at St Claude, where he no doubt enjoyed the fishing in the mountain rivers, as one of his characters was to do in a later novel, *Pied Piper*.

At St Claude he received a telegram to say that Watt had sold the film rights to *Ruined City* to an American film company for $35,000, the equivalent at the exchange rates of the day of about £7,000. He struggled to take in what he read, for his financial security had suddenly increased from five to ten years. This doubtless confirmed his belief, resulting from the success of *Ruined City*, that he could now earn a living as a novelist and he had the financial security to ensure that he had the time to develop his writing. However, the payment he received for the sale of the film rights raised its head a couple of years later in regard to the payment of tax. Watts had advised him that this sale was of a capital asset and therefore not subject to income tax. Shute wrote to the Society of Authors asking for their advice on the matter and was told that the sale would most certainly be regarded as part of his literary income and therefore taxable. The Society's tax advisor was quite definite on this point and Shute wrote back, accepting this and saying that there was little doubt he would have to pay up. At income tax rates then current, the tax payable would have been around 35% or nearly £2,500.

Although the rights were sold, the film was never actually made, but preparations for its production were put in hand. On 25 April 1939 the *New York Times* reported[1] that MGM had announced that the film of *Kindling* (the American title of *Ruined City*) would star Robert Donat. The film's title would be *Roman City* and it would be filmed in England. The filming did not go ahead. Whilst this happens in many cases, there may be a possible explanation as to why this was so. In 1934 a film called *Red Ensign* was released, directed by Michael Powell, which has a similar plot to *Ruined City*; a director of a British shipyard builds new ships in the midst of economic depression and resorts to forgery to secure a loan. He is caught and goes to prison but later becomes a public hero. Perhaps *Roman City* was dropped because of this similar predecessor.

Motoring back through France, Shute would have passed through Dijon, Angerville, Pithiviers and most likely through Chartres and on to the cross-channel ferry from St Malo, subconsciously storing up information that would later be used in *Pied Piper*. Once home from France the topic for his next novel was not long in coming. This was the time of the Munich crisis in the autumn of 1938 when war with Germany seemed imminent. Air raid shelters were being built, public buildings protected with sandbags and Air Raid precautions were issued. It was these precautions, issued to his wife as a doctor, that angered Shute with their emphasis on the dangers of gas attacks from bombing. He believed that the enemy would not use gas bombs for fear of reprisals and that by far the greatest danger would come from damage caused by high explosives and incendiaries. He felt he had to get this message across to the public and this was what led him to write one of what he later called his "socially useful" novels, *What Happened to the Corbetts*, which had the original title of *Overture*. By "socially useful" he meant a book that was written without regard to sales, to put a message across to his readers and as a novel for a large audience. For greater impact he set the story in a real city, Southampton, and to an ordinary middle class family, the Corbetts. He foretells vividly the destruction caused by precision bombing and how the family copes and escapes. He reckoned that the bombing would be achieved by aircraft using pinpoint celestial navigation, not knowing, of course, that such accuracy would later be achieved by the Luftwaffe using intersecting radio beams such as Knickebein.

In the novel, the Corbetts escape to sea in their yacht and, reworking material used in an earlier unpublished short story "The Uttermost Parts of the Sea", they rescue airmen in a downed aircraft from the carrier *HMS Victorious*. For the sailing aspects of the book, Shute drew on the weekend sailing trips made with his young family in the Solent, bathing at Seaview in the Isle of Wight, anchoring in Wooton Creek and Yarmouth. Also, Peter Corbett puts into action a plan that must have been evolving in Shute's mind of despatching his wife and children to the safety of Canada before himself volunteering to join the Navy.

As he was writing this book Shute's father Arthur was admitted to Portsmouth Hospital where he died on Christmas Day 1938 at the age of 79. In its obituary, the *Times* recorded Arthur's career at the Post Office, his books and that when he retired in 1920 his colleagues felt "that a man of real distinction had disappeared from the service."[2]

Already he had ideas for another novel. He had read Fridtjof Nansen's book about Polar exploration and the crossing of Greenland, and was also curious about his Nordic ancestors and the fact that they were probably the first to discover America. Later he wrote that the year he spent on researching and writing this book was a pleasant year and gave him a distraction from the build-up to the war. The book also gave him the opportunity to include the details of a transatlantic flight that he had carefully researched back in 1932 in a proposal to Sir Alan Cobham.

In April 1939 *What Happened to the Corbetts* was published both in Britain and in the United States under the title of *Ordeal* and in England Heinemann distributed, on publication day, a thousand copies free of charge to workers in Air Raid Precautions.

Since *Ruined City*, with the American title of *Kindling*, had sold well in the United States and also because he wanted to visit the Cape Cod area where the Vikings had landed, he undertook a trip to America and sailed from Southampton aboard the *Ascania* on 25th March 1939. His destination port was Halifax, Nova Scotia in Canada. Whilst in Canada he deposited some money in a bank account. This deposit was to ensure that, if it came to evacuation, his wife would have funds to draw on in that country.

From Canada he journeyed south to explore the Cape Cod area before going on to New York where he was entertained by his American publishers and gave the first public speeches of his life, no easy matter for a man with a stammer. One meeting he spoke at was a Tuesday lunch in New York attended by around 200 writers, journalists, newspaper executives and theatre men. The French writer, Andre Maurois, gave a talk on French politics and he was preceded by Shute. Maurois was so impressed by what Shute said that he gave an account of the speech as follows:[3]

> Before me, an Englishman, Neville [sic] Shute, author of a novel which has had great success over here (*Ordeal*) gave a courageous and brilliant paper. I do not have the text, but the meaning was something like this:
>
> Gentlemen, I have been in your country for several weeks. Naturally, I read all your newspapers with ardent interest. I see that most of them extol the doctrine of isolationism. In their articles I learned that a living coward is worth more than a dead hero, that America would be wrong to plunge even its little finger into the boiling cauldron of European politics and that, moreover, Germany and Italy might have a right to their living space. Your arguments struck me, I have reflected and come to think that you are right. . . . Yes, isolationism is a splendid doctrine; my ancestors knew this already in the nineteenth century and I intend, upon returning to London, to preach this doctrine again to my compatriots.
>
> Certainly we English should isolate ourselves from the American continent and refuse to plunge even our little finger into the boiling cauldron of politics in the United States. . . . Why should we involve ourselves in quarrels which don't concern us directly? Since the totalitarian states need living space, let us give Canada to the Germans, the British colony to Japan, the Antilles and Bermuda to the Italians. By so doing we will have resolved the European problem, provided them with excellent bases of departure, the three totalitarian powers will be able to strive towards the methodical conquest of America in raw materials and riches, a conquest much more interesting for them than that of sorry little Europe.
>
> Then, through the fog, seated on cliffs in comfortable trans-atlantic armchairs can we catch glimpses in the distance of the dictator's fleets hurrying to your shores. Then can we command with a light heart the virtue of isolationism. Then will the House of Commons be able to say: "Not a man, not a penny for an American war."

Then we too will be able to praise the living coward at the expense of the dead hero. . . . I expect to derive great pleasure from all of that. . . . and who knows? perhaps, at last will we be able to take our turn at earning some money by selling guns and aeroplanes to you and if we feel generous and tender-hearted we might even lend you a part of these earnings thereby guaranteeing ourselves an eternal and plausible cause of complaint against you. . . .

Gentlemen, I thank your press for the precious education it has given me.

During this speech, delivered, Maurois recalls, "calmly and surely in a style which reminded him of Disraeli at the time of Peel, I was a curious observer of the audience. In the beginning, the faces showed surprise, a little anxiety, a shadow of resentment, then the quality of irony and also the correctness of the critique touched them and they smiled. When he finished, they applauded him. That day I felt that isolationism is a fragile, vulnerable doctrine and one which will not long survive events."

It is a testament to Shute's courage that he was prepared to make this speech to an audience that could be expected to be hostile given the current feeling that America should not get involved in a European war.

Shortly after that lunch Shute suffered what was probably his first heart attack and which he recounts in *Slide Rule*. After a dinner and dance, at the Rainbow Room in New York, he was accompanying his hostess to Grand Central Station. There he was seized with a stabbing chest pain that made walking and breathing difficult. He had to wait motionless until the pain eased and he managed to get himself back to the Hotel Chatham where he was staying. The following day a doctor took a cardiograph and pronounced that he had "strained his heart", but not very badly and would recover with rest. No doubt the strain of his journey, travelling long distances, making the speeches, not to mention the combination of unaccustomed alcoholic drinks combined to bring on the attack. Shute did note that it was six weeks before the pain entirely disappeared.

Early in May Shute sailed for home aboard the Cunard liner *Britannic*, arriving back in Southampton on 14th May. He was no doubt glad to be home after the rigours of his American trip and could resume the writing of *An Old Captivity*, with the detail that he had acquired from his visit to the Cape Cod area.

About this time, or perhaps even before his American trip, Sir Dennis Burney re-entered Shute's life. Ever the entrepreneur and inventor, Burney had obtained Admiralty backing for the Toraplane and Doravane. The former was a gliding torpedo, the latter a gliding bomb, but it was the Toraplane that was of interest to the Navy. What Burney wanted was Shute's aeronautical expertise to help with the Toraplane design and development. Shute became an unpaid consultant to the project.

Being an ex-naval officer, and given his background in World War I, it is not surprising that Burney's attention turned to methods of aerial attack on ships. A perceived problem with attacking ships with torpedoes dropped by aircraft was that, because the aircraft needed to get close to stand any chance of hitting the vessel, it would be vulnerable to the vessel's anti-aircraft fire. Torpedoes also had to be dropped from low level (less than 100 feet) to avoid damage on hitting the water. Although the Admiralty Torpedo Design Committee had considered gliding torpedoes, very little work on them had been carried out. In March 1939 Burney offered to provide the Admiralty with gliding torpedoes to his design for trial purposes. These would be built at his own expense if the Admiralty would undertake to co-ordinate the tests and thus began the story of the "Toraplane" as Burney christened it.

The idea was simple enough—fit wings, a tailplane and rudder to a standard 18-inch diameter torpedo. When released it would thus glide for some distance before shedding its wings just prior to hitting the water. Then it would behave as a conventional torpedo and run underwater to its target. This would mean that the torpedo could be launched further from the target while the aircraft was beyond the range of anti-aircraft fire. Burney's Broadway Trust Company designed and built the Toraplanes but used the workshop facilities at the Torpedo Development Unit, RAF Gosport near Portsmouth. By mid summer 1939 Shute was working actively on this project and others that Burney had in hand. It was a part-time job for Shute but he was to devote a good deal of time to it, increasingly so as the months passed, whilst writing *An Old Captivity* in his spare time, though spare time would be in short supply given the work on the Toraplane.

With the financial settlement from Airspeed and royalties from *Ruined City* and *What Happened to the Corbetts*, he was in a position to buy a new yacht and commissioned David Hillyard at Littlehampton, just along the coast, to build him a boat. What he ordered was a 40 foot 7 berth yacht, schooner rigged, from a boat builder with a good reputation for producing sound, well-founded boats. It was perhaps inevitable that she would be named *Runagate*, which means renegade or rebel, for it was a name he had used in an early novel, *Pilotage*, and also in the short story "The Uttermost Parts of the Sea." *Runagate* was delivered during that summer of 1939, a boat that would take him anywhere. But he had little time for sailing before the outbreak of war, although he and Frances were sailing *Runagate* off the French coast when war was declared on Sunday 3 September. They were fogbound but managed to get back to Portsmouth the following day. Thereafter *Runagate* was laid up in Birdham Pool at the top end of Chichester Harbour, her sails removed and the boat sheeted over. There would be no more pleasure sailing for Shute during the wartime period.

He spent an increasing amount of time with Burney working on the Toraplane. First there was the design of the wings with Sydney Hansel, ex-Airspeed, whom Burney had recruited to work on the project. The method of attachment of the wings to the torpedo and the design of the paravane mechanism had to be thought out and designed. The paravane was Burney's invention from the First World War, a small aerodynamic shape with inverted wings that was reeled out on a wire trailing from the Toraplane after launch. The paravane hit the water just before the torpedo shearing a bolt in a clamp that held the wings to the fuselage. By this means the wings and tailplane separated from the torpedo as it entered the water. The torpedo then ran in the conventional manner to its target.

From the outset Royal Aircraft Establishment (R.A.E.) Farnborough were involved in the Toraplane. They had had a gliding torpedo project in hand for several years but had done little or no work on it. It was Burney's activity that had stirred them into life and the R.A.E.'s Dr Harris was involved in working with the Burney team. In July Shute and Hansel were at meetings at Gosport discussing the height and aircraft speed on release and the many factors involved in preparation for launch tests from an aircraft. The Toraplane work involved meetings and visits to the Torpedo Development Unit at Gosport, towing trials on the paravane in the Solent and a considerable degree of development. The R.A.E. staff were inclined to criticise the Burney team and imply that they were unscientific in their approach to the development. Burney, a man with contacts in high places, arranged a meeting chaired by Air Marshall Tedder at Harrogate in September 1939 at which Shute was present. At that meeting Burney said that he wished to dispel any impression that might exist that his calculations had not been carried out scientifically. He explained that the design of the Toraplane wings "was the result of careful preliminary calculations by Messrs Norway and Hansel."[4]

Burney had also secured the enthusiastic support of Admiral Sir William James, Commander in Chief, Portsmouth for the Toraplane. This support was crucial in providing the Burney team with the Naval facilities required.

By early August they were almost ready to test the Toraplane, using Swordfish aircraft from Gosport. Arrangements for ferrying observers to the trial area east of the Isle of Wight were made, including two destroyers to ensure that the drop zone was secure and free from shipping. On the morning of 14 August a Swordfish took off from Gosport for the first trial. It released the Toraplane at 2500 feet. After a short glide it entered the water correctly and the wings separated. The trial was a success, no doubt much to the relief of the observers at sea, of whom Shute was probably one. This was but the first of more than 50 trials that followed over the following months, sometimes two in a day, more often with gaps of several days. Early trials were promising but not always consistent. On occasions the time of glide was too short or, worse, the torpedo failed to release properly from the aircraft. Each trial was observed from trawlers out in the Solent and even from observer aircraft, often with either Hansel or Shute doing the observing.

When war was declared on 3 September six trials had been completed and some progress made towards repeatable performance. The following day Winston Churchill was appointed First Lord of the Admiralty and made Professor Frederick Lindemann his scientific advisor. Lindemann visited the Burney team on 19th November. He wrote that Burney was "wreathed in smiles" after a particularly successful trial that day. On that day Admiral James wrote to Churchill that "Professor Lindemann's visit has been of the *greatest* value . . . I arranged for all the fellows connected with the Burney experiments and trials to meet him and talk things over."[5] No doubt Shute was one of the "fellows" who met Lindemann.

However the R.A.E. had in parallel been developing their own version of the Toraplane. Wanting to keep the project for the Admiralty, and to encourage co-operation, Churchill wrote to Admiral James that he had agreed with the Air Ministry to set up a joint committee at which Air Marshall Joubert would represent the Air Force and there would also be "a scientist, Professor Thomson, of high repute." G.P. Thomson was indeed a distinguished man, son of J.J. Thomson who discovered the electron. G.P. was Professor of physics at Imperial College London and a specialist in aerodynamics. Later he would chair the MAUD committee on the feasibility of the atomic bomb.

In proposing the setting up of a Committee, Churchill had written to Sir Kingsley Wood, Minister of Aircraft Production[6] "I now propose that Admiral James, who is extremely keen on this matter [the Toraplane] . . . should be Chairman of this Committee . . . to drive things ahead day after day. That the Admiralty should bear the charge upon their vote. . . . The invention promises to be helpful to the Navy and Fleet Air Arm . . . [it] all turns on whether the explosive charge can be accurately directed from a distance. Burney declares this is so and in view of his credentials I feel we are bound to find this out at the earliest moment."

So was formed the Toraplane and Doravane Development Committee, or TDD for short. The first meeting was on 30 October at Admiralty House, Portsmouth with Admiral James in the chair, Air Marshal Joubert, Professor Thomson and both Burney and Shute present.[7] So Shute, the unpaid consultant, found himself in a meeting at a very high level discussing a project that was considered of great importance. In the minutes of that meeting Shute is referred to as "Mr Norway, Assistant to Sir Dennis Burney". In minutes of later meetings he is "Mr Norway BA, F.R.Ae.S."

At that first meeting Admiral James read out Churchill's letter in which he wrote "I do not want a report, but a result. If it is found to be of no use condemn it [the Toraplane]. If it is all right, make it, so that we can enter production at the earliest moment." So the pressure was on to produce a reliable weapon. The minutes of that first meeting contain no record of a contribution from Shute. Rather Burney did the talking pointing out that his costs on the Toraplane were running at £1,000 per month. It was agreed that the Admiralty would meet the costs from that time on.

Whilst the trials continued with an equal measure of success and failure, Shute's main job was to design and produce an aiming sight for the Toraplane. Working with specialists at the Gramophone Company near London he developed a gyro-stabilised sight or "computer" as it was referred to. By December the design had been completed and in January 1940 at a TDD sub-committee meeting chaired by Professor Thomson it was reported that "Mr Norway produced a sight designed by the Gramophone Company and explained that the aim was to produce an accurate gliding angle and that the computer could be operated by the second member of the crew. On the Swordfish the sight was situated on the starboard side of the windscreen. Also "three of these sights were being manufactured and one would be ready for trial in an aeroplane on 17th January. The other two were expected by the end of January."[8]

Whilst the design was patented, the equipment was found to be too large to fit into a Swordfish. In the spirit of co-operation, elements of this aiming sight were incorporated into a rather more sophisticated sight developed by R.A.E. and this was subsequently used in trials, being fitted in a larger Blackburn Botha aircraft.

By late 1939, despite his increasing involvement with the Toraplane, Shute had finished *An Old Captivity* and sent it off to the publishers. About that time he started writing a novel entitled *The Lame Ducks Fly* but only got as far as the end of the first chapter and then abandoned it. At a TDD Committee meeting in December[9] he probably heard of the attack on a British submarine by an RAF Anson that mistook it for a German U-boat. He adapted this real life event for his next novel, for with his writer's eye he had absorbed the characters and settings of the Toraplane project, the rivalry between the Navy and Air Force as to which service Coastal Command should belong, and from that the plot for *Landfall* evolved. This must have supplanted "The Lame Ducks Fly" because the *Landfall* story was more immediate and he had so much more material from his own real-life work that could be woven into the novel.

Nearly all of Shute's novels draw on his own experiences and the characters in them by people he met. With *Landfall* the connection between events in the novel and reality is even more immediate. In the novel Jerry Chambers is posted to the "Marine Experimental Unit" at Titchfield to pilot an aircraft on trials of a secret weapon. Meetings are held at Admiralty House, Portsmouth chaired by "Admiral Sir James Blackett"; Professor Legge is the scientist, a character most likely modelled on his other mentor, Barnes Wallis. Trials at sea are observed from a trawler. However for obvious security reasons Shute could not mention the actual weapon—the Toraplane—so he based the fictional work on magnetic influences around a ship used to trigger a weapon. Shute may well have known of the use of coils fitted to a Wellington bomber for detecting submarines by their magnetic field, work on which Barnes Wallis had been involved.

One can imagine Shute attending meetings and working closely with both Naval and Air Force people, observing events and characters and storing them away to be woven into his novel. Trawlers were used to ferry observers to the trials, and Shute may well have seen and overheard the naval divers preparing to recover torpedoes after dropping which he used in *Landfall* when divers descend to the *Caranx*.

It was clear to Shute and many others that Portsmouth and its Naval dockyard would be a strategic target for German bombing, and his home at Helena Road, Southsea was fairly close to the dockyard. Therefore in late 1939 the family moved to Langstone Mill, owned by Flora Twort. The family lived there for a few months before moving on again to Langstone Place, both locations being further away from Portsmouth and its dockyard.

As the autumn and winter of 1939 dragged on, Shute was busy with the design and making of the aiming sight, observing Toraplane trials and attending monthly meetings of the TDD Committee. By that time the R.A.E. version of the Toraplane was getting ready for trials. At the third TDD meeting on 28 November,[10] in addition to Burney and Shute, Dr Harold Roxbee-Cox, Superintendent of Research at R.A.E., was also present with some of his staff. For Shute this was probably ironic, since Roxbee-Cox had been his opposite number at Cardington on the *R.101* project, doing the calculations on that ill-fated airship. In a number of important ways the R.A.E. design was superior to Burney's. It had its own gyro and ailerons, which gave it better control. Trials on the R.A.E. Toraplanes began in early January 1940 and at once gave better results than the Burney design—in one trial when dropped from 5000 feet the R.A.E. Toraplane flew for 5 miles. Gosport made a film of the Toraplane which combined footage of both the Burney and R.A.E. designs being assembled and also from the trials at sea, for most of the trials were filmed, and shots of both the successful trials as well as those which were failures were included. Indeed Shute had made time in October 1939 to visit Gosport, writing to his contact there that[11] "I have not seen the cinema records of the last two flights and would like to come in on Saturday morning and see them if this is convenient to you."

Trials on the Burney Toraplanes were still continuing but it remained inconsistent in performance and it was impossible for the Admiralty to support both. In a note of May 1940 Admiral James summed up the situation as follows:[12]

The development has followed the usual course of development of a scientific weapon; there have been many disappointments intermixed with striking successes. The early hopes that the Burney type of wing would, by trial and error, soon be perfected were not fulfilled. This was particularly disappointing as in the Burney design the torpedo's gyroscope was also used for controlling the flight in air, and production in quantity would therefore not present a difficult problem. In the autumn of 1939 the R.A.E. establishment entered the field with their design, and in the course of time it became evident that the R.A.E. design was producing better results than the Burney design.

There comes a moment in development of this nature when it is necessary to focus attention and work on one design, particularly in war time when time presses, and there is not an unlimited supply of torpedoes, or unlimited supply of skilled workmen, or unlimited opportunities for flying and releasing gliding weapons. So in March 1940, at a meeting at the Air Ministry, attended by the T.D.D. Committee, it was decided to focus all attention on developing the R.A.E. design.

Effectively there would be no further work on the Burney Toraplane even though the Admiralty had expended many thousands of pounds on it, including the loan of the Admiralty yacht *GRIVE* which had accommodated Burney and his team in some luxury for the sea trials. By then Burney, in typical fashion, had moved on to other things, one of which was the Burney Amphibian. This was a huge six-engined aircraft designed to be an aircraft carrier of the sky from which smaller "satellite" aircraft, armed with bombs or torpedoes, could be launched and retrieved. Through his American contacts Burney had got estimates that such an aircraft could be built for 1.5 million dollars and he tried, through Lindemann, to sell the idea to Churchill, with the hope that Churchill might try to persuade President Roosevelt to back the idea. According to Hansel, Burney tried unsuccessfully to get Shute involved with this design, so it was Hansel who did the design and initial drawings, and on the drawing board it stayed, never to see the light of day. The Air Ministry thought the whole concept and specification "fantastic" and refused to pursue it.[13]

Shute's reaction to the whole Toraplane episode can only be guessed at. Naturally he would have been disappointed that all the work on the Burney design had come to nothing, but he would have had to accept the superiority of the R.A.E. design as the one to be taken further. It had, however, given him a grandstand view of the workings of the Services at a high level. As it turned out, the whole Toraplane project faded away. Although a Squadron was formed in 1941 to use the Toraplane it never got beyond the trial stage. The official records contain a memo of June 1942 to the Chief of the Air Staff saying that "at long last the Ministry of Aircraft Production are recommending that the work (on the Toraplane) should be abandoned because of the inaccuracies found by trial due to the errors in flight path and to windage during the time of descent."[14]

The "phoney war" which Shute so epitomised in *Landfall* was about to come to an abrupt end. On 10 May the German army invaded Holland and that same day Churchill became Prime Minister. No doubt Shute, like millions of other British families, listened to his "Blood, Toil, Tears and Sweat" speech broadcast on the wireless on 13th May. By the end of May Holland and Belgium had been overrun and the British Expeditionary Force was trapped at Dunkirk. Operation Dynamo began to rescue as many as possible from the beaches. Whether Shute thought of being one of the armada of little ships that rescued so many, is not known. However the fine Admiralty yacht *GRIVE*, which had been used for the Burney Toraplane trials, was sunk by enemy fire whilst taking part in the Dunkirk evacuation.

After Dunkirk he, like many others, knew that England was in imminent peril of invasion and he decided that he must enlist to fight the enemy across the Channel. He had no pressing work to keep him from enlisting; his work on the Toraplane was at an end. He would never have dreamed of just carrying on as a writer at this crucial time. He had no respect for any writer who thought they could best serve their country in time of war by sitting still and writing. The Royal Naval Volunteer Reserve (R.N.V.R.) had put out a call for "elderly yachtsmen" to join up, and Shute answered the call. For him the Navy was the obvious choice being a yachtsman and familiar with handling boats and navigation. At 41 he was too old for aircrew and it was many years since he had piloted an aircraft. As if mentally preparing himself for war, he made arrangements for his wife and small daughters to go to Canada. Frances and the girls travelled to Liverpool and departed for Montreal on the 24 June aboard the *Duchess of Atholl*. So, in real life, he put into the action the plan, of evacuating his wife and children, that he had written into *What Happened to the Corbetts*. At that time both Shute and Frances assumed that, when he joined the RNVR, he would, after training, join a ship and serve his time at sea. It must have been a wrench for Frances to leave her home, her country and her husband at this time and travel to Canada.

By June Shute had finished writing *Landfall*. Later that year George Orwell reviewed the book and wrote: "The present war, owing to its peculiar character, has not yet produced a literature of its own, but Mr. Nevil Shute's Landfall is a beginning. It is a straightforward, convincing story, and I shall keep an eye open for Mr. Shute's books in future."[15] After giving a resume of the plot Orwell continues "the author ... sees the young airman's point of view, because, presumably, he has at some time shared his experiences. He can stand inside him as well as outside him and realise that he is heroic as well as childish, competent as well as silly. The result is a good, simple story, pleasantly free from cleverness and at times genuinely moving."

Having enlisted, Shute was sent to H.M.S. King Alfred, the shore-based training establishment at Brighton to begin his basic training. He had only been there a few days when he was pulled out of the squad, asked questions about his previous work and technical background and sent off for an interview in London with a Commander Goodeve. This was all before he had even acquired his uniform. He was, he later wrote, "furious . . . I had just abandoned technical work on gliding torpedoes to go and fight." Now he found himself being interviewed by Goodeve and "threatened with a posting to a new experimental department, the king of which was interviewing me."[16] He was not reassured by Goodeve's appearance, a young man with snow white hair, very blue eyes, and a nervous, restless manner. Shute's first impression was that he was a crank who had duped the Admirals into setting him up with a staff to mess about with graph paper and slide rules. However to refuse this posting meant being cashiered, thus ending his Naval career before it had even begun. In a matter of days he completed basic training, was commissioned a lieutenant in the RNVR and sent up to Goodeve's office in London to work on secret weapons. His training for the Navy was so brief that when he did venture on board ships he had the dread of perhaps being the senior officer on board and having to do something. He was he said "the only executive lieutenant-commander in the Navy who had never attended Sunday Divisions and didn't even know what happened at that ceremony."[17]

So he found himself separated from his family, living at his Club in London and going to the office each day with, as he put it "occasional excursions to sea to attend trials of my toys."[18] He was yet to realise it, but his practical approach to problems, aeronautical background, and his work on the Toraplane, with the initial enthusiasm and ultimate failure, would prove an ideal preparation for the weapons he would help to develop and test over the next four years.

For Shute, and for the thousands of others who joined up, life, both in war and peace, would never be the same again.

7
To See My Things Go Wrong

The embryo department that Shute joined in June 1940 occupied offices in Central London and was at that time part of the Navy's Inspectorate of Anti-Aircraft Weapons and Devices (I.A.A.W.D.). This group was originally under the command of Admiral Somerville but he had been ordered to sea, to confront and later sink, the French fleet at Oran in North Africa. The running of the department was left in the hands of Somerville's deputy Charles Goodeve. Goodeve, a Canadian, trained as a physical chemist, was a lecturer in peace time, had obtained his D.Sc. at London University and was one of the few Canadians to be elected a Fellow of the Royal Society. Before the war, he enlisted in the RNVR, being keen on the Navy, and had served at HMS Vernon, a shore-based establishment responsible for mine clearance. With his deputy F.D. Richardson, he had developed the double-L sweep for making ships less susceptible to magnetic mines and was later to develop the "de-gaussing" method, passing an electric current through cables drawn along ship's steel hulls for the same purpose. Goodeve knew that applied science would be an essential requirement for the wartime work of the Navy.

At 35 he was younger than Shute but had asked officers at King Alfred to look out for technically qualified entrants. Shute, with his engineering and aeronautical background and his work on the Toraplane, must have seemed to Goodeve like God's gift. Shute was just the man he was looking for to provide the practical engineering for his projects.

To begin with, the department had just a handful of Naval Officers and scientists; by the end of 1940 this number had grown to 60 and was to expand to over 200 by the middle of the war. In addition to Goodeve and Richardson, another recruit who joined about the same time was Edward Terrell, a barrister in peace time, who was working on plastic armour for shipping—steel plates coated with bitumen and granite chippings which were found to absorb the impact of bullets. Writing later Terrell said of

Shute that "his broad, benign beam made him a friend."[1] It was only later that he learned that Shute had an aeronautical background and was also a successful novelist.

Throughout late 1940 and into 1941 Shute lived at the Oxford and Cambridge Club in Pall Mall, whilst working at the office in London. He experienced at first hand the Blitz when, night after night, the Luftwaffe bombed the capital causing the extensive damage and disruption that he had predicted in *What Happened to the Corbetts.* He saw how, for the most part, that people carried on with their daily lives as best they could, remaining calm and with very little panic. "London can take it" became a slogan and Shute saw for himself how, indeed, it did.

In those early days, a pressing requirement was to equip merchant ships with defence against attack and also to provide them with some form of early warning of air attack. One of Shute's first jobs was the development of the Acoustic Warning Device for merchant ships. Sensitive microphones were placed high up on the mast which, coupled with amplifiers, could give early warning of approaching aircraft. Shute worked on this with his old friends at the Gramophone Company at Hayes in Middlesex. The microphone had to be insulated against wind noise, and various materials were tested by wrapping them around the microphone which was mounted on a whirling boom. The best material apparently was mattress ticking. The amplifier tuning was set to pick up sounds between 150–200 Hertz in frequency, roughly the noise frequency of an aircraft engine. The unit gave a red alarm light and a bell warning on the ship's bridge. Early trials on the quaintly named M.V. "Titlark" were satisfactory and in 1941 the Gramophone Company were given a contract for 500 of these units to be fitted in merchant vessels at a cost of £265,000.[2]

In service, the device was plagued by spurious warnings with a tendency to pick up shipboard noises and, with coastal vessels, onshore sounds. One captain of a coastal ship plying the Thames and east coast complained bitterly that the whole thing was a waste of money. He was sick of endless false alarms. The device was altered to listen only without the warning light and bell. It might pick up the sound of an approaching aircraft but there was no way of knowing whether it was friend or foe until it had been sighted. With the greater availability of radar from 1943 and the reduction in attacks on merchant shipping, the acoustic warning devices were gradually removed from ships.

In 1940 there were no surplus guns available to equip merchant ships for defence, so rockets were used. The application of rockets in various devices was to occupy much of Shute's time throughout the whole of his wartime service. To quote Terrell,[1] referring to Shute, "He was learning by painful experience a lesson that we all had to learn in turn—namely that it was one thing to produce a prototype that functioned on land, but an entirely different thing to make it, with all the varied movements of the ship, work at sea. . . . Nevertheless with dogged determination as soon as one rocket weapon failed to show enough promise he started designing and developing another and went from projectors based on land for defence against invasion to yet another system of rockets for the defence of ships. Although at first promising, once again the result was failure. Still he went on testing, trying and failing. But as a result of the groundwork of research carried out in these first few months, the Rocket Landing Craft, with its devastating power of attack . . . was ultimately produced and proved successful, used both in the Mediterranean and Normandy landings."

An early device designed by Shute was christened Pig Trough, a pivoted launcher resembling an umbrella stand, capable of a firing up to 14 rockets vertically from the deck of a ship as a counter to aircraft attack. This was followed by the Radiator, a gimballed multiple rocket launcher, the Harvey Projector and the Pill Box. With these three designs the launcher could be rotated and elevated, giving some means of aiming them.[3]

The rockets themselves were developed at the Projectile Development Establishment, located on the coast at Aberporth in Wales, run by Dr Alwyn Crow. Rockets or unrotating projectiles were not particularly sophisticated devices, being essentially long steel tubes filled with cordite plugged with millboard at one end, fitted with guiding fins, and ignited with an electrical fuse.

Of the more successful applications the Rocket Spear deserves a mention, a rocket fitted with a fluted cast iron spear at its head capable of puncturing a hole in a submarine's hull. This was the outcome of Shute's attendance at Committee meetings chaired by Professor Blackett to consider all possible means of attacking submarines. Initial tests by the RAF using a Hurricane fighter showed promise, but there was little urgency to use it in action until one of Admiral Sir Max Horton's staff witnessed a demonstration at Boscombe Down. He was greatly impressed and urged its adoption. Horton, who was directing the Battle of the Atlantic, wanted every means to be used to counter the U-boat threat and, as a result, a flight of Swordfish aircraft operating from an escort carrier was equipped with Rocket spears and achieved success against U-boats in the Atlantic, and this within weeks of its introduction.

A later success in this field was the Rocket Grapnel, which Shute devised in response to a requirement for cliff face assaults. Here a four-pronged grapnel was fitted to the top of the rocket with 500 feet of rope attached. Successful trials on the Isle of Wight cliffs led on to the combat use of the Grapnel by US forces on Omaha beach on D-Day.

Shute was working in the spirit of "never taking no for an answer and of never accepting without question the opinion of generally accepted authorities on any matter."

In 1944 he wrote an article which includes this explanation on the use of rockets for defending merchant ships:[4]

Early in this war, I used to have a lot to do with merchant ships. We used to put comic weapons on them, when there were no guns. In the summer of 1940 we worked desperately to design weapons that could be manufactured very quickly; most of these were rocketty things for which the "gun" consisted of a couple of bits of angle iron and a flash lamp battery. We rushed these gadgets out and took them to the merchant ships at the ports, and started training classes in their handling, and did our best to persuade gloomy masters that they were "almost as good as a gun." I had quite a party on this work in the winter of 1940/41, all young officers of the Royal Naval Volunteer Reserve. We used to go to sea to fire the things and get the crews steamed up about them; mostly they made a good big bang in the sky which stimulated the ship's crews—if it did not occur too close because of a defective fuse. Some of my officers shot down a German aircraft on these trips, and some of them got sunk. Nothing ever happened to me. The merchant ships were properly armed long ago, and most of the rushed substitutes for guns have gone to the scrapheap.

Christmas 1940 found Shute on his own, with his family on the other side of the Atlantic. He stayed with Harry Roberts and his friends at Oakshott near Petersfield. According to Flora Twort, who was also there, "fresh from the Admiralty he entertained us with stories of escape."

She later recalled,[5] "He was always writing about men and women aged about 25. I told him for goodness sake write about a different age group. He came up with Pied Piper—a story revolving around an old man and children. I think it was his best book."

This comment of Flora's must have planted the seed for his next novel. In 1941 the plot came to him on a slow train to Aberporth for a meeting at the Projectile Development Establishment. According to Goodeve he and Shute shared a sleeping compartment on that train. Goodeve had a good sleep on one side but on the other side Shute did not. Over breakfast and whilst waiting for their car, Shute told Goodeve the outline of the story in some detail and asked for 3 days leave to dictate it to his former secretary. Despite his heavy workload he had finished writing the book by late July. In her diary for 27 July 1941 Flora Twort wrote[6] "Norway came for breakfast, brought typed copy of Pied Piper for me to read."

Pied Piper made Nevil Shute a household name. In America it was serialised in *Collier's* magazine, appearing in November 1941, just before Pearl Harbor. The following year it was made into a popular film to add to the stock of mildly propaganda films of the time. It was produced in the United states at 20th Century Fox by Nunnally Johnson, directed by Irving Pichel, and starred Monty Woolley, Anne Baxter, Otto Preminger, in perhaps his only acting role, and a very young Roddy McDowall, as one of the children led to safety through war torn Europe. The heart-warming story of determination and courage appealed to the public. It is also the only one of Shute's books to have been translated into French twice, first with the title *Coeur Genereux* (*Generous Heart*) in 1945 and later with the ironic title of "Bonnes Vacances Mr Howard" (Happy Holiday Mr Howard). Goodeve reputedly called it one of the most successful by-products of their work.

In 1941 the Directorate of Miscellaneous Weapons Development (DMWD) was formally established with the appointment of a Director, Captain G.O.C. (Jock) Davies. He was, according to Shute,[7] "a burly R.N. Captain with a strong sense of humour who intended to retire from the Navy at the conclusion of the War." He apparently had private means, something that always appealed to Shute, implying that the person did not have to toe the line and think of their pension. Davies was quite prepared to incur the wrath of his seniors if need be, and it probably was incurred as he got to grips with this growing group of civilian scientists and volunteer officers who seemed so intent on bending the rules, committing the Department to expenditure in a totally unauthorised fashion.

So the Department developed and in March 1941 Shute was promoted to the rank of Lieutenant Commander, as were both Richardson and Terrell. Shute headed the Engineering Section whilst Richardson looked after projected wire devices and Terrell plastic armour. Projected wire devices were another defensive measure against aircraft using a rocket to fire a long cutting cable attached to a parachute into the sky, the idea being to entangle and hopefully bring down attacking aircraft. Terrell supervised the manufacture of plastic armour on an industrial scale, many tons of it being fitted to protect warships. At the end of the war Terrell was awarded £10,000 for his invention. However in the beginning the Department of Naval Construction was not at all convinced of the benefits of plastic armour and dismissed it as a waste of time. This attitude changed when the First Sea Lord paid a visit to DMWD and samples of plastic armour were put out for his inspection. Just before his visit Shute, with an impish sense of humour, pinned a note to one of the samples. The note read "PLASTIC ARMOUR—THE ONLY ARMOUR THAT WILL TAKE A THUMB TACK."

By 1941 the DMWD required its own site for testing the many devices that it was developing. In February it requisitioned the pier at Weston-Super-Mare at an annual rent of £375. In June 1942 the pier became HMS Birnbeck, probably the only pier to become an official naval establishment! With the high rise and fall of the tide it allowed devices to be tested and the remains recovered at low tide.

Two other events of 1941 were notable for Shute on a personal level. In February he again suffered severe chest pain on a train going up to London and went to see a Navy doctor who had rooms in Harley Street. He told the doctor all about the circumstances of his attack in New York. After examining him, this doctor pronounced that he had not had a heart attack. What he had suffered was a bad attack of wind. He told him to take prescribed powders which would cure the problem. This diagnosis is surprising given that the symptoms Shute describes are the classic ones of a heart attack.

Late in 1941, with the threat of invasion over, his wife and daughters returned to England. When they had arrived in Canada, Frances had practised medicine for a time in Hamilton, Ontario. However she had apparently not been able to access the funds in the bank account that Shute had opened—he may have forgotten to add her name as a drawee. Frances and the girls left Canada and lived for a time in Bermuda before returning to England.

Shute had been living at his Club in London and, with the family returning, they needed a home. In September Shute bought Pond Head House on Hayling Island, a large house with five acres of land and gardens running down to Chichester Harbour. This was to be their much loved family home until they emigrated to Australia in 1950. Pond Head House was a fitting home for a man with a young family and a rising literary income—by then he had earned over $30,000 in royalties from America alone. The house provided a separate study, room for a model workshop and a jetty for mooring *Runagate*. Shute's daughter Heather recalled happy times at Pond Head, with frequent visits from young Naval officers who would play with her. She remembers also going to sleep to the sound of her mother playing classical music softly on the piano. The family also kept poultry and pigs to supplement wartime rations. One night an invasion exercise took place near Shute's home. That night a company of signallers camped out in the garden underneath the trees. Their young officer, a rather puzzled captain, asked Shute privately what part of England he was in.

As well as rockets, Shute and his section adapted flame throwers, mainly for defensive purposes. Flame throwers had been developed before the war and an early task for the DMWD engineers was the Cockatrice, a flame thrower was mounted on a Bedford truck to provide mobile defence for airfields. This fearsome weapon projected a flame 100 yards long, consuming several gallons per minute of flammable mixture. Shute went to demonstrations of flame throwers and saw for himself their power. The Petroleum Warfare Department also experimented with many mixtures of petrol, diesel, tar, heavy oil and even dispersed solids such as caustic soda and crepe rubber, all designed to stick the burning mixture to its target. Shute later wrote:[8] "Of all the weapons in a modern armoury, a flamethrower is most misleading to the Staff. A big flamethrower in full blast is a very impressive sight, and very terrifying. Everybody who sees it working for the first time is utterly appalled by the sheer horror of the weapon." Shute's worry was that Staff Officers might become "flame-minded" and want to use them in action. To test the effectiveness of such weapons Shute and his team used caged mice in a boat that was towed through a the blast of a flame thrower mounted on a jetty. The boat with the mice on board passed through the blast four times and they were alive and well at the end. Not all the mice had been used, some were left at the hotel where the team were staying. When they got back they found that two of these mice had died, presumably of fright at the apprehension of their fate. The officers spared the remaining mice, gave them a good feed, and slipped one under each bedroom door in the hotel that had one pair of ladies shoes outside for cleaning. Even the grimmest aspects of their work had its lighter side.

Flame throwers were tried out for defence of ships. A Naval pattern vertical flame thrower, resembling a large boiler with a vertical stack, was mounted on an old French fishing boat *La Patrie* and Shute was on board to witness the test. The weapon was capable of sending up a vertical jet of flame 100 feet high. An RAF aircraft made several runs at the vessel, seemingly undeterred by the flame, and on one run the wingtip brushed the flame. Questioned later by Shute, the pilot thought that whilst the aircraft might not be damaged by the flame, the pilot might be mesmerised by it. The pilot did admit that before the war he had driven a car at a fair and was quite used to passing through flaming hoops as part of his act.

From this work emerged his next novel *Most Secret*, which had the original title of *The Other Side*. In the book he relates the stories of four men, Simon, Rhodes, Boden and Colvin who come together for a secret mission to mount a raid on a Brittany harbour using a French fishing boat fitted with a flamethrower. The interwoven story technique was a new one for Shute, contrasting with the linear plot of *Pied Piper*, but it was a style he would use again in later novels. Many years later he wrote that, from a strictly technical point of view, *Most Secret* was the best formed book he ever wrote and that it was written to perpetuate the mood of bitterness and hate which evolved in England in the latter stages of the War. Certainly it has a sinister theme. It also has a cameo role for his Housemaster at Shrewsbury. One of the characters, Charles Simon, arrives in England by an unconventional route and is required to establish his credentials. Simon was at school at Shrewsbury and asks to see his housemaster, known as "The Beak". Mr Scarlett (a thinly disguised Basil Oldham) is summoned from the school to vouch for Simon's identity which he does saying that "I was his housemaster for four years . . . if that's not knowing him well I'd like to know what is."

By August 1942 he had written *Most Secret* and submitted it to the Admiralty censors for publication. It failed to pass the censors and, Shute claimed, was being suppressed by a policy of inactivity.[9] This angered

Shute and he wrote to his publisher in January 1943 that he was resigning his commission in protest. The precise reasons for refusal are not known, but it was probably not for writing about flamethrowers—the Germans had them—but possibly for writing of the clandestine operations across the Channel in aid of the French, for such operations did take place out of Dartmouth, where the book is set. These operations used high speed boats rather than French fishing boats. Whatever the reason, Shute, as a serving officer, had to accept the ban and swallow his annoyance. His resignation would have been pointless anyway, as the ban would still have existed. *Most Secret* was finally published in 1945 after the War.

By this time Shute had more than 60 working in his Engineering Section. Lieutenants Abel and Biddel looked after aeronautical and electrical aspects respectively and there was Ian Hassall, son of a famous cartoonist, who was to become a lifelong friend along with Alec Menhinick, another member of Shute's team. According to Goodeve, Shute managed to supervise his team without section heads or deputies, relying on inspiration rather than organisation. People liked working for Shute, as he had a very practical approach to problems. He gave his staff a free hand to go away and get on with it, to come back either when the job was done or when they wanted help. James Close, another member of DMWD, wrote recently[10] that "it was in the nature of the way DMWD was run that we were given our individual projects and ordered to get on with it and only report back when we had success or final failure."

Another project was the development of fresh water stills to make drinking water for ships lifeboats. According to the official record[11] "The work was commenced without official requirement on the instructions of Lt.Cmdr. N.S. Norway RNVR whose foresight anticipated the arising of the requirement." Several different types of still were developed —to distil fresh water from seawater by evaporation and also to recover fresh water from engine exhaust gases. The more conventional fuel-heated stills were designed and developed by one of Shute's engineers, Lt. J.H.G. Goodfellow, a very able engineer, who incidentally produced extremely good engineering drawings. His terms of reference were to produce a still which would convert seawater to fresh water at the rate of one gallon per hour. This was to occupy him through 1942 and 1943, producing several marks of still, steadily increasing their efficiency.

The second method, of recovering water from exhaust gases, was Shute's baby, but the development was carried out at Southampton

University under the direction of Professor Tom Cave-Browne-Cave. He had been involved in an apparatus to produce drinking water from the engine exhaust gases on the *R.101* airship. Development made slow progress, one of the problems being the filtration of the recovered water and this type of still did not come into service during the War.

For gunnery practice, aircraft were used to tow targets, but this was inefficient, tying up aircraft for this work. A simpler method for deploying targets was needed. Shute went to the firm of International Model Aircraft (IMA) in Morden. Here he met Joe Mansour a director of IMA and also Bert Judge, who had recently joined the firm. In 1936 aged 19 Bert had won the Wakefield cup in the USA with a 4 foot wingspan rubber-band powered model. Shute decided that this was just what was needed and so it was adapted for the target glider and developed into a rocket-propelled glider, supplied complete with a portable launching catapult which could launch the gliders up to a height of 200 to 300 feet. Once the rocket had burnt out the glider would spiral down to earth, taking about 90 seconds to do so and it was during this period that it was used for target practice. The Technical History[12] records Alec Menhinick as the principal officer involved. Wrens were trained to set up and deploy the target gliders because Shute insisted that DMWD officers could not be spared for this work. Perhaps this is why a Wren is shown in the background of one of the photographs in the Instruction manual. Bert Judge remembers a long, slow train journey up to Scotland to train Wrens on how to set up and launch the gliders. Interestingly, the gliders were made from impregnated paper with wood stiffening sections because "Timber Control would not sanction the use of balsa," presumably because it was a scarce imported commodity during the War. The gliders were painted bright orange for visibility, with the instruction that they must be handed into the police by the finder.

From 1943 onwards DMWD turned from the defensive to the offensive as plans for the invasion of Europe gradually took shape. Shute and his engineers were at full stretch during this period; he wrote nothing during 1943 but in early 1944 produced a series of six short articles with the title of "Second Front". These are generally supposed to have been written for the Ministry of Information, but this is doubtful since some are marked as possibly being suitable for publication in *Collier's* or other magazines. These articles were probably written to record his personal observations of the preparations for D-Day. Mindful of security, and the prohibition on the publication of *Most Secret*, the articles were written in very general terms without reference to specific places or events. These six articles, with two rather technical essays on Beach Assaults and landing craft, were never published.

In 1944 he did find time to write another novel, *Pastoral*, which he later rather dismissed as "a trivial book written in a hurry." Although it was no doubt written in a hurry, given the pressure of work, it is as carefully crafted as all of his other novels. Set in an imaginary bomber station in Oxfordshire, it tells the love story of a bomber pilot and a WAAF officer. Years later he classified it as one of his entertainment books, written at a time when the war seemed to be going on for ever and it looked as though all the joy and fun had gone out of the world. He wrote *Pastoral* to show that it hadn't. It contains excellent descriptions of bombing raids over Germany and the interaction of the Wellington crew. It is a book in which fishing plays a significant role, reflecting a pastime that Shute had enjoyed since his time at the Dragon School. He finished the book before D-Day and it was published in August. *Pastoral* sold well both in Britain and the United States and he evidently thought enough of it to attempt a film script of it the following year.

Shute's engineering section was involved to some extent in very many of the devices that DMWD devised in preparation for Overlord (the code name for D-Day), probably far more than is credited in the official Technical Histories. No doubt those involved with floating harbours, for example, would have asked for advice or help from Shute or his engineers. However there were two main projects in the lead up to D-Day for which Shute had overall responsibility.

The first of these was the Swallow glider[13] or pilotless aircraft, which was to take him to the Beaulieu river on many occasions and not only provide him with background for later novels but also give him a grandstand seat to observe D-Day preparations at first hand. The Swallow project was also probably one of the most complex and technically challenging of any that DMWD undertook.

The origin of this project went back to 1942 with a proposal by Barnes Wallis that such a pilotless aircraft should be developed. The idea that he had was set out in a memo of June 1942. The invasion exercise at Dieppe in August 1942 showed that a frontal assault on defended beaches could result in very heavy casualties, and such was the case on this occasion. The Dieppe Raid was planned by Combined Operations and championed by Lord Louis Mountbatten, although the Prime Minister, Winston Churchill, had serious reservations about attempting it, haunted as he was by memories of the disastrous Gallipoli campaign in 1915 when he was First Lord of the Admiralty. The Canadian forces that took part in the Dieppe Raid, although only on shore for some nine hours suffered very heavy casualties. It was immediately apparent that the lessons learned from this had to be incorporated in the plans for the full-scale invasion of France. One factor that was considered desirable was the laying of a smoke screen to hide the invasion force from land defences. To attempt to do this with piloted aircraft would have been almost suicidal from heavily defended positions, hence Wallis's ideas for a pilotless glider were resurrected and it fell to the DMWD to take on the task of the development of the pilotless aircraft. The Staff Requirement was stated by Combined Operations in a document of 1942. Firstly the aircraft should be capable of laying a smokescreen upwind to a height of 600 ft; it should travel not less than ¼ mile before beginning to emit smoke. Then it should turn 90 degrees and generate smoke for a distance of at least ¼ mile. In addition the aircraft must be capable of being launched from an L.S.T1., L.C.T. or Giant R-craft. and also that 1000 of the "gliders" were required by 1 April 1943! The planners in Combined Operations were perfectly serious and the Requirement was confirmed in August 1942 and given "High Priority".

Having agreed to take on the development, DMWD had already made preliminary investigations as to where facilities were available. The choice for the landing craft tests was the Beaulieu river in the New Forest, Hampshire.

So was born the Swallow Project. The aircraft themselves were called "Swallows" and though they were often referred to as "gliders", they were not. They were rocket propelled pilotless aircraft and did not glide until their useful function had been achieved. Shute was in overall charge and co-ordination of the Swallow project, whilst Alec Menhinick took charge of the trials. Lieutenants Abel and Biddell were responsible for the aeronautics and electrical design respectively.

In 1942 the British aircraft industry was at full stretch meeting the requirements for aircraft of all types. All aircraft production was co-ordinated by the Ministry of Aircraft Production (M.A.P.) and it was desirable to find a firm outside the M.A.P. "ring" to take on the design and building of the Swallow. Having worked with International Model

Aircraft on target gliders they were Shute's choice to build the Swallow, which was to be much larger than any model aircraft ever built by I.M.A. At the suggestion of the DMWD, Sydney Hansel was engaged as a consultant aerodynamic engineer

The Swallow had essentially two elements to it: the development of a suitable catapult for launching the aircraft from the deck of a vessel, and the design of the aircraft itself. The aircraft were built by IMA, and the rocket-powered catapult was in the hands of the R.A.E. The Swallow's prime purpose was to lay a smokescreen, and the smoke was generated in a cordite-operated smoke canister (S.C.I.) unit which weighed 300 lbs. The design that emerged was a high wing monoplane with a twin boom fuselage and a tailplane with two fins. Beneath the wings was a nacelle housing the smoke unit, four propulsive rockets, a gyro, air bottle and other equipment. The Swallows were made of wood, with the wings having spruce main spars, plywood ribs and a covering of thin plywood. The wings could be folded back and attached to the booms for easy stowage, and because of course the whole aircraft had to be loaded onto an LCT by manpower alone. The tailplane was one piece and pivoted on the booms at its centre, and a coil spring at its front edge. Beneath the wings the nacelle had a steel tubular framework, covered in thin steel sheet and with the curved nose made from a pressing of impregnated buckram. The upper part of the nacelle was a detachable wooden cover to allow the smoke canister to be fitted. A hatch between the booms gave access to the gyro, which was a standard Mark VI B unit. Beneath the canister and gyro were four racks each taking a 3" wrapped charge rocket designed to give a thrust of 50 lb for a specified length of time. The rockets were made by the Low Pressure Ballistics section of Woolwich Arsenal.

Within the tailplane was a compartment, housing a clockwork mechanism rotating a cam. The clockwork motor was similar to that in a gramophone, but of greater accuracy. Once started, the rotating cam actuated various switches in sequence to activate the gyro, fire the propulsive rockets, switch on the smoke canister etc. The wing span was 19 feet and the chord of 2 ft 3 in, giving a wing area of 42 sq ft. Since the all up weight, ready for launch, was 820 lbs the wing loading was just over 19 lbs per sq ft. This meant that the launch speed had to be quite high and also that the aircraft, unpowered, would have glided like a brick. The combined thrust of the 4 rockets, some 200 lbs, was necessary to keep it flying. Some additional thrust was provided when the smoke emission began through the emission nozzle which pointed rearwards and downwards under the nacelle.

Being pilotless, the Swallow had to have some means of automatic control when in flight. This is what the gyro was for. Compressed air from the bottle spun the gyro, which was mounted in gimbals, and gave the absolute reference. The gyro was electrically linked to an actuator motor in the tailplane which, through a disc with a slot, varied the incidence of the tailplane by pulling against a coil spring. The initial tailplane incidence, which was always negative, could be set by adjusting the nuts linking the disc follower to the tailplane. By this elementary control system the pitch of the aircraft was controlled, governing the climb and level flight. The idea was to achieve a steady climb to 300 feet and then fly level. The wings had ailerons controlled by electrical actuators so that the aircraft could bank and turn.

For the land trials the catapult had a track with 80 feet of steel rails with a trolley and cradle into which the Swallow fitted. The motive power was provided by solid rockets of the type used by the DMWD on the parachute and cable device. The trolley could hold up to 20 such rockets giving the several tons of thrust needed to achieve a flying speed of over 80 mph in a short distance. The rockets were fired electrically from firing boxes mounted alongside the track. At the end of the track the trolley had to be decelerated rapidly. This was achieved by having a steel ram pierce a metal disc on the end of a water filled cylinder. The trolley was brought to rest within less than 4 feet of travel by the hydraulic pressure built up in the cylinder.

Depending on the wind strength at the time of launch, both the launch run on the catapult and the number of rockets used could be varied. The rockets were heated to so called "magazine temperature" according to the thrust required. So for each launch these parameters were decided upon to suit the conditions at the time.

Later, the catapult design was altered to suit launching from a Landing Craft. A better and lighter trolley was built so that a launch run of around 40 feet could be used.

To test the concept, land-based trials preceded those from a Landing Craft. So quickly did the team work that by December 1942 the first Swallow was ready for flight trial. The site selected for this was at HMS Kestrel, a shore-based Fleet Air Arm station at Worthy Down, just north of Winchester in Hampshire. This location provided sufficient room for a flight of up to 1000–1500 yards to take place within the perimeter. Everything was ready for the first flight trial on 19 December 1942. Because things would happen very quickly, two ciné cameras were used to record the trial. An Admiralty photographer deployed a slow-motion and cine camera to the left of the Swallow whilst an RAF photographer from Boscombe Down positioned a high speed camera to provide data for plotting the complete flight in plan and elevation.

At its first trial the Swallow launched successfully, climbed more steeply than intended, and landed after a flight of about 500 yards. Bert Judge, who was present at the trial with Shute, remembers that the noise and blast of the rockets was awesome and that the flight was straight and largely successful. The second trial ten days later did not go so well. four seconds after the launch two of the propulsive rockets exploded, causing the Swallow to lose height rapidly and crash land. At this stage, Farnborough took over development of the Swallow, with DMWD being responsible for the conduct of the tests. It was hoped that from then on the project would follow a straightforward development programme, but events were to show that the development would be anything but straightforward.

Seven further land trials took place over the following two months, and in all cases the Swallow hit the ground after distances between 110 and 200 feet from the point of launch, dismally short of what was required. After these trials a new R.A.E. representative took over the trials and did a careful analysis of the previous trial data and film records. He found two main problems—the cam follower in the control became detached due to the high acceleration on launch. This meant that the coil spring pulled the tail down to its maximum negative angle of incidence (-14 degrees), which caused the Swallow to climb too steeply and then crash. Also, photos showed that the tail booms required stiffening to prevent "whip". The cam follower was made positively locating and steel struts were added to stiffen the tail booms. A test on 25 March 1943 with these modifications was successful with a flight of over 1000 yards and a height of 150 feet. This was the last test at Kestrel—the next phase was to be test launches from a Landing Craft.

In February 1943 the DMWD had requested an LCT be allocated for the trials, but this could not easily be done. LCTs were in short supply and a barge landing vehicle was placed at DMWD's disposal. Although this might have been suitable, its use was ruled out because it had petrol engines—not a good idea with explosive rockets on board. Eventually a diesel powered Mark 5 LCT was found in Scotland and sailed to the South Coast in June. By mid-August, work on fitting out the LCT with launching rails was proceeding slowly and DMWD pointed out that progress was not quick enough and, for Combined Operations, the Swallow project was still an urgent requirement. Following an intervention by the Vice-Controller of the Admiralty the modified LCT was ready in October.

The official record states that DMWD surveyed various sites for the LCT trials and selected the mouth of the Beaulieu river as "this locality offered the required degree of security and a suitable stretch of straight water to allow varying lengths of run." It would also have been an area known well by Shute who had sailed in the Solent and was very familiar with its harbours and rivers.

In a Second Front article written at this time,[14] Shute talks about testing inventions: "I keep a private L.C.T. on the south coast of England for the trials of things like that. Landing Craft (Tank) are in considerable demand these days for—if the Censor will allow me—landing tanks. We wanted one for an experiment some months ago and we were given a poor bastard ship, herself a bit of an experiment that had not turned out quite so well. Too weak to go to war on operations, she was good enough for what we wanted her to do; we took her gratefully and got to work on her with experimental hardware."

The experimental hardware that was installed on LCT 2119 was a redesigned catapult trolley from R.A.E. which was lighter and more efficient than that used at Worthy Down. It was capable of carrying twenty 3-inch rockets and a water cylinder was carried at the front. This track was mounted on the port side of the LCT and inclined upwards at an angle of about 7 degrees. It was also mounted well forward on the LCT deck to give clearance for the rocket blast between the trolley and the bridge.

Before full-scale Swallow trials could be carried out, the characteristics of the trolley on the LCT had to be measured, in particular the speed achieved at the end of the run. Because only a limited number of Swallows were available, the speed tests were done using concrete blocks of the same weight as the Swallow. Dr Hatfield, a DMWD scientist arrived with electronic gear to measure the speed. This apparently gave erratic readings and numerous blocks were hurled into the river before repeatable and believable measurements were obtained.

By early November 1943 the DMWD team were ready to do a trial launch from the LCT. All the preparations were completed with assistance given by the staff of HMS Mastodon (formerly Exbury House), which was a hub for activities on the Beaulieu river. Shute would have briefed certain Mastodon staff on the project and what the requirements were, and Boats Crew Wrens ferried DMWD staff to and from the LCT. In this way Shute became familiar with Mastodon and was a frequent visitor. He came to respect the Boats Crew Wrens, cheerful young women, competent in a skill he admired, handling boats in the confined reaches of the Beaulieu. And, no doubt, they would have saluted him and called him "Sir".

He wrote,[15] "I travel down from London to this experimental ship about once a week and spend a day or two in her. . . ." In the spring of 1944 he wrote, "I drove out of London in my truck one day towards the end of February with a couple of hundredweight of experimental hardware at my back, mildly explosive." From this it is reasonable to assume that he was transporting the rockets for the Swallow trials from Woolwich to the Beaulieu river.

The first LCT trial was carried out on 2 November 1943 and went reasonably well. The trolley performed well; the Swallow separated cleanly but landed short of the designated target. It also developed a pronounced "phugoid" (porpoise motion) believed to be due to the gyro not being spun up properly before the rockets were fired. Nonetheless it was a promising start. But the next two trials in November and early December were failures, the first caused by structural failure of the fins which resulted in a flat dive into the water and the second by a gyro failure.

For the next tests, rockets with a burning time of 40 seconds were fitted to the Swallow to give the required range. Tests on the 10th and 17th December were "almost perfect".

However the next test was not successful. The initial climb was good but was followed by a spinning turn to port and a crash. The cause was believed to be a break in the airline between the bottle and gyro. Later it was discovered that one of the bearings on the gyro had become unseated, probably due to the launch acceleration (8 g). R.A.E. did a modification to this bearing for all subsequent trials.

A notable success was the trial on 14 February 1944, the first with smoke—previously a weighted canister had been fitted in place of the smoke generating unit. A good smoke curtain was laid "satisfactorily close to the target." Although the Swallow was perhaps 100 feet too high, obscuration at the water level was excellent. Stills from the film taken that day show the launch from the LCT, separation from the trolley and the smoke curtain being laid. Success had been obtained, the Swallow could be launched satisfactorily and a useful smoke curtain laid. But it had to be repeated reliably, for if it was to be used in the Invasion, many such gliders would be needed. Time was running short. So the trials continued through March and into April but there were problems with every test; if the flight was good either the smoke emission was late or the Swallow's flight was poor and, in some cases the Swallow lost height and crashed. For Shute it must have been frustratingly similar to the Toraplane project where so many factors had to be right to produce a successful trial.

By 15 May a total of 29 trials had been made of which 18 were from the LCT but repeatability had not been achieved; there were just too many parameters which had to be right in order to achieve good flight with correct smoke emission.

It was inevitable that the Swallow team would get mixed up in the invasion preparations, even by accident. One evening when LCT 2119 was moored up on the Beaulieu, preparing for a trial next day, a Canadian officer drove up in a jeep and told Shute that his eight guns, self-propelled twenty-five pounders mounted on a tank chassis, were on the road immediately behind him, and was he ready to embark them? Shute said that he was not. The officer said he must; there could be no mistake; and showed him his signal. It said that at that time and place an LCT would be found upon the hard which would embark his tank-like guns for an exercise. Shute told him that his LCT would be staying where it was all night, and in the morning he would be letting off something that would make a lot of blast and flame on the deck, and if the officer was a wise man he would not have his eight petrol driven tanks in the LCT while all that was going on. While the misunderstanding was being sorted out, the Canadian officer came aboard for a pink gin. Later another LCT came alongside and embarked the guns.

There was a gap in the trials around the time of D-Day; the last trial before D-Day was on 15 May and resumed on 20 July. This was inevitable given the scale of preparations for the invasion. By May the Beaulieu river was packed with craft all preparing for D-Day. Development test work such as the Swallow was of a very low priority.

The fate of the Swallow project was decided at a meeting held by

DMWD on 5 July 1944 at which all the parties involved were present. The situation was that DMWD could provide more rockets for trials and M.A.P. said that the defect with the smoke equipment had been fixed and smoke emission would probably be more satisfactory than before. Shute said that, subject to the decision of the meeting, the plan was to hold the next trial on July 17, when it was hoped to shoot off three Swallows in succession.

Combined Operations indicated that very considerable discussion had taken place upon the requirement and as a result of that discussion the staff requirement for a pilotless aircraft for the laying of smoke screens had been withdrawn. Further, it was not envisaged that the Swallow would be required for operations in the Far East.

There were five Swallows left and three were launched in succession on the same day. The first one was a failure because the Swallow rolled to port, possibly due to aileron controls being crossed. The next two were much better but smoke generation was not perfect. The final two trials in late August and on 1 September resulted in two good flights but with less than perfect smoke screens. There being no more aircraft, the project came to its end.

Work on the Swallow was not entirely wasted, for Farnborough carried on with the development of radio controlled pilotless aircraft. Development over the years led to the sophisticated Unmanned Aerial Vehicles of today.

At the same time as the Swallow, there was the Great Panjandrum, the large rocket-propelled wheel for beach obstacle demolition.[16] Of all the DMWD projects this is the one that is best remembered.

The established version of the requirement for this device was that it was designed to breach the "Atlantic Wall", a concrete wall 10 feet high and 7 feet thick which had been built at the head of beaches along the coast of France. Breaches in the wall would be necessary for tanks, vehicles and troops to move inland. To breach the wall it was estimated that a ton of explosive would need to be detonated against the wall. The problem was how to get the charge in place without risking lives on heavily defended beaches. Shute was pondering this problem in 1943 when he had a visit from Group Captain Finch-Noyes from Combined Operations. He brought with him an innovative design. This comprised two large wheels some 10 feet in diameter with a drum of explosive held between them. Slow burning cordite rockets would be placed around the metal rims of the wheels to drive them in the manner of two large Catherine wheels. Shute thought about it and decided it had possibilities and christened the device Panjandrum. It was intended to be launched from a landing craft, reach speeds of up to sixty miles per hour, crash into the wall and explode. Under contract, Commercial Structures Ltd of Leytonstone in East London built Panjandrums in September 1943. Under great secrecy they were transported to the North Devon coast where Combined Operations had their experimental headquarters.

On 7 September on the beach at Westward Ho, in full view of the public, the first trial was carried out. With 18 rockets Panjandrum travelled just over 600 feet along the beach. It was slow and evidently lacking thrust so, with local improvisation, the number of rockets was doubled. Two days later they tried again, this time with *Panjandrum* launched from a landing craft directly up the beach. It made a spectacular sight spewing flame and spray as it traversed the shallows but was slowed up by soft sand on shore, just reaching the head of the beach. It was suggested that stability might be improved by having a third wheel. When this was tried Panjandrum swerved off course and tilted over buckling an outside wheel. At the same time rockets became detached and skittered along the sand, chased by a dog.

The next step was to try and control the path of Panjandrum by attaching cables to each side. These would be paid out from winches with brakes which would hopefully steer the device. Shute and his colleague Williamson tried this out on the 24 October 1943. As Panjandrum gathered speed with the two men paying out cable on each side, one of the cables broke and flipped back over the operators, causing them to duck. A month later, with stronger cables they tried again. This time Panjandrum pivoted to the left, and the starboard wheel distorted. In a final test the following January, with Admiralty top brass present, Panjandrum with 66 rockets began its run but veered off in a tight spiral, narrowly missing the cameraman who was filming it, and turned on its side to expire in a cloud of smoke. That spelt the end. The whole project was halted and no more was done on it. The surviving film records and its notoriously erratic behaviour ensured that Panjandrum became the best remembered of the DMWD projects.

The assertion that it was intended to breach the Atlantic Wall is probably incorrect and has led to speculation, given that it was tested in public view, that perhaps Panjandrum was somehow part of Operation

Fortitude, the code name for the deception plan to fool the Germans into thinking that the invasion would be across the Pas de Calais region where concrete walls had in fact been built to resist invasion. However the Technical History of Panjandrum has the title "Beach Obstacle Demolition" and this was undoubtedly its intended purpose as a device to be launched from an landing craft and demolish beach obstacles to clear a path for the vehicles and troops. There were plenty of these beach obstacles such as the steel tetrahedrons which often had mines attached. Shute was well aware of these obstacles and also of the night-time cross Channel trips by Naval frogmen to the invasion beaches. These men risked, and often lost, their lives to bring back vital information on the beach defences.

Shute's work with the Swallow aircraft on the Beaulieu river gave him a close up view of the preparations for Overlord and he wrote about various aspects of these in his Second Front articles, including a description of the desperate bid to rescue the driver of a tank that had flooded and sunk when driving off a landing craft on the Isle of Wight. In the third of these articles he casually mentioned that he had recently been on an invasion exercise. In fact he took part in Exercise Trousers, the full scale rehearsal by the 3rd Canadian Infantry Division that took place at Slapton Sands in Devon on 12 April. Quite how he came to be aboard an LCT loaded with tanks and guns on that exercise is not clear. He may have been one of the LCT officers, for he knew these craft well, but from his description it appears he was there merely to observe and write about the exercise.[17]

For Trousers they sailed all night in a great fleet and at dawn came to the assembly point where the Infantry Landing ships were disembarking troops for the assault. His LCT went in to bombard the coast in a rehearsal for softening up enemy defences and it was a piece of coast that Shute knew well. In peacetime he had anchored his yacht here to bathe and he had travelled down there to see the actor Clive Brook act out his part when *Lonely Road*, was being filmed.

The LCT fired as it closed in to the beach and Shute watched, through field glasses, the shells bursting inland. Slapton Sands and the surrounding villages had been completely evacuated from December 1943 so that it could be turned into a practice area for beach assaults and all forms of rehearsal exercises. There is no doubt that the gunners on the LCT were firing live rounds, for Shute describes the shells causing damage to a house set on a hillside, landing in the drawing room, destroying the coach house and laying waste to a walled garden with fruit trees. His LCT finally beached so that the guns and tanks it carried could disembark to carry on their assault on land. The assault landing craft were also putting the infantry ashore to fire from the sand hills. The men and vehicles were, as he put it,[18] "going through their lines on the beachhead as other actors in a petty play had before them." Some vehicles and tanks got stuck on the shingle of the beach and had to be towed out, but ninety five percent had got ashore alright and had gone on to complete the exercise successfully. The Canadians acquitted themselves well on that exercise and it was a resounding success, much to the relief of Generals Montgomery and Dempsey, who watched the whole thing.[19]

Once the exercise was over and manoeuvres completed, the LCT re-embarked the Canadians, formed up in a convoy and set course for home. Shute was full of admiration for these gunners who lived on board the LCT for several days during the voyage to and from Slapton. An LCT is little more than an open barge with a bridge at the stern. The gunners lived, cooked their meals, washed, shaved and slept alongside their vehicles out in the open. "They had reduced the art of living to the simple essentials without losing very much; under all circumstances they knew what to do, and they did it well and cheerfully."

So they left that "assaulted and devastated coast", as Shute describes it, and sailed back to where they had come from. In Shute's case, this was the Beaulieu river and Lepe Hard where he left the LCT on the morning of 18th April. What he encountered next is best described in his own words:[20]

I left that LCT at the same hard as the Canadians, and got into my truck and drove away. Only a few miles on I came on an enigma of this curious war, in a small country lane with fields on either side, very near the sea. A German aeroplane, a Ju 188, had crashed across the road that morning; it had spread itself all over the field in the manner of a modern aircraft, so that no part of it was recognizable or more than one foot high above the ground, save for the rudder. There had been fire, of course, but no explosion, for it was not carrying bombs.

I got out of my truck and talked for a time to the young Air Force officer who was doing a technical examination of the black, burned wreckage. It had come in from the sea at an altitude of only about a thousand feet; it seemed a suicidal venture at that height, and in broad daylight. It crossed a spit of land with several batteries firing at it, crossed a channel, and came into a more heavily defended area still. One gunner captain in the district swore that he personally put seven Bofors shells into it. Then four Typhoons returning from a fighter sweep caught up with it and gave it their squirts, and so it came to ground across this lane, not far from salt water. So perish the King's enemies.

All the occupants were killed outright save one, who died ten minutes later without speaking. And when they came to count the bodies there were seven; seven men in an aeroplane that normally is manned by four, that only had seats for four in a cramped cockpit, with no other space in the machine. They must have been sitting on each other's knees. All of them were non-commissioned officers.

What duty brought the seven NCOs to England in full daylight, without bombs, and at that suicidal height? Why seven? Or had they stolen the machine, and were they trying to escape to England to surrender? It may well be that we shall never hear the answers.

That scene and the descriptions he received stayed with him over the years and were to form the core event of two novels, only the second of which was published some 11 years after the event.

A call was put out for members of the Royal Observer Corps to volunteer to serve on merchant ships on D-Day. Each ship would have two observers to help identify aircraft—a vital task to distinguish friend from foe. The Corps consisted of part time members who had other occupations. They manned 1400 posts and reported all aircraft sightings to central locations. It was, had he known it, the Observer Corps on the Isle of Wight who had first spotted the Ju 188 shot down on that fateful morning of 18th April. Shute's attention to these observers was drawn on a visit to an officer on a defensively equipped merchant ship. He followed up the story with a visit to their headquarters at the Royal Bath Hotel in Bournemouth. There he found elderly men being prepared for shipboard life with volunteers from many walks of life. He heard of a hotel proprietor who had closed his hotel, sacked the staff, to answer the call. The Secretary of the Society of British Aircraft Constructors—an organisation well known to Shute from his days at Airspeed—decided that the aircraft industry could get along without him for a while and volunteered.

Men of 50 to 60 years old, veterans of the First World War were there relishing the prospect of making a useful contribution to the invasion. Shute found in these men the Dunkirk spirit which had burned bright in 1940, but had dimmed over succeeding years. They renounced personal ties, family and went with laughter to a life of hardship and the possibility of death aboard ship—and they were very glad to get the chance. It was, he said, "a grand and stimulating party; I am very glad I met them."

On D-Day itself Shute sailed with Force L, a follow-up to the main invasion force. He went, he said,[21] "as a naval officer with no duty but to write what and when I chose, and with no responsibilities. Looking back upon it now, it was the perfect assignment." Shute was at Farnborough on 1st June watching the trial of a "difficult gadget" when he got a call to report next morning for a briefing. The "difficult gadget" was the Swallow which was undergoing tests at R.A.E. He had then to dash around to collect his gas mask, blankets and other gear before the briefing. At the briefing he learned that he was to sail with Force L, a follow up to Force J and would sail from the Thames. He was disappointed not to sail with Force J from the Solent, since that force included the Canadians with whom he had shared the Trousers rehearsal. He consoled himself by reflecting that he would be safer with the follow up force.

So the following day he reported on board to Captain Shaw of the US Navy and boarded his American flagship where he learned that they would sail for Juno Beach opposite the town of Courseulles Sur Mer, and would arrive in the evening of D-Day. Before embarking Shute bought two books for the voyage, *The Grapes of Wrath* by John Steinbeck and a book of modern poetry. He received a friendly reception from Captain Shaw and his crew and found that the food was greatly superior to that served on British Naval ships. On the Sunday before departing Shute attended a short service conducted by a young Canadian padre. The service was conducted on deck amidst the tanks and scout cars.

After a postponement of 24 hours due to bad weather, the crossing to Normandy was uneventful. The invasion force followed channels well swept for mines. They arrived off the French coast and anchored at about 5 o'clock on 6 June. The following day—D+1 he was able to go ashore and spent time assessing the situation, inspecting a gun emplacement and German dugouts before walking on into the town of Courseulles Sur

Mer. At that time the front was about 4 or 5 miles inland, but there were still snipers about including, he learned, two German girls who lobbed shells onto the beach from a mortar hidden behind a hedge. He spent the night in a slit trench but got little sleep because of intermittent air raid warnings and anti-aircraft fire. The following day he inspected the town, which was in a condition of light blitz and spoke in halting French to the occupants of an *estaminet*. By late afternoon he was back on board his ship, which had been beached to offload its vehicles. That night as the tide came up the ship floated off and set course back to England.

Shute had seen for himself the initial outcome of the D-Day landings into which he and his engineers had put so much work over the previous two years, devising measures to increase the chances of the landings succeeding. Shortly before the invasion he had written:[22]

> We who have worked on weapons for this thing throughout the last two years know something of the value of our work, and we see it in proportion. We know that all our effort has done no more than to transform an utterly impossible task in to one which may now be brought to success if men have sufficient valour and self-sacrifice and determination—and luck. . . . The most that we engineers have been able to achieve has been to lift the venture out of the impossible in to the barely possible class. By virtue of our work, men instead of fighting an inglorious blockading war from England, with light casualties, may strive to land in France and to know the bitterness of exhaustion, wounds, and death which such an operation must entail. No weapon that we have made for them holds the promise of victory, any more than a wood chisel holds the promise of a Chippendale chair. Without the chisel the chair could not be attempted, without the weapons the assault on France could not be attempted. That is all we have done.

Shute was also involved in the early development of the Grasshopper, a landing craft adapted to fire multiple rockets.[23] He designed the projectors for the rockets and was involved in the ripple firing system. Ultimately this became the Rocket Landing Craft—LCT(R) which could fire over 1000 rockets in salvos. Once DMWD's development work had been completed by about the end of 1942 the Naval Ordnance Department took over production of the craft themselves. Unlike Swallow and

Panjandrum, these were successfully used on D-Day to produce a hail of fire on enemy defenders to stun them at the time when troops were coming ashore. Given his arrival late on D-Day he would not have seen them in action.

Back in England he continued with the Swallow trials and later in June travelled up to Scotland to witness the flight of a Fairey Swordfish which took off from "Lily Pad", a floating airfield that DMWD had helped to develop. By late 1944 his work at the DMWD was all but over. Although some staff were transferred to the Far East, Shute was not one of them. There would be loose ends to tie up, reports to be written but no new projects on the horizon. In December 1944 he left DMWD, was demobilised, and assigned to work for the Ministry of Information as a war correspondent.

It was Shute's misfortune that many of the projects he was involved with were largely abandoned. Shute himself summed up his feelings on his time with the DMWD:[24]

> I have sometimes been a little despondent about my war service as we worked on such a lot of things that proved to be useless either because they would not work ... or because by the time the long development was over and the thing was working satisfactorily the staff requirement had become obsolete and they were not wanted or because by the time development was completed the war had moved on and that particular device was no longer required. Some of the things of course were some good and I suppose one should be satisfied if one in ten of those projects turned out to be really useful.

In May 1945 the War in Europe was over, but in the Far East the Japanese were being pushed back from Burma, and Shute would be there to observe and report on British operations in the Far East. The war and his work at DMWD with its hectic pace, had left their mark on him. He had aged noticeably, his hair thinner and his face more gaunt than that of the lieutenant who had signed up in 1940.

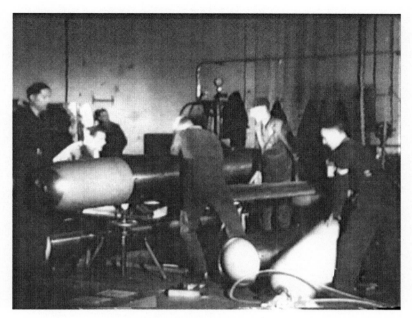

Toraplane—Assembly of wings onto the torpedo. Gosport, 1939.

Toraplane trial 42, 5 January 1940. The Toraplane, with the trial number on its fin, is suspended beneath a Swordfish aircraft.

Lieutenant Nevil Shute Norway, R.N.V.R.

A tank-mounted flamethrower undergoing tests.
"A big flamethrower in full blast is a very impressive sight, and very terrifying."
(National Archives)

8
And Turn Their Faces East

Shute left the Navy on 20 December 1944 and was demobilised. Although he had some regrets that many of the projects he worked on had been abandoned and not used in service, he was probably glad to leave the service. The D-Day invasion that he spent two years working for, and had witnessed at first hand, had been successful. Although the Allied advance into Europe had come to a halt with the German counter-attack in the Ardennes, it seemed, in that winter, that the war in Europe would soon be over. Shute had been seconded by the Ministry of Information to go out to the Far East and write articles on the campaign there.

The Ministry of Information was a government organisation set up at the beginning of the war to counteract the highly efficient German propaganda machine. To begin with, the reaction of the press was hostile, fearing a return to the level of censorship experienced in the First World War. The Ministry had three heads in quick succession before it settled down under Brendan Bracken, a slightly eccentric MP and a friend of Churchill. It was the Ministry's function to present the national case to the public at home and abroad. It is probably best remembered today for its poster campaigns such as "Careless Talk Costs Lives" and "Keep Calm and Carry on", but it also produced booklets on the various campaigns of the war. Early in the war it set up and ran the Crown Film Unit which produced propaganda films such as *Target for Tonight*. Given that *Pied Piper*, the book and film, had been propaganda successes it is perhaps not surprising that Shute was sought out to be released from DMWD duty and given the assignment of reporting the war in the Far East. Shute was to report to George Grafton Green, one of the Ministry's editors. Green had been involved in film making as well as publications, and was later to join the Rank Organisation. What he wanted was not objective reporting, but articles on British successes in the Burma campaign.

Shute entered on a period of waiting in early 1945 whilst the administrative machine ground its way through the arrangements for his credentials and his passage to the Far East. He occupied this time on two specific writing projects. He might have described *Pastoral* as a "trivial book" but he thought enough of it to produce a film script. The film rights had, or were about to be, bought by Alexander Korda. Although two of his novels had already been turned into films, Shute had not previously written the scripts, so writing one for *Pastoral*[1] was a departure for him. That he did this probably indicated that he wanted the film to reflect the book accurately and not be altered by an outside script writer. During January he produced a 90 page script which faithfully reproduced *Pastoral* as a film, with dialogue, descriptions of scenes and shots as well as non-verbal interaction between the characters. By the middle of January he sent the script to Carol Reed, who was to direct the film. Reed was a well established film maker with films such as *Night Train to Munich* and *The True Glory*, but is best remembered for his 1949 film *The Third Man* starring Orson Welles.

In late January Shute received a letter from Ian Dalrymple, with comments and suggestions on the script. Dalrymple was also well established in the film industry and had worked in the Crown film unit, but in this instance was working as assistant to Korda. Dalrymple's opening comments on the script were that it successfully reproduced the flavour of the book and it was not necessary to say he liked it, because he liked the novel more than somewhat. For him the great attraction was the human story. The physical scenes, good of their kind as they were, had been done before. The domestic side of an Air Force station with its atmosphere, characterisation and excellent dialogue were what made the film a proposition in war or peace. He followed these comments with several pages of suggested alterations, mostly minor and designed to enhance the film—no major changes were suggested.

The film, of course, was never made. Had *Pastoral* been written earlier in the war it might have been attractive as a propaganda film as *Pied Piper* was. Now, towards the end of the war, the need for such a film had passed.

The second piece that Shute wrote in this waiting period was *Vinland the Good*,[2] the only one of his published works that is not in novel form. It is a script for a play or film. In the foreword he tells us that he read several books on the Norse discovery of America, including Edward Gray's book *Leif Eriksson, Discoverer of America A.D. 1003*. This author speculated about the possible Viking landing at Martha's Vineyard and Cape Cod and Nantucket. He also mentions the Gaelic 'scouts' among the Vikings.

Shute said that he had put a little of the story into *An Old Captivity* written before the war but the story stayed with him as one of the best he knew. It appealed to him because it was not the history of great people and the Spanish Royal Court, but about an ordinary man, a farmer, who set out to get a load of lumber and discovered America on the side. He had told the story in wardrooms and messes during the war and kicked himself for writing only a small piece of it before. Now he wrote it as a script, possibly because he thought that was the best way to tell it and maybe because he had just written the *Pastoral* script, so the technique of script writing was fresh in his mind.

As if to emphasise the difference in the historical aspect, the first scene is set in an English school, perhaps modelled on Shrewsbury, where the Headmaster is talking to masters who are all elderly and awaiting the arrival of Major Callender, a former pupil who has had an interesting army career in the War—serving in North Africa, Italy, Normandy and Arnhem no less. Callender is to teach history and that of the United States to the Upper Fourth and Lower Fifth forms. What follows is Callender's lesson interspersed with scenes from the Nordic saga of Leif Eriksson and the young Scots Haki and Hekja, the runners who had featured in Ross's dream in *An Old Captivity*.

Throughout, the Headmaster is listening sceptically behind the door. The last scene shows that the boys enjoyed the lesson with its unconventional teaching of history. The Head though, seems less than pleased with Callender's implication that Kings and Princes are just froth, that Thorgunna had a baby and that the boys themselves are going to make history. He says, with a touch of sarcasm, that as a first lesson in United States history it was certainly original. It was certainly quite different from the way Shute would have been taught history at Shrewsbury.

It is the only one of Shute's published books that was never re-printed and languished in semi-obscurity until it was re-published in 1998.[3]

By April the necessary arrangements had been made and Shute travelled out to India by the B.O.A.C flying boat service. Also on that flight was Dr Davies the V.D. specialist for the Burma forces. The flight stopped over in Egypt and the two dined together at the luxurious Mena House Hotel near Cairo and visited the Sphinx. When he arrived in Calcutta, Shute was attached to the RAF Public Relations Section run by

Group Captain Dodd. So he began his stint as a war correspondent. He sent his first article to Green on 30 April based on what he had learned from talking to various people in Calcutta. Sergeant Allen took him to get his inoculations. Allen had been in Calcutta for over three years and his main concern was not about the war—that seemed to be going well enough—but that when he returned to England all the marriageable girls would have married Poles or Czechs or Americans. In all his time in Calcutta he had never been out with a girl and he seemed to Shute to be rather bitter about this and, with others of his type, inclined to get into fights with Americans on a Saturday night when they had had a skinful. Apparently he was known as "Round The Bend Allen" in the office.[4]

From talking to other officers, Shute got the view that most serving men wanted to get the job done against the Japanese as soon as possible and get home. They were grateful for American help both in this theatre of war and also in Europe. One officer thought that the war against the Japanese ought to be prosecuted to the bitter end and the towns and cities in Japan razed to the ground to teach them a lesson. This officer's view was that we couldn't rely on any peace treaty with the Japanese. Whilst in Europe the view was that the Germans could be rehabilitated after the war, it would not be possible to do that with the Japanese, since their philosophy was so different from that in the West.

Shute wrote that the following day he would be moving to the Forward Area, to Burma itself. He would fly in an American Dakota and noted that the Americans were providing many of the transport aircraft used to supply the advancing British and Indian armies in the Burma campaign.

Following the conquest of Malaya and the fall of Singapore in early 1942, the Japanese armies had moved quickly north into Burma taking over the whole country until their advance was halted at the Indian-Burmese border in 1944. The tide turned in the Allies favour after the battles at Imphal and Kohima, and the British 14th Army under General Slim began re-occupying Burma in a steady advance southwards through Mandalay, often in appalling conditions. Simultaneously, Fifteenth Corps was attacking down the coast towards Arakan, one objective being the capture of the islands of Ramree and Cheduba, where airfields could be constructed for air support for operations in central Burma. So when Shute arrived in the forward area the British were on the verge of taking Rangoon and attempting to cut off the Japanese retreat eastwards from Pegu.

In his second article of 2 May[5] he describes the air supply operations needed to sustain the advance of the 14th Army in its long narrow salient. He flew in a Dakota manned by Canadians in a supply drop and describes the event in vivid detail. The Dakota took off from Akyab and flew over the mountains to the drop zone just behind the front line. They carried about 3 tons of petrol in cans attached to parachutes. They flew in a tight circuit over the drop zone already littered with parachutes. When the pilot rang a bell, Shute and the Indian regulars sweated to manoeuvre the heavy loads down the cabin to the door and push them out. Then the bell stopped and the aircraft banked steeply for another run over the zone. In several passes the load was dropped, and the aircraft climbed on course for base whilst the following aircraft lined up for its drop. He sat back, dripping with sweat and feeling sick on the flight back. It had been an exhausting trip. Once back at Akyab he left the crew who were already loading up again for another airlift. This airlift went on continuously, for it was the only way to keep the advancing army supplied, since road to the front was impassable for trucks because bridges had been blown.

The aircrews preferred to do long days of intensive flying followed by a day or two relaxing and bathing in the warm Indian Ocean. Each crew did no more than 110 to 120 hours a month and there were 2 or 3 crews for each aircraft. Only in this way they could supply the advancing army at the rate of 165 tons each day.

Shute went to the briefing for the airborne part of the air-sea landings at Elephant Point at the mouth of the Rangoon river south of that city. This was part of Operation Dracula to silence the coastal batteries and allow naval minesweepers to clear the river for shipping. It was to be the first operation of airborne Indian troops in American aircraft with British jumpmasters. The operation was a complete success and served, Shute wrote, to show the happy integration of forces from all three countries.

Minesweepers swept the channel and were followed by Landing craft which landed men of Fifteenth Corps on both banks. Meanwhile in Rangoon itself, 1200 prisoners of war in Rangoon Jail, who had been there since 1942, found that the Japanese had gone. Climbing up on to the roofs they painted the words "JAPS GONE". Fearing that this might be interpreted as a Japanese trick they added the words "EXTRACT DIGIT" on another roof. The message was spotted and photographed by an Allied aircraft. Shute wrote about the condition of these prisoners after 3 years in prison. Most were suffering from beri-beri; they had also

suffered many indignities but had not been starved. They had received
no Red Cross parcels but said that conditions had improved somewhat
in recent months as Japanese discipline relaxed as their morale declined
with the Allied advance.

So Rangoon was liberated, or rather the Japanese abandoned it, a
characteristic, Shute wrote, that they displayed whenever overwhelming strength was deployed for attack. Shute pondered on the Japanese
mentality, where they hardly ever surrendered, but in some cases fought
like devils till the end came. To Shute the Japanese mentality had queer,
uncharted areas of weakness and strength judged by Western standards.
If we could understand the way the Japanese behaved in war we stood a
chance of doing something with them in peace.

Shute despatched his third article on 12 May.[6] In his covering letter he
told Green that he was in Rangoon and would make it his headquarters
for a while. At the moment there was little war to write about but he
expected things to liven up soon. He ended by saying that he was keeping
very fit and enjoying it all very much. The article begins with a description of the Buddhism of Burma, that the people were literate, there was
no caste system and no *purdah*. Women looked at men fearlessly and did
most of the business dealings. They also married at a natural age, and had
freedom of choice in marriage, and even after marriage a woman did not
change her name. He had met no officer of the British administration
who did not have a great liking and respect for the Burmese. On their
part they had a good understanding of the good points and failings of
the British.

Before the war, the Civil Administration was divided equally between
the English and Burmese. Many of the Burmese administrators had been
taken away by the Japanese, making administration difficult at a time of
great need.

Shute travelled with a young English Civil Affairs officer, a Major,
who had been in Burma before the war and spoke the language. They
went to visit a local village where the headquarters was a thatched basha,
serving as a court, police headquarters and municipal offices as well as
the home of the Major. Shute asked what the people wanted and was
told that they wanted to be left alone; they had been so messed about by
soldiers over the last three years. Shute observed the officer talking and
sharing jokes with the Burmese who came to the basha. He signed their
chits for labour and materials—they were very short of cloth. Many things

were in short supply, including cattle, and it would take time to build up stocks. But the people were improvising, making their own inferior cloth and finding ways to transport cattle and other livestock.

Shute visited the local hospital run by an Indian doctor, a native house with army camp beds on the floor. The patients had their wives living with them to tend their needs. That afternoon Shute went with the Major to investigate a problem with soldiers from the Royal West African Frontier force. They found eight to ten black soldiers cutting bamboos for a basha as shelter from the approaching monsoon and they were cutting the bamboo on private property. The officer gave them a good dressing down and the soldiers moved off sullenly. Shute commented on these black soldiers who had come from West Africa and who did not appreciate that they had fought the Japanese to liberate the Burmese, not to conquer them too. They believed that they had conquered Burma and were therefore entitled to the spoils of victory. To make a fuss over a few bamboos seemed to the black soldiers to be incredibly small-minded, as were the harsh punishments meted out to them in cases of rape. Shute ended his article by observing that the Civil Affairs officer was seldom short of work.

Shute's next article was about the state of Rangoon just after the evacuation by the Japanese.[7] Believing that they would be in Burma for good, the Japanese had thought nothing of circulating their own currency. In fact they printed the worthless notes by turning a handle of a small press making the notes on the spot. When the Japanese left, the banks had been broken open and stacks of notes were lying in the streets. The worthlessness of the currency was brought home to Shute when he tried to buy some bananas in the market and offered one Indian rupee. The girl seller did not understand that 1 rupee was real money, more valuable than the Japanese notes. This, to Shute, was one more problem for the Burmese, the replacement of worthless currency with one that had real backing.

During the occupation the Japanese were thoroughly disliked by the native population for the brutality of their soldiers and their crude behaviour.

In 1942 the Burma Independence Army had fought alongside the Japanese, believing that they were freeing Burma from British rule. They quickly realised they were merely assisting in the conquest of their country by another great power, and a less tolerant one. The Independence Army was disbanded after Japanese occupation, but secretly re-formed later and helped the advancing British forces by providing intelligence.

Turning to religion, Shute wrote that the Japanese were keen to reduce the number of Buddhist monks or pongyis, and that some of the temples had been desecrated, though not the Shwe Dagon pagoda. The Protestant Cathedral in Rangoon had been turned into a distillery for sake. Only the Roman Catholic priest and nuns had remained throughout the occupation, although they were imprisoned to begin with, but later released. He visited a Mother Superior at a convent, an elderly Irish woman who told him of their suffering during that time, with dysentery, beri-beri, malnutrition and lack of medicines. Shute was shocked by what she told him, but much impressed by her serene courage and faith. He ended his article with these words: "A faith like that, after three years of privation, suspicion, disease, and death. The universal comment here is 'They've got something. You just can't deny it'. I can't deny it, either."

Shute sent this article on 17 May, adding in his covering letter to Green, that he had typed it on both sides of the paper because paper was in short supply. Also he had not heard from Green about the earlier articles, but as he hadn't had any mail for three weeks that was not surprising.

A couple of weeks later Shute was on board a Naval Fairmile launch, part of an armed fleet of gun boats lying in wait to ambush the Japanese landing craft that they used to escape down the Irrawaddy Delta. The Fairmiles kept to the river banks, covered by trees, listening and waiting for the Japanese to come. It was an eerie vigil through the night. The Japanese gunboats came at dawn and the Fairmiles opened up on them, turning broadside on to bring all their guns to bear. The Japanese returned fire viciously but it was all over in a few minutes. One by one the Japanese boats were set on fire and headed for the mudbanks. Any escaping Japanese on the banks were swiftly dealt with by the Burma Independence Army with their steel dahs. In all, over 300 Japanese were killed in that engagement for two wounded on the Fairmiles.

Shute was impressed by the Burmans who crewed these boats. They were, he wrote, incredibly good types judged by any standard. They were fearless, disciplined and very good with machinery. The officers were Burmese or English and the work of the boats was carried out in English and, because they all had the same sense of humour, they were happy ships. Two of the officers came from Henzada and Shute attended several parties there where he met and talked to a number of the Burmese girls who were invited. These girls were very pleasant, well-educated and spoke good English. They were anxious for news from the west and asked Shute about Mr Churchill, the film stars Deanna Durbin and Rita Hayworth. Shute assured them that Mr Churchill was well and that Rita Hayworth seemed prettier than ever. When the girls asked after President Roosevelt, Shute broke the news to them that President Roosevelt had died in April.

Some Burmese who visited the ships spoke of torture by the Japanese Kempe Tai, the equivalent of the German Gestapo, and gave hints of collaboration by others. Shute heard stories of the uncouth behaviour of some Japanese soldiers: eating food from a bedpan and one who ate furniture polish as jam and liked it. Whilst the Japanese were thoroughly disliked, the Burmese did have some grudging respect for their soldiers who carried everything they needed on their backs and had conquered a country with so little equipment. Yet the Burmese had no doubt that the Japanese would be defeated by the British and Americans with their superiority in guns, trucks and aeroplanes.

At Henzada, Shute and the Naval officers were among the first to arrive after the Japanese evacuation. Here he met the local railway superintendent, who told him that he had removed certain parts from the locomotives and buried them. Believing that the locomotives were useless, they had been left alone by the Japanese before they left. The man said he could get the railway running again in a couple of days and there was plenty of rolling stock. He asked Shute if he should start running the railway up to Bassein. As a war correspondent, Shute felt it was not a matter for him to decide, so he talked to the RNVR officers with him. They believed the 14th Army were only about 15 miles away and wondered how the soldiers would feel being met by the Navy and being offered a ride on the railway the rest of the way. They told the superintendent to get the locomotives working but not to run the railway until he had further instructions.

Henzada was bombed and blitzed because it had been the Headquarters of a Japanese division. Much of the town had been burned down; the market stood empty and deserted. Shute paid tribute to a 75 year old English Mother Superior who had stayed on during the occupation, confined to her quarters. She and her Burmese Sisters had endured starvation and disease. The Japanese had dug slit trenches for the air raids, but there were none for the Mother Superior and the Sisters. Bombs fell very near but they were not injured. A Burmese gentleman said that the holy angels were flying above the house all through the raids, shielding the Mother with their wings. Shute wrote that he must remember to ask the Hurribomber pilots about that. He and the Naval officers left tinned food, biscuits and soap for the Sisters and a couple of days later in Rangoon made arrangements for the evacuation of the Mother Superior. Shute had great respect for this lady and even more for the Burmese sisters who served her with a devotion seldom seen elsewhere.

The covering letter for this fifth article was dated 29 May.[8] Shute said that the war was completely static and might remain so for some time. In that case he warned Green that he could not expect one article a week if there was nothing to write about. He was also concerned that his articles were not getting through. He had asked Green to cable him with his reaction to them but had heard nothing. However when he got back to Rangoon, a cable from Green was waiting for him with his reaction to the first three articles. The first article from Calcutta was disappointing because it was too objective, the second on the airlift to the 14th Army was out of date. However the third on Civil Affairs hit the target, although Green did say in a separate letter that he would cut the references to the West African troops because there was a good deal of sensitivity on that subject, and there were some people who were always ready to seize upon any excuse to accuse us of exploitation. Green added that he would prefer Shute to concentrate on stories of definite British achievement. In his reply Shute warned Green that there was no British achievement going on in this theatre of war at the moment and unlikely to be for the remainder of his stay. Indeed, General Leese had just told war correspondents that they could take six weeks leave and would be recalled if anything seemed likely to happen. In articles 3, 4 and 5, Shute had written about civil affairs but didn't think he could get any more out of that, adding that Green would probably find articles 4 and 5 rather objective. He was, he said, trying to get a story about the difficulties of flying in monsoon conditions.

His sixth and last article was about just that.[9] He met a Spitfire squadron on the island of Ramree, a hot, dry, dusty location with an airstrip, hot enough to fry an egg on a Spitfire wing, one of the few amusements the crews had. There was a perpetual hot wind blowing the grit about, which got into the oleo legs, the engine oil and on the seat and controls of the aircraft. It got into the eyes and stuck to sweat on the body. A Spitfire, wrote Shute, sitting lower to the ground, was more vulnerable than the larger Liberators. Yet in spite of these hardships the squadron had 12 out of its 14 aircraft serviceable and ready to scramble. These scrambles were to give close air support to the advancing army fighting in the jungles of Arakan. Approaching the target a matter of minutes later, ground radio would give the target, and the aircraft would attack Japanese strong points with cannon fire, bombs and rockets, knocking them out in advance of the troops. He met the same squadron again at Mingaladon aerodrome outside Rangoon. The runway was in poor shape owing to attacks by Allied planes in the advance to Rangoon. Only one runway, the shortest, could be used. Spitfire pilots returning from sorties, tired from flying in monsoon conditions, frequently overshot their landings and veered the aircraft off the runway at the last minute to avoid blocking it, damaging the undercarriage. Then the weary fitters would begin the task of collecting jacks and slowly raising the aircraft so it could be put onto a truck and moved to the hangar for repair. Cannibalism then came into play, the fitters taking serviceable parts from one aircraft to make the repairs on the other. Working with limited tools, they would replace the parts, pushing out bent cowlings and covers. So one aircraft could be made fit to fly, a little shapeless in places perhaps, but good enough. By the time it was ready, another pilot might well have crash landed and the long slow process began all over again.

There was also frequent danger from flying in monsoon weather, where monsoon clouds had very strong vertical currents quite capable of flipping an aircraft over on its back. Even larger aircraft had got into trouble in this violent weather and had crashed. It was not always possible to fly around or above these monsoon clouds; many pilots had bailed out or made belly landings in paddy fields, possibly in enemy territory. Shute ended his article with these words:

> These are the conditions in which the R.A.F. has fought its war in Burma. It has been a war of victory, for the Japanese Air Force has been driven from the air and utterly destroyed in combat. It has been a war of heat and dust and dirt and slogging, weary work on blazing airstrips, far from the green fields of home. It has been a war in which for six months of the year no pilot has gone out upon a distant mission with any confidence that he would not meet death from the sheer danger of flying in fantastically bad weather.
> It is a war that has been won.

Shute despatched this article on 26 June. In the covering letter he said that he had received the instruction to return to England and would get back as soon as he could obtain a passage. A month before that he had written to Group Captain Dodd requesting permission to join with Ian Morrison, the *Times* correspondent, to drive back to Calcutta, borrowing a trailer from the 14th Army and driving up part of the Burma road to see how far the infiltration of the Chinese in the north of Burma had gone. Could Dodd obtain his SEAC accreditation and allow him to go? The answer was a suggestion that a trip to Ceylon might be a good idea. The planned trip never happened nor did a visit to Ceylon—Shute thought it a waste of time since there would be nothing to report from there.

So his trip to India and Burma came to an end and he was home probably in late July. Whilst he had been away the British General Election had returned a Labour Government with a very large majority with a programme of nationalisation and state control. Rationing of most commodities was in force and would remain so for the foreseeable future. His articles were not used by the Ministry of Information and remained unpublished in his files. Why the Ministry did not use them remains unknown, perhaps they were too objective or localised in their coverage, or out of date.

In August the War against Japan, which many had feared might drag on for months or years, came to an end after the dropping of the atomic bombs on Hiroshima and Nagasaki. The instrument of Japanese surrender was signed on 2 September.

The 14th Army was known as the "Forgotten Army". Its campaign in Burma against the Japanese in heat and monsoon weather and jungle terrain was much less reported than the Allied victories in Europe and the Pacific. The war cemetery at Kohima bears the inscription, "When you go home, tell them of us and say, for your tomorrow we gave our today." Shute had played a small part in telling them of us. His time as a war correspondent was over. He had nothing tangible to show for it, but his experiences remained with him and his adventure in Burma gave him material stored up for use in his next novel.

He was returning to a Britain victorious but almost bankrupt, weary after five years of war and to an era of hardship, rationing and austerity under a Labour Government.

An early Swallow on its test track at H.M.S. Kestrel, Worthy Down.
(National Archives)

Panjandrum trial on the beach in North Devon, 1943.
(National Archives)

Pond Head House on Hayling Island.
Shute bought this house in September 1941.
(Author)

Runagate in full sail on the Solent.
(Heather Mayfield)

9
Frustration and Fatigue

Back home at Pond Head, Shute could pick up the threads of domestic life and resume writing as the full time career he had hoped for when he left Airspeed in 1938. Since then he had doubled the number of published novels and established himself as a best-selling author and a household name. His dollar earnings alone in royalties since 1938 totalled over $80,000, with probably a similar figure from Britain and other countries.

At home he was re-united with his wife and two daughters, both then at boarding school. That year Heather went to Sidcot School in Somerset, a co-educational Quaker school. Her parents believed it would be good for her to be educated alongside boys as well as girls. In 1943 Shirley, aged eight, began at Bedale's School, another independent co-educational school near Petersfield.

At Pond Head he had a considerable domestic establishment, his own separate study, five acres of grounds, the workshop and boathouse down by the jetty. He could get *Runagate* back from Birdham Pool in Chichester Harbour, where she had been laid up during the war, fit her out again, moor her at the jetty and go sailing as he pleased.

With the end of the war the Admiralty embargo on the publication of *Most Secret*, which had so angered him at the time, was lifted and the book was published in 1945. His trip to the Far East had broadened his outlook and given him experience of competent peoples from other countries and cultures, notably the Burmese, and a wealth of material stored up for a novel.

On his return he read *A Rising Wind*, written by Walter White[1] which impressed him greatly and provided another stimulus for a book. White was the Secretary of the National Association for the Advancement of Colored People (NAACP). Although blue-eyed and blond, White was of colored origin, had graduated and done a number of jobs before working full time for the NAACP in New York. In 1944 he had made a trip to England specifically to study the racial problems between black and white US troops stationed in England in the build up to the invasion of Europe. General Eisenhower's staff gave him freedom to go where he wanted and investigate anything. *A Rising Wind* was the product of this visit. Before leaving he had heard rumours of trouble between black and white American soldiers. A distinguished British family had invited American soldiers for dinner and dancing. Everything went smoothly until one black soldier danced with an Englishwoman, was assaulted by a white soldier from the South, and a free-for-all ensued, with the British taking the side of the black soldiers. He had also heard of a pub where the landlord posted up a sign saying "THIS PLACE IS FOR THE EXCLUSIVE USE OF ENGLISHMEN AND AMERICAN NEGRO SOLDIERS."

What might well have struck Shute in reading the book was the case of a Negro soldier accused and convicted of rape in Portsmouth and this letter from the people of Portsmouth, Shute's home town:

Sir:

Please pardon the liberty I take in writing you. We are concerned at the unjust sentence passed on Joseph Ballot, a young American Negro soldier, who was stationed here in Portsmouth. He was arrested in February last while on his way to camp about twenty minutes before midnight.

The arrest was made because a girl said she had been molested. There was no evidence to prove this, for at the trial neither the girl nor the policeman recognized the young man. Yet he was sentenced for natural life; no doubt on account of his color.

The people of Portsmouth were horrified at the sentence and suggested something be done. My husband prepared an appeal. I obtained 276 signatures and could have got many more had I the time. The German bombers at that time were paying us some attention and we were afraid the list might get destroyed, for some men wanted to take it into the dockyard and another to a factory. People in all walks of life talked about the injustice of the sentence. My husband sent the appeal with an accompanying letter through military channels. We got no news.

I then wrote to General Eisenhower, who referred my letter to a Brigadier who more than ever confounded us by saying the lad had been sentenced for rape. There had been no mention of this at the trial. It was supposed to be attempted assault.

All that happened to the girl was something to the face, whoever was guilty.

Sexual desire is not confined to the Negro soldier. Every young person, no matter what rank or color, is liable to succumb to the desire.

Crime should be punished, but let there be justice for all.

We are asking ourselves why we stood up to the nights of terror in 1940 and 1941 if it was not for the freedom, justice, and rights of all men?

We are hoping most sincerely that you will be able to do something for this unfortunate young man.

All that we have accomplished is to get the sentence reduced to twenty years.

A white American sailor, tried for murder, received a sentence of only ten years!

With all good wishes from the citizens of Portsmouth.

Here, together with his Burma experiences, were all the elements of a good story, which he began writing in September in a book written with a purpose, to promote racial tolerance and to expand his reader's awareness of inter-racial marriages. Shute worked steadily on the book throughout the winter and into the spring of 1946 and entered into correspondence with Walter White, sending him a copy when it was published as *The Chequer Board*.[2] As with *Most Secret,* he used intersecting story lines, brought together by the central character, John Turner, in his search to find out what happened to fellow wartime survivors, hospitalised after an aeroplane crash.

The book also contains a courtroom trial where one of the characters, Duggie Brent, is on trial for attempted murder. To write this, Shute may well have recalled the case brought by Stack and Turner against Airspeed in 1934. He had been present for that three day trial in court at the King's Bench Division.

Of *The Chequer Board* he later wrote that it was a book written with sincerity, but he genuinely thought it would ruin his American sales with the story of conflict between white and black soldiers in England during the War. It did not and was a *Literary Guild* selection and eventually sold over 600,000 copies.

The Chequer Board combined both wartime and post-war themes and had the topicality that Shute always strove for. Another theme from the War that was to occupy him was its effect on young people. Those straight from school, drafted into the Services, had an experience that broadened their horizons, giving them a different training and perspective than they would otherwise have had. For many, wartime had been a highlight of their young lives, not because of their experiences through it, but because it coincided with their youth. It gave them a comradeship and a common purpose. This was also something that made adjustment to peace all the more difficult for them.

It was with this in mind that Shute wrote *The Seafarers* after completing *The Chequer Board*. He drafted out the plot in 4 typewritten pages and followed it up with 52 pages of the complete story of the romance between Donald Wolfe and Jean Porter, he an RNVR officer and she a boats crew Wren, who find happiness together only when they return to their mutual love of boats and the sea. In writing this, Shute might well have had in mind his friend and colleague from the DMWD, Alec Menhinick, who had married Dorothy Jackson, a boats crew Wren known as Spiffy, in 1944 and lived aboard a yacht after their marriage. In writing the book Shute drew on his own experience of sailing in the English Channel and off the Channel Islands, but the book also has an account of Donald's single-handed crossing of the Atlantic, his fear of sailing alone and terror during an Atlantic storm. For whatever reason, he set the book aside and it was not published until 2002 with minor re-writes by the Nevil Shute Foundation.[3]

At this time Shute entered a period of some frustration, for it was about that time he first applied to the Ministry of Fuel and Power for an increase in his petrol allowance. Petrol rationing had been in force in Britain since the beginning of the War, and for his car Shute was issued with coupons allowing him 20 gallons a month. The Ministry of Fuel and Power declined his application for a supplementary petrol allowance. In 1946 both bread and potatoes were rationed, which they had not been during the war and to add to the misery the winter of 1946–47 was one of the coldest on record. The petrol ration curtailed the motoring that Shute could do and he increasingly found it a constraint and an irritant in not being able to use his car for travel to collect material for his books. He would also have had to pay super tax at 19 shillings in the pound (95%) on the top end of his income. His earnings from his published novels provided him with an income of well over £5,000 a year. Churchill, who had resumed writing after the war, was another who famously balked at paying super tax.

The following year Shute planned a visit to the United States, with the purpose of meeting ordinary American citizens—the man in the street. He may also have made the trip with a view to seeing if he could emigrate there, such was his growing disillusionment with England. He wrote to Walter White to say that, anticipating adverse criticism of *Chequer Board*, he was coming over to the United States "to stand up and be shot at, which should be great fun."

First though, he had to obtain sufficient dollars for which there were strict rules under Exchange Control regulations. He made a case to the Bank of England for the visit, stating his dollar earnings for the 9 years since his previous visit. He told them that there was no special appointment for this journey. He wanted to freshen up his ideas about America and keep in touch with his reading public. He proposed to make a speech or two and give a few lectures, and he proposed to spend about three weeks in New York, buy an old car and tour in it for about a month. He wanted to take his wife with him to help him in the fatigues of entertainment and to help him make contact with women. For this trip he got a dollar allowance equivalent to £600 for two months, which was ample for the two of them.[4]

In May 1947 he and Frances flew in the new B.O.A.C. Stratocruiser service across the Atlantic, his first flight in such a new all-metal aircraft. They flew via Gander and, on landing at Boston, the undercarriage failed on one side, a serious occurrence but without injury to crew or passengers. Shute bought a car and over a seven-week period travelled through Pennsylvania, Ohio, Michigan, Kentucky, Tennessee, North Carolina, Indiana, New York, New Jersey, and Connecticut. He avoided the lecture circuit and literary circles as much as possible, although he did lecture on India at Fisk University. They stayed in motor camps and ate in small town restaurants or Greyhound bus stations. Shute saw the Indianapolis 500 motor race and fished in the Smoky Mountains. He bought newspapers in every town or village where they stayed, and took every opportunity of getting into conversation with ordinary Americans. Throughout this tour, he said, he never heard one word of criticism of Britain. Many people asked him if England was going Communist. This question was always asked courteously and from a genuine desire for information, and not from animosity. There was universal sympathy amongst ordinary people for Britain in regard to rationing: "Gee, it's been tough for you. We're mighty sorry." In working class circles, as at one factory on strike at Louisville, Kentucky there was admiration and envy of Britain in regard to its administration. Someone said to him, "You folks over there are doing all right. You've got a Labour Government." He formed an impression of great goodwill towards Britain and did not read one newspaper article that was disparaging of Britain. Early in his trip he visited his American publisher in New York, who assured him that if Britain wanted another loan of any amount, the American people would approve it. At the time he discounted this as mere politeness to a visitor. Having travelled through the country and spoken to many people, he came to believe that it was true.[5]

Shute had returned to England by the end of June. His American trip, whilst giving him a good impression of American's goodwill to Britain, had been unproductive so far as new material for novels was concerned. At this time a plan was forming in his mind of buying his own plane and flying out to the Far East and Australia. He wanted to undertake such a long flight, emulating those of his old friend Sir Alan Cobham and Amy Johnson. He felt that if he went out to those places, particularly outback Australia, he would find new material.

His first step was to buy an aeroplane. Percivals at Luton were selling their Proctor V aircraft for £3,300.[6] This was a low wing monoplane of wooden construction with a de Havilland Gypsy engine, very suitable for his purpose. It was a four seater in the style of a contemporary motor car, with red leather upholstery. He ordered one from Percivals and had a long range fuel tank, an air thermometer, VHF radio and a better compass fitted as extras. In July he took delivery of the Proctor, painted silver with the registration letters G-AKIW in green. In the phonetic alphabet of the time she was George Able King Item William and quickly became known as Item Willie for short. Shute kept her at Portsmouth aerodrome, the same one where Airspeed—now a subsidiary of de Havilland, had their factory; a very familiar location from his days running the company and convenient to his home on Hayling Island.

At that time, he had clocked up about 180 flying hours spread over the period from when he gained his pilot's licence in 1924. He had not flown since the early days at Airspeed and would not have been familiar with wireless procedures used at the time. So Shute set about increasing his flying hours, which, he said, were done by flying to France to avoid the restrictions on fuel imposed by the Air Ministry. Instructors at Portsmouth Aero Club helped him with wireless procedures, and ground engineers at Air Service Training Ltd stood over him whilst he did airframe and engine overhauls for them to sign for in the log book.

Again Shute needed foreign currency and he asked the Bank of England for £260 for the various hard currencies encountered on this route, and he got it without any argument or difficulty. It was supplied in the form of a Letter of Credit, which could be negotiated at banks in the countries he would visit.

In late 1947 and through 1948 he meticulously planned the trip, poring over maps, plotting the stages, flying times, stop-overs, fuel consumption and obtaining the necessary kit, equipment and spares. The Shell Company provided him with a carnet enabling him to obtain fuel on credit all over the world from their network of agents. It seems that the Chairman of Shell, on hearing about Shute's planned flight, gave instructions that his managers and agents were to give him every assistance on his journey. Many of them were to prove very helpful, not only in providing fuel, but arranging accommodation and other assistance along the way.

On the literary front, his mind turned again to the effects of the War and he wrote a draft of a novel, *Blind Understanding*,[7] about a Wren, Janet Payne, who shoots down a Junkers 188 over the Beaulieu river, possibly killing a German student who studied before the war with her father, a don at Oxford. The plot also includes not only the Junkers incident, the aftermath of which he had witnessed in 1944, but many other elements from his Second Front articles, the drowning of a Sherman tank, the Wrens at HMS Mastodon, the Royal Observer Corps. He also included indications of the austerity of post war England, the student driving his car "on the meagre drain of petrol granted to him for research." He has another character, Lieutenant Craigie, engaging in sly trading of cars and black market weapons. He wrote the complete text but seems to have been unable to conclude it to his satisfaction and the manuscript, dated 8 March 1948 remained unpublished.

Shute always had his model-making as a relaxation and had kitted out the boathouse down by the jetty as his workshop. He began subscribing to the *Model Engineer* magazine, published weekly, which covered all aspects of his hobby. He had been working, on and off, on a model petrol engine since the end of the war and by 1948 the model was complete. He invited

Donald Stevenson of the *Model Engineer* down to Pond Head to have a look at it.[8] When Stevenson arrived, Shute was on board *Runagate* making adjustments to the radio. He showed Stevenson, who was also a yachtsman, over the boat before they looked at his workshop. The workshop was divided into two main areas, the first Shute described as the "dirty" workshop, where there was a forge, a grinder and a long woodworking bench with an electrically-driven circular saw. Behind this room was the metalworking shop with a lathe, pillar drill and an assembly bench. All the lathe and hand tools were neatly stored away in cupboards on the walls. As Stevenson noted, there was a place for everything and everything was in its place. Ever methodical, Shute kept a timesheet recording all the hours he spent on each project.

The model Stevenson had come to see was a 1/8th horsepower horizontal petrol engine made from Stuart Turner castings but with considerable modifications. Shute had added a driven oil pump in place of the usual bearing oilers. He had made the carburettor from a description given in the magazine. Stevenson was most impressed with the quality and fine workmanship of the model. It started easily and ran beautifully. As they strolled back towards the house, Shute pointed out where they kept the bees and the pigs, which were housed in a sty made from an old air raid shelter.

Shirley would sometimes come and sit on a stool in the workshop and watch her father as he turned parts on the lathe. He would give her some of the turnings which, as a youngster, she thought he was making specially for her.

If the model making was progressing well, his two unsatisfactory attempts at novels, *The Seafarers* and *Blind Understanding*, must have added to a sense of frustration. This was compounded by the post-war austerity conditions in Britain. Yet even as he was planning for his flight to the East, he had ideas for another book, which would evolve into one of his most popular novels. The germ of the story may have occurred to him during the long transatlantic flight to America and the undercarriage failure at Boston. He had had a long association with R.A.E. Farnborough and had visited the establishment many times, both whilst at Airspeed and during the war. As Shute was a Fellow of the Royal Aeronautical Society, its publications would have kept him abreast of current work on fatigue in aircraft structures. He knew many of the people at Farnborough, including Roxbee-Cox and Pugsley who had both worked on the

R.101 and also P.B. Walker, then head of the Structures Department at Farnborough. Indeed, according to Sir Peter Masefield[9] he "took my old friend, Percy Walker, of Farnborough, as a somewhat over-painted central figure as the prototype boffin, Mr Honey. Norway based part of the plot of that story on his discussions with Percy Walker about the increasing recognition, at that time, of problems of metal fatigue." In 1949 a Royal Aeronautical Society Meeting on fatigue in aircraft structures took place[10] and Dr D. Williams of the Structures Department at the R.A.E. stated that "Specimens of the same component having a mean life of 10,000 hours could depart from that mean by thousands of hours. This was not only known to metallurgists but had been proved at the Royal Aircraft Establishment on built up structures such as tailplanes" and also "cracks in the skin were easily seen but a stringer could break clean through without immediately betraying the fact."

Given that he was aware of all this, Shute wondered what would be the effect of fatigue failures on aircraft already in service, the possibility of a crash, and the suspension of a transatlantic service whilst the failure was investigated. The narrator of Shute's new story is Dennis Scott, newly appointed head of the Structural Department at Farnborough. Whether Sir Peter Masefield is correct about P.B. Walker being the model for Mr Honey in the book, Shute had probably encountered many of the "boffin" types there who became so immersed in the theoretical aspects of what they were working on that they forgot the practical consequences of their work. Shute has Mr Honey producing an atomic theory of fatigue failure. Honey uses fatigue tests on the tailplane of the (fictional) Reindeer aircraft that has just gone into service to test the theory. Shute was probably unaware that, coincidentally, another Farnborough scientist Dr A.A. Griffith, had laid the theoretical foundations for crack growth in metal fatigue some years earlier.

With this material, and with his gift for using his own real life experience and knowledge, Shute wrote the novel in 1948 with a working title of "The Mental Fight" taken from Blake's *Jerusalem*, later changed to *No Highway*[11] from a poem by John Masefield, a poet for whom Shute had great admiration. Once again he produced a good story combining topicality with a warm human dimension. As a footnote, *No Highway* became a favourite of Shute's daughter Heather. For the first time, she read the manuscript before it went for publication and so got a preview of the book in which Mr Honey's daughter Elspeth is one of the characters.

Two years after publication Twentieth Century Fox made the popular film
No Highway in the Sky starring James Stewart and Marlene Dietrich. In
the early 1950s there were crashes of the new de Havilland Comet which
had recently entered service with B.O.A.C. The subsequent enquiry and
investigation revealed that the cause had been metal fatigue, around the
windows, not the tailplane. This served to give *No Highway* and Shute the
status of being prophetic. Many years later when asked about prophecies
on metal fatigue in *No Highway* he replied,[12] "You think that was my own
idea? Look I'm getting a little embarrassed about being hailed a prophet
of metal fatigue. It really happened this way. Someone sent me a couple
of technical papers by Professor Pugsley and he forecast the whole thing.
I thought it was a fascinating idea for a novel, so I wrote it. If anyone was
the prophet in that book it was the Prof."

By about the middle of 1948 Shute had finished the book and sent
it for publication. That September the book was about to be printed but
at the last minute, there was a serious potential libel problem. In the
book Shute had British Overseas Airways Corporation (B.O.A.C.), a
real company, as the operators of the new Reindeer aircraft. B.O.A.C.
picked this up in the pre-publication press notices and claimed that the
book constituted a serious libel of the company and its Chairman and
threatened legal action. On 20 September there was a top level conference at B.O.A.C.'s headquarters[13] at which Shute agreed to delete all
reference to B.O.A.C. and substitute the fictitious "Central Air Transport
Organisation" (C.A.T.O.) instead. For good measure, Sir Miles Thomas,
B.O.A.C. Chairman sought, and got, assurances that the change would
be made in all editions and translations, and that any film of the book
would be made in a manner approved by B.O.A.C. Thus disaster was
averted at the last minute, but it was not the last time that the possibility
of libel would hold up publication of one of Shute's novels.

At this time, Shute was also making the final preparations for his flight
to Australia, and had increased his flying hours to around 250 and had
become thoroughly familiar with the Proctor. He wanted a companion
to go on the journey with him. In the autumn of 1947, at R.D. King,
who had been an agent for Airspeed aircraft, he met James Riddell and
they talked about Shute's planned journey by air to obtain material for his
books. On 28 March 1948 he wrote to Riddell telling him of the aircraft
he had bought and the preparations he had made. He asked Riddell if
he would be interested in coming along. Riddell read the letter—and,

he said, did no work for the rest of the day.[14] He jumped at the chance to go on the trip.

Ever practical, Shute wrote that any expenses to do with the aircraft would be his responsibility, but he would expect Riddell to pay for his own hotel, food and personal expenses.

Riddell was not a qualified pilot but was to be navigator and able to take the controls for a spell. He was a sportsman and a champion skier who had been British national champion in 1935 and vice-captain at the 1936 Winter Olympics at Garmisch-Partenkirchen. During the Second World War, he was based in Jerusalem and Syria. In 1942, he was seconded to the Australian 9th Army to set up the Middle East Ski and Mountaineering School at the Cedars of Lebanon above Beirut. He was awarded the MBE for his work, teaching upwards of 20,000 soldiers the techniques of mountain mobility and survival. While working at the War Office, he was pasting cuttings for a snowcraft manual when he inadvertently pasted together the head of a dog on the body of a camel. From that came the idea of "Split" books for children, a series published in many languages. So Riddell came to write children's books, and his and Shute's literary interests did not clash.

By 22 September everything was ready for their departure. In Shute's words, "we were probably as well prepared as anyone could be who had never made a flight longer than two hours."[15] He wrote to a friend that the only part that wasn't new and serviceable was himself, now two-thirds worn out.[16] Item Willie was at Portsmouth aerodrome, the back seat filled with luggage, tool kits, spares and medical supplies, a rubber dinghy and two life belts—and Riddell's neatly rolled black umbrella which caused a certain amount of amusement. The Proctor stood spick and span, fuelled and ready to go, but seemed to Riddell incredibly small for the long journey ahead. Shute acted just as though he was going to take a short flight, which he was, to Eastleigh airport to clear Customs. Farewells were said and then they were off on their adventure, on what Riddell called a *Flight of Fancy*, that was to take them half way across the world.

Heather (in front) and Shirley with their pets.
(Heather Mayfield)

Shute in his workshop at Pond Head.
(Heather Mayfield)

1947 advert for a Percival Proctor V; price £3,300.
(Flightglobal archive)

Shute in front of his new Proctor G-AKIW (Item Willie).
(Heather Mayfield)

10
A Flight of Fancy[1]

So they set off on their flight, crossing the Channel to Dinard in France, with Jimmy wondering what on earth he was doing, having exchanged his comfortable life in England for this possibly risky adventure. They had no trouble with Customs at Dinard where everyone seemed very pleased to see them. Then they flew, in the summer evening, to Tours, where they were welcomed at the Aero club. They slept at a local hotel following a good dinner in a restaurant.

Next day, somewhat later than planned, they shopped in Tours for a picnic lunch in the air and for blackout material to reduce the windscreen area. The course to Australia would mean mostly flying into the sun, and the machine would be quite hot inside. They flew via Lyon, finding that the maps of France were rather inaccurate and many roads and railways were not shown at all. They found the airport at Cannes with slight difficulty due to haze and they proceeded on a course over the hills, following the coast and giving Toulon a wide berth as it was a prohibited area. They landed at Cannes after this flight, quite tired from the noise. They refuelled the machine at once and got every-thing ready for the flight to Rome the following day and took a taxi to the Hotel Montana.

The following day they flew on to Rome but did not actually take off until 10:45. They tried wearing headphones to reduce the noise, using the radio to communicate. It worked well for Shute and he was much less tired at the end of the flight. Jimmy did not care for them and found they gave him a headache. It was a lovely flight, about 1000 feet all along the coast. They circled both the Leaning Tower of Pisa and Rome then headed for the airport. The following day they were up at 5 a.m. on the flight to Brindisi and Athens. There was a forecast of cloud over the mountains so they decided to go south past Naples and across the bay of Taranto. They flew over Naples and had a good view of Vesuvius, followed the coast round and so on to Brindisi where they landed just before lunchtime.

They could not find any food or drink and so Jimmy foraged around while Shute did the formalities and returned with two large cheese rolls which he had got at a military barracks. Crossing the Adriatic they flew over Corfu, where Jimmy had spent six months. It was a beautiful coast and a lovely warm afternoon; they went up to 6000 feet after Corfu in perfect weather and landed at Athens airport which is 16 km from the city. After a fruitless trip in to Athens, where all the hotels were full, they found the hotel Rex within half a mile of Athens airport. The accommodation was about six to one room, each with one washbasin and they could see Item Willie parked on the airport from the balcony of the hotel. Having no drachma and it being a Saturday night, the landlord paid the taxi and trusted them until the banks opened on Monday. The following day they rested and took the bus into Athens so that they could visit the Acropolis. Jimmy thought the Parthenon was one of the most beautiful buildings he had ever seen. Shute said he preferred the Rockefeller Plaza, holding that it was a complete work of art, whereas the Parthenon was handicapped by being a ruin.

Shute reckoned that they had done themselves very well at the Rex Hotel. Just before taking off from the airport the cable on the brakes of Item Willie broke. This was a weakness on the Proctor where too hard an application of the brakes could cause the small nipple of the Bowden cable to break free. This time the manager of the Greek airline re-soldered the nipple for them and charged nothing. This delayed take-off for Rhodes until half past one, making it too late to go on to Cyprus as they had planned. They flew over the sea and the many islands in sunny, bumpy weather, which Shute reckoned was good training for the crossing of the Timor Sea. The airport at Rhodes had quite a strong cross wind for landing, but Shute put her down fairly well and ran straight, but on taxiing, the brake cable failed again. They had intended to go on to Nicosia that day and had the brake cable repaired. But the town seemed so lovely that when Shute went to the bank he decided to stay another day. At the hotel they met Dr Ralph Bunche, a black American, who was the United Nation's Chief Mediator working on a settlement in Palestine. Shute thought him a fine chap, intelligent and very competent and he talked about his work trying to mediate a settlement of the Arab-Israeli conflict.*

They took off after checking on the radio at 118.1 megacycles and flew over the sea towards Cyprus at a height of about 2500 feet. Working out the fuel consumption gave a figure of around 11 gallons per hour, which Shute thought reasonable. They landed at the large aerodrome which they found without difficulty and were met there by the Richards family, with whom they stayed for the next two days, being entertained and taken sailing and swimming. Shute sent messages ahead giving their arrival at the next stop and also arranging for the 30 hour engine overhaul to be done at Baghdad. Whilst at Cyprus Shute got news of Mrs Morrow-Tait, who had passed through Nicosia two weeks earlier in her Proctor aircraft. She was making her bid to be the first woman pilot to fly an aircraft around the world.[2]

On the morning of departure Shute gave a joyride to two people who had been their hosts. However on landing, the brake cable failed yet again, and once more delayed their departure. After yet another repair they took off and flew to Beirut in an hour and 20 minutes. They circled the city and landed on the runway that was short and downhill, afraid to use the brakes too much. However all was well and they stayed at the Hotel St George. Jimmy was in his element and knew many people, having been stationed in the Lebanon during the war. Lebanon was full of wealthy people and large new American cars, but they were unable to discover where all this wealth came from speculating that perhaps some of it came from the sale of hashish to America. The following day they were up at 5 a.m. and took off soon afterwards. The mountains between Beirut and Damascus rise to about 7000 feet, so they climbed over Beirut and set course over the airport. After clearing the Lebanese mountains they passed over Damascus, talking to air traffic control on the VHF radio. The route onwards was not obvious, but from H.3, a remote point on the oil pipeline, they found a tarmac road leading eastwards towards Baghdad, where they landed after about an hour and a half. On the last part of the flight the desert, from the air, looked yellowish-pink in colour, which Shute found rather beautiful.

In Baghdad they met Mr Tull, the de Havilland agent, who was very helpful and lent them money until the banks were open. The following

---

* Dr Bunche was awarded the Nobel Peace Prize in 1950 for this work, the first black American to be so honoured.

day Shute went to the aerodrome with Tull to start work on the 30 hour engine overhaul but found at once that number three cylinder was blowing at the gasket. They stripped the engine and found that the cylinder barrel was too badly burned to put back. They did not have a spare, so it looked as though they might be delayed for up to a week waiting for a spare to be flown out from England. However Mr Tull got to work and located a replacement cylinder at Habbaniyah, an RAF station some distance away. After a hair raising flight to Habbaniyah in another aircraft, Shute collected the spare cylinder and returned to fit it into Item Willie's engine. The following day they worked on the engine and got it running in the afternoon and made a short test flight just before sunset, which he described as being rather lovely over the drab earth coloured city. That evening they were invited to a party on a riverboat, eating fish that were caught that day and grilled on an open fire. There was a sing-song on the way home and Shute was amused by quite respectable young women of the party singing "Roll Me Over" with gusto.

The next day they took off about nine o'clock and flew over very hot desert all the way to Basra, where they refuelled in the heat of the day, finding the metal of the aircraft almost too hot to touch. They flew on over the Persian Gulf and located Bahrain without difficulty. Because the brake cable had failed yet again, Jimmy had to take off his shirt and taxi the aircraft on the wing tip. Shute noted that Bahrain was a good place, much better than he had been led to expect. There were about 800 people, mostly American oilmen, living there. The place was hot but very healthy. As there was no hostel accommodation they stayed with Squadron Leader Lewis in a fine spacious house which was very comfortable.

The following day the brake nipple was re-soldered by one of the RAF people. They had a refreshing swim and lunch and took off for Sharjah at about 12:30, flying as high as 8000 feet so that it was cool. On nearing Sharjah they heard air traffic control calling on the radio, which made this the most efficient control they had so far met. They were accommodated at the local hospital, where the water tasted horrible and there was little beer. They dined with the C.O. of the small RAF staging post. Shute thought the town of Sharjah lovely at a distance with dhows and flat-roofed houses and veiled women peeping out at them from barred first-floor windows.

Shute learned that Mrs Morrow-Tait had passed through some days earlier. The RAF had no comment on her flying but plenty to say about the briefness of her shorts, the diaphanous nature of her jersey, and that she had kissed her navigator in full view on landing safely!

After a night stop they flew on towards Iran, flying at 5000 feet to clear the mountains but having to reduce height because of poor visibility. They picked up the Persian coast near Jask and flew on to Jiwani, another small RAF staging post, where they refuelled. This little post had 15 RAF men, who did a six month stint there and had their mess about 3 miles away. They set off again, heading for Karachi flying parallel with the coast which Shute described as plain hell—bare jagged mountains falling straight into the sea with no beach at all. It was certainly not somewhere for a forced landing, a factor that was always to be considered when flying a single-engined plane like Item Willie. On they went and flew past Karachi airport, finding that radio reception was difficult and visibility poor due to dust haze. They reversed course and spotted the large airship hangar alongside the airport. Once again there was a cross wind but they landed safely. As at Athens they eventually found accommodation in a dormitory at a nearby hotel. Next day a taxi took them into Karachi to the bank and then to the de Havilland agent because Shute wanted to get No.3 cylinder tightened down. However they were referred to Orient Airways, whose General Manager was Neville Stack. Shute was pleased to hear that he was available but uncertain what reception he might get because it was Stack and Turner who had brought the lawsuit against Airspeed in 1934 which Airspeed had won. However Stack was delighted to help and he arranged for the work to be done the following day.

They found Karachi a spacious, decent town with everyone optimistic that Pakistan would eventually get on its feet, having recently gained its independence from India. The hotel they stayed at was good, convenient for the airport, and Orient Airways did an efficient job on the aircraft. Shute was content to let them get on with it after an hour or so watching their engineers at work, although he later admitted to spending a rather dreary evening listening to the exploits of Stack.

They tried for an early start the next day but were delayed until 10:30 because of endless formalities at the airport; officials were suspicious of anyone going on to India. They flew at 7000 feet towards Ahmedabad, hoping to refuel there and go on to Bhopal. However, over the desolate Ran of Kutch the engine coughed and spluttered once or twice, which frightened them both. They made Ahmedabad and landed in the heat of the day, resolved to clean jets, change petrol filters and change plugs before going on. Once again red tape and the leisurely ways of the East held them up and they stayed over night at the local Bombay hotel, which was shabby, dirty with inadequate water supply and primitive sanitation.

Next morning they flew on to Bhopal in perfect weather at about 7000 feet, landing at 11:45. The Control officer telephoned the secretary to the Nawab of Bhopal asking if two English authors could stay at the Palace guesthouse. The reply was that they would be most welcome, so they parked Item Willie in the Nawab's hangar and were driven to the guesthouse, where they were accommodated in great luxury with their own suite of rooms and servants to wait on them. They were given a tour of Bhopal which impressed Shute with its colleges, hospitals, maternity homes and industry on a scale suited to the community. A trip to Sanchi was laid on for the following day to visit the Buddhist ruins.

They took off early next day for the flight to Calcutta with good weather to begin with, but they encountered a heavy rainstorm later on, the tail end of the Monsoon and a waterspout right in their track, to which they gave a wide berth. They arrived in Calcutta in the evening and handed over the aircraft to Airways (India) Ltd for the airframe and engine maintenance schedules. Although Calcutta was crowded, a friend of Jimmy's met them and took them to the Great Eastern Hotel, where they got a room. Shute was pleased to be back in the city where he had stayed in 1945 at the beginning of his time as a war correspondent.

There then followed three days in Calcutta, being entertained and meeting many people and being wined and dined whilst work on Item Willie was carried out. Shute was surprised and pleased that the work was done well and he was charged only for materials used—they did not charge for the labour.

On October 20 they left Calcutta at noon on route for Akyab in Burma, which Shute had visited on his trip in 1945. He found the airstrip littered with crashed aircraft and unexploded bombs from the war. A Mr Baroni met them on their arrival and drove them to the Convent where they were met by the Sisters, who remembered him from his previous visit and gave the two travellers a warm welcome. The following day they flew down the Burmese coast, passing Ramree Island, which Shute had visited in 1945, and climbing over the hills at 9000 feet to arrive at Rangoon after a flight of 2½ hours from Akyab. They were met at Mingaladon airport by friends and driven to the city. At that time Burma was in a state of internal strife, with various armed factions and Shute learned something of the country's troubles from friends he met. However they did manage some sightseeing, visiting the Shwe Dagon Pagoda. They also visited U Prajnananda, an English Buddhist monk, formerly Major Fletcher of the Royal Engineers. He talked to them at his ashram for over an hour and told them that a new Teacher would begin his teaching in about 1960 or 1970 and would be of Tibetan-Russian-Chinese stock, educated in America.

The next flight was southwards to Bangkok, and the route took them over the notorious Burma-Siam railway built by the Japanese with prisoner of war labour, with one life being lost for every sleeper that was laid. At first the railway was visible and being used but it then disappeared but for a faint line in the jungle. Shute described this flight as being by far the most beautiful and enjoyable so far; early rain had given way to clear sunny weather, and the jungle scenery below was spectacular. After some 3½ hours they landed at Bangkok airport where they planned to stay for a few days.

Shute described Bangkok as a most lovely place, all that the East ought to be but seldom was. There was no rationing, but there were masses of consumer goods and an ordered, clean city where everyone seemed to smile. As at previous stops they were entertained and dined with friends of both Shute and Jimmy. After 5 days they set off again for Songkhla in northern Malaya, a flight of over 500 miles. During this flight they encountered low monsoon clouds and rain, which forced them down to 100 feet flying along the beach. Fortunately the weather cleared as they neared Songkhla and they did a circuit at about 600 feet, flying over a small hill and putting down on a runway of hard packed sand and taxiing through pools of water to a palm-leafed basha which served as the control office.

They were met by Captain Dennis, a retired Naval Officer, acting as the British Consul and he accommodated them in the Consulate, a good house in a lovely position by a bathing beach. Captain Dennis intended to make his life in Songkhla; he liked the Siamese people and had fallen in love with Kum Chada, a Siamese lady who was the daughter of a Minister in the Siamese government. Dennis hoped to marry Kum Chada whom Shute had met in Bangkok, but Dennis seemed unsure of what to do about a proposal of marriage.

It rained heavily during the night so they were doubtful whether Item Willie would start after a night out in the open, but she did and they received a good weather forecast so set off to fly to Penang. They found Penang without difficulty, landing just before a monsoon shower and were able to taxi right into a hangar to get out in the dry. They stayed at the local hotel, but during dinner an engineer from Malayan Airways came to tell them that Item Willie had a flat tyre. Shute and the engineer worked all the next morning to remove the tyre and fit the spare, a difficult job. They also changed spark plugs, checked petrol filters and tightened the cylinder head nuts.

Shute and Jimmy flew next day to Kuala Lumpur where they were to stay with the Headleys, friends of Jimmy. Here they spent a rest day which was marred when Shute found that the tyre on Item Willie was flat again and he had already used the spare. This meant that they would be stuck at Kuala Lumpur until the tyre could be replaced. He also needed replacement brake cables that had been ordered earlier from R.K. Dundas. So the following morning they took the flight down to Singapore in a Dakota and got a room at the Adelphi hotel. Shute got two rather doubtful inner tubes from the RAF in Singapore and took them to Liddel at Dunlops. The outcome was that he had one rather doubtful inner tube and a tyre. He got a local garage to do an experimental repair on the tube and asked Liddell to cable Sydney to send two tubes by air, which he hoped would arrive in a couple of days. At Singapore his mail caught up with him—three letters from Frances and one from Heather. A parcel from Dundas had also arrived with contact breakers but no brake cables.

Shute flew back to Kuala Lumpur on the Dakota and had the spare wheel fitted and next day flew down solo to Singapore, where Jimmy had stayed. There the press caught up with him and he gave interviews. He also met Ian Morrison, the *Times* correspondent whom he had met in Burma in 1945. Another acquaintance he met was Dr Davies who flew out with him in 1945 and now had a large general medical practice in Singapore. Once again he and Jimmy were well entertained with dinner engagements and a visit to a Malay opera, which Shute found interesting with beautiful dancing by the main character, the Moon girl. In general, though, Shute found Singapore disappointing, perhaps because of some rather dull people he met and boring discussions with them about Malay politics. He had no complaint about the work that Malayan Airways carried out on his aircraft, nor their bill of £30, which he paid without query, having, he said, paid nothing for the work done at Baghdad or Calcutta.

On November 14 they set off once more, bound for Palembang in

Sumatra. En route they had to deviate from the course two or three times to avoid local monsoon storms. They found Palembang by locating the river on which it stands and flying up the river from the coast. They found they were not expected, and having no local currency, KLM gave them lunch. They asked for permission to fly on to Batavia (now Jakarta) on Java, but at the last moment permission to fly was refused. Once again the KLM people came to their rescue and took them to a hotel for the night. At that time there was a full scale war going on between the Dutch and Indonesian rebels. In the course of their flight to Java and on to Bali and beyond they encountered hostility from Dutch officials, with the KLM airline people being as helpful as they could. Jimmy had brought with him a letter of introduction from Prince Bernhard of the Netherlands and on more than one occasion this helped to smooth their passage.

They continued on through Batavia and Surabaya in Java and, in hazy weather, crossed the Bali strait and arrived in Den Pasar airport. Now, at last, they had arrived at this tropical island which Jimmy, in particular, had been anxious to see and explore and where they intended to stay for several days. So Item Willie was parked, the cockpit covered over and sumps drained. While Shute attended to this and got them rooms at Den Pasar, Jimmy went to see the Governor with Prince Bernhard's letter, which worked wonders, with cars laid on and people to show them the island.

During their stay on Bali they both came to appreciate these simple and artistic people, their feasts and festivals. One evening they saw a special dance performance performed by local girls and were also taken to visit Theo Meier, a Swiss artist married to a Balinese woman and were served an excellent Balinese meal prepared by Meier. That evening they were present at a local trance dance where girls, seemingly in a trance, danced until they dropped, going through the most complicated moves as if in a hypnotic state. This went on for some hours until it was stopped by Meier who thought the girls had had enough.

They visited some of the local shrines and temples and Shute thought the religion was a mixture of Buddhism and animism. The Balinese said prayers to various gods and left gifts in the shrines. After the visit to Meier, Shute took their hosts, Mr & Mrs Dronkers, for a joy ride in Item Willie. Dronkers was a keen photographer and wanted views of ravines, temples and volcanic craters. Shute obliged but commented that he did things on that flight that no sane Proctor pilot would do just to please his host and returned to the strip after 90 minutes of the most unwise flying.

On 22 November they said goodbye to Bali and flew on eastward once more, this time carrying a jerry can of petrol, being unsure of what fuel might be available on the next leg. On landing at Soemba Basar they found the airport organisation in chaos and again their arrival was unexpected. However the Army did produce some petrol to refuel them and accepted a signature against the Shell carnet in return. After 2 hours they took off again for Koepang in East Timor, landing there in a cross wind after a two hour flight. Shute described Koepang as a "bloody place", all the buildings being old Japanese barracks with no proper sanitation or decent accommodation. This did not give the rest required to tackle the next leg of the journey—the crossing of the Timor Sea to Australia. This was a stage of the journey that probably most concerned Shute, a flight of over 400 miles across the open sea. This was by far the longest crossing of open water in the whole trip.

So the next morning they left Koepang and set out for Wyndham in Australia, a flight of 474 miles, nearly all of them over the Timor Sea. Both Shute and Jimmy were nervous, alert for any signs of engine trouble, counting the hours and anxiously peering ahead for the first sight of land. Item Willie performed perfectly and after about three hours, to their relief, they sighted Eclipse Island off the coast, flew over the Drysdale River Mission and found Wyndham without difficulty, landing on a large airstrip. They were supposed to go on to Darwin immediately for immigration formalities but Shute struck at the idea and declared they would night stop at Wyndham and would fly on the next day. They were both tired with the strain of the flight and stayed at the local hotel. The temperature was well over 100 degrees and the countryside was, he said, just like Arizona with spacious bare distances and brown hills across salt flats. They spent the rest of the day lying down and drinking copious quantities of water, with the sweat pouring off them. However they had arrived in Australia at last, 61 days out from England.

The next day they flew to Darwin in about 2½ hours, where they found that the Customs officer insisted on looking through everything on board. The Shell representatives, by contrast, were very helpful, driving them to their Darwin hotel, changing money for them, and even fixing up to get their washing done! The great heat, plus sweating and drinking lots of water gave Shute an upset tummy. This, and the forecast of dust storms in Central Australia, meant that they stayed in Darwin for the next two days, during which time Shute gave a number of interviews to press people, learned about the Aborigines and about Darwin itself. He described Darwin as an attractive place though hot and humid, but spoiled by the relics of a meat works and the ruins of the war effort.

On November 17 they flew from Darwin, intending to get to Tennants Creek. When they landed at Daly Waters to refuel, the weather report there warned of dust storms and deteriorating conditions, so they stayed at the local hotel, which was quite busy, being a stop over for the trucks and buses travelling between Darwin and Alice Springs. A dawn start the following day took them to Tennants Creek, which had a large 3 runway aerodrome but little else. Then on to Camooweal. They had to wait until later in the day when the heat had abated a little, reducing the bumpiness of the air, before flying on to Cloncurry, another outback town where they stayed the night. Shute noted that, because of their late arrival, they missed tea at the Post Office hotel where they were staying and there was no beer available. They went to bed in a temperature of 102 degrees. Shute noted that his bed had bed bugs but Jimmy's did not.

After an early start next day, they flew to Townsville on the Queensland coast, a distance of 510 miles, which they did in 3 hours 35 minutes due to a tail wind. They found Townsville a charming place, prosperous with a population of about 40,000, with plenty of employment and a standard of living similar to England. They were entertained by many local people and gave radio and press interviews. As it was time for another 30 hour schedule maintenance on Item Willie, this was put in hand by Trans Australia airways. Shute visited Customs in Townsville, finding that his was the first case of a foreign tourist visiting Australia in his own aircraft with no intention of selling it in the country. There was no provision in Customs regulations at all for such a case. As a result, he was required to keep an inventory of everything to do with the aircraft and to present it when required so that a check could be kept by Customs.

On visiting a bookshop he found that *Pastoral, Chequer Board* and *Most Secret* were on sale and was told that his books sold out very quickly. Shute greatly enjoyed a boat trip arranged for him to Magnetic Island, a real tropical island with palms down to the waters edge and clear blue water. On the way back the girls in the party, on a hot sunny evening, in shorts and bathing dresses sang Christmas carols. He was glad to have seen young Townsville disporting itself.

He flew up to Cairns next day over beautiful countryside, all mountains and water, not unlike the West coast of Scotland, and then over sugar farms with small fields in various stages of cultivation, giving a patchwork not unlike the fields of England. At Cairns he was met by Arthur Wadsworth, the Shell representative, who arranged his accommodation and took him for a drive in the countryside. Wadsworth also introduced him to Reg McAuliffe, an agent for insurance. Reg spent a good deal of time in the Gulf Country and explained the business of poddy dodging or cattle rustling. Shute was very keen to spend some time in the Gulf country where he expected to gather material for his books. So he arranged to fly with Reg and the local doctor to the Gulf country the following week. Jimmy was not well and Shute had a long talk with him about their plans. Jimmy confessed he was bored with this country; however he was keen to see the Barrier Reef but would probably fly down separately to Sydney to stay with friends there and catch up with Shute later. However he cheered up when he met Beatrice Borst, an American author whose first novel *Nearer the Earth* had won a $1000 prize from the publisher, and who was touring round Australia.

The next day Shute, Jimmy and Beatrice went, as part of a group, on a trip to Green Island some 15 miles off the coast. Shute described it as a very pleasant day of yachting, bathing and looking at the coral and wonderful marine life through a glass-bottomed boat. He did get badly sunburnt on the legs through wearing shorts.

On 11 December Shute, Jimmy and Beatrice flew up to Cooktown. This was again a lovely flight up the coast to the bay where Captain Cook had beached his ship, *Endeavour*, in 1770 for repairs to damage sustained on the Great Barrier Reef. Shute talked to the local schoolteacher, Mr Hudson, who taught about 70 children who came from up to 200 miles away and stayed locally in term time. In some cases it took them up to 4 days to get home for the holidays by air, jeep or packhorse. Mr Hudson had a 15 foot long model of *Endeavour* in his classroom and Shute asked him if he would like a picture of Whitby in Yorkshire, where she was built, to go with it. Mr Hudson said he would. Later Shute sent a note to his secretary, Mrs Bessant, asking her if she could get hold of a print of Whitby to send out to him. Mr Hudson showed them the hard where Endeavour was laid up. Shute described it as a lovely place fringed with mango trees and a beautiful white beach just across the river. They flew back to Cairns in the afternoon and met Reg, who had their Gulf trip all lined up for the following Saturday. Reg was camping with his family but when he joined Shute for dinner at the hotel that evening, he had to borrow a coat and tie. As Shute noted, hotels would not serve guests who turned up without a jacket and tie.

On that Saturday Shute said goodbye to Jimmy, who was catching the morning flight down to Sydney. He then collected Reg and Dr Marcus Clarke who was coming with them on the Gulf trip. Marcus was a 35 year old doctor currently doing a locum at Cairns and was shortly going to England.

Cairns to Georgetown is about 184 miles, which they did in 1 hour 35 minutes—a lovely flight at about 5000 feet. The country was desolate and almost impossible for landing. First there was the coastal range of mountains, then the Tableland, about half cleared and farmed; then the country became wild ranges and scrub plains. At that time of year it was very brown and dried up, and all the water courses dry. Georgetown was a corrugated iron town of about 150 people. In 1900 it had been a gold mining centre, and it was said that it then had 30,000 inhabitants. Certainly the roads showed that it was once a much larger place. Now it was just a cattle centre, a place with a bank and a hotel where the ringers came in for a drink. They re-fuelled Item Willie and drank beer, then went into town in the trucks for three or four more beers before breakfast, which was steak with two fried eggs in the usual country style; then more beer and so all through the day. This beer drinking was not specially harmful: the great heat and the light quality of the beer seemed to make it innocuous. In these circumstances men got talkative but not drunk. Shute drank shandy all day and reckoned this did not count but he thought, it must have been 20–25 glasses, say a gallon and a half.

He learned a lot more about poddy dodging from the ringers from stations as large as 4000 square miles, parts of which were visited only once or twice a year. Poddies were the unbranded calves and the technique was to ride out on a neighbour's land and drive off as many poddies as you could onto your own land and corral them in a secret place. They were left without food or water for four or five days, then let out and given food and water. The calves would then stay put and were branded. Shute learned that the man who was most expert at driving his neighbour's cattle onto his own land was the man who got on.

Dr Clarke was busy with two pregnant women, who were very pleased that there was a doctor there to deliver their babies. Both gave birth during the night. Reg gave a Golden Casket ticket to the first mother, and Shute presented Mrs Wilcox, the second mother to give birth, with another ticket as a consolation prize. The Golden Casket was a lottery scheme to raise money for the Flying Doctor and other outback services.

Next day Shute, Reg and Marcus flew on westwards to Croydon in about 50 minutes. Item Willie had been parked at Georgetown with the cattle but there was no damage. Croydon was another corrugated iron town of about 150 people, variously reputed to have had between 8000 and 39,000 people, and 92 hotels, in its time. It had certainly been a big place at one time. The one-way strip used by the Dakota was earthen and in quite good condition. In this country it was usually dead calm in the mornings, but the wind might get up later in the day with the intense heat. The landing technique was to circle low over the town until someone, usually the local storekeeper, came out in a truck to meet you. When you saw him coming you went in to land. The doctor spent the morning with his patients, Reg with his insurance prospects, and Shute thinking what a shame it was that all the capital taken out of this country in the form of gold was not now available for water catchment schemes, for drought was a constant problem on many stations. At the bar he had a long talk with ringers about the shortage of girls. The ringers were all young men, good types, but there were no young women at all. The girls all went off to the cities and got jobs or got married there. This was understandable, because in a place like Croydon there was absolutely nothing for a single girl to do. But the boys would go where the girls are, and the future of North Queensland, Shute thought, might lie in the provision of jobs and amenities for women.

They lunched at the hotel, and took off for Normanton at about 2 PM. It was very hot indeed, impossible to touch the metal parts of the machine. In the air the climb was very bad, but they gradually got up to 7000 feet, the air temperature was still 30° C.

Normanton was another similar town, once much larger. It had a first-class 2-runway aerodrome put up in the war, and here Shute put up the worst show of the whole flight by making quite a good landing down a 20 mph wind. Wind socks in this country were very difficult to see, a white sock against sun baked earth: there were two but he could see neither from the air. Conditions were very bumpy and hot and he decided to land, judging the wind direction from smoke about 3 miles away. On landing, Item Willie ran and ran. At the end of the runway, still going about 30 mph or so, he ground looped the aircraft deliberately and pirouetted to a standstill in a cloud of dust. Fortunately he had checked tyre pressures at Cairns, and there was no damage. Marcus wanted to send a telegram to his mother, who did not know about this flight. Having considered this landing, they drafted it: "Making flight to Gulf with world-famous pilot, etc!" Shute thought that he might be world-famous, perhaps, but not as a pilot! They thought this a good compromise, satisfying to his mother while sticking to the truth.

They went to the hotel, which was the usual wooden and corrugated iron building with deep verandas. Normanton was very hot and humid indeed, with vast numbers of mosquitoes which almost certainly carried malaria. There was the usual deep drinking with absolutely no effect, the sweat poured out and the beer poured in and nobody seemed to get drunk, or not very. He visited the Bank Manager and after supper spent the evening talking to Fred Dawnbush, the local policeman.

On 16 December they took off for Augustus Downs, a large cattle station with an airstrip, taking Fred Dawnbush with them: This made four in the Proctor, so they took little luggage. Shute had to change the port set of plugs before starting. Augustus is about 100 miles south west of Normanton. It had one good tarmac strip laid down by the R.A.A.F. in the war, and one transverse grass runway. The tarmac strip was rather on the narrow side.

Augustus proved to be a showplace, one of the best run stations in the Gulf, covering 1500 square miles. It carried about 30,000 head of cattle valued at £4 10 shillings each, so the stock value was about £140,000. It was managed by Mr Nissen and his wife, who were very pleased to see them and gave them lunch in the homestead.

This vast property had just one house on it, a three bedroomed wooden house with deep verandas, spacious, but quite modest. There was an outstation about 40 miles away, but this was only a tented camp. Mr Nissen employed about 18 ringers or stock riders, about half of whom were Aborigines. This was all the staff employed to run this huge estate.

They took off after tea and flew to Burketown, about 60 miles north-west on the Gulf Coast. Burketown had two runways of hard earth, quite good but unusable by large aircraft in the wet. They picketed Item Willie down for the night, and drove into town.

Burketown was another ghost town, once a big place, in part supplying the gold rush towns as far away as Cloncurry. Now it had a population of just 50 permanent residents. There was a hotel and the store and a police station and a school, and that was about all. Station managers came in for their stores and took them out in a truck before the wet season, when they might then be isolated for three months till the earth roads were passable again. There were several such people in town, and many ringers: Reg sold a lot of insurance. Shute thought this was a bad thing, because he talked them into life insurance, taking all their spare cash for premiums.

In talking to the station managers he learned that the owners appeared to be reactionary. Many cattle died in the drought in the Gulf country each year, as many as 5,000 on one station alone. Managers wanted to spend money on water catchment schemes, building dams and pools and were confident that the expenditure would pay for itself in a few years in stock saved. Some station owners were reluctant to spend money on such schemes when the land was leased and the lease was up for renewal.

At Normanton Shute met Jimmy Edwards, the station manager at Glenore, about 15 miles out. He and Marcus arranged to go out with him that night in his truck and spend the next day with him. Jimmy was a cheerful tough, humorous Australian of 35 or so, just married, but his wife was away. He had been a prisoner of the Japanese, as had the doctor, and Shute heard some extraordinary stories of their time in captivity. Jimmy had been tied to a tree by the Japanese for several days as punishment for stealing food. He had been tied with wire pushed through the palms of his hands.

They drove out with Jimmy in his Ford truck about 11 PM over an unmade road that was often little more than a way across country between the trees. They got to the homestead about midnight and went to bed: Reg was busy with insurance, and stayed in Normanton. Glenore station was similar to the others described. It was about 1500 square miles, the furthest point of the property being about 100 miles from the homestead. Jimmy ran it with about 10 men, mostly Aborigines. The yard and equipment and outhouses round the homestead were similar to those of a 400 acre farm in England: the house was rather worse, though suited to the climate.

The following day, about mid-morning, they set out in a Ford truck to shoot alligators, wild pigs, wallabies or anything else that came their way. Trucks had a hard time in this country, but Jimmy's truck had a harder time than most. They drove for an hour straight across virgin country through the bush, threading their way between the trees and knocking down the small ones with the bumper like a tank. It was a rough ride. They came on a few pigs by a creek but the pigs escaped before they could get in a shot. They were greyish black in colour and shaped like a wild boar, with a very long face.

They drove on through the bush looking for pigs, and about midday met their doom, when a stump that Jimmy had not seen hit the bottom of the radiator and tore it out. This was quite serious, because they were 5 miles or so from the homestead and if they had had to walk home they would have been exceedingly thirsty by the time they got there. However, Jimmy, like most of these men, was a superb bush mechanic. He set to work with the tools carried in the truck and took off the radiator of the engine, and the fan. Then he plugged the filler cap and put the radiator back upside down, so that the damaged bottom was on top. They lashed it in place with a rope and wooden wedges, made a sort of mud and rag bandage for the damaged part, and filled it up with two gallons of water they carried. The whole job took about two hours. This water was sufficient to take them two miles to the nearest water hole, where they filled up and got home without further trouble. That afternoon Shute and two others rode out to shoot wallabies, which were too prolific. Shute had not ridden for 20 years and didn't know which had sweated most, him or the horse! Back at the ranch, Jimmy had made a fine improvising job of fitting the new radiator, mounting it on a baulk of timber higher up so that no stump could hit it again. They drove back to Normanton in the dark, and drank all the evening. There was no other recreation normally available in Normanton, but once a week there was a movie show and very occasionally a dance.

That was Shute's first meeting with Jimmy Edwards whom he greatly admired and who was to be the model for Joe Harman in *A Town Like Alice*. They kept in touch and remained firm friends for the remainder of Shute's life.

At the hotel in Normanton Lois, the waitress, asked if the doctor was free as she was feeling ever so ill. Marcus saw her and told her she was pregnant. Lois's comment was, "Gee Pa will be wild: he'll beat the daylights out o' me." Her sister had had two children before marriage. There was nothing much that they could do to help her.

On 19 December they flew to Dunbar Station via Galbraith. Dunbar had a good 2-runway aerodrome of packed earth and gravel. The station people came out to meet them in the truck, and they were very drunk. The property was the largest and the most efficient they had seen. It covered an area of 3,770 square miles, had about 30,000 cattle with 20–30 stockriders. The stockyards were beautifully laid out and equipped. The house was the best they had seen, surrounded by a garden of flowering trees and a lawn, and masses of crotous. They had got their Christmas supplies of drink a few days before and had been drinking solidly ever since. The manager, Noel Irwin, could hardly articulate. There were three others in equally bad condition, all very pleased to see them. They seemed to have slept where they fell the night before, and had been wakened by the noise of the aircraft. They had smashed all their glasses, so they plied their visitors with drinks in teacups. They were drinking beer, rum, port, whisky, and crème de menthe, and switching merrily from one to the other. The contrast between the efficiency with which Dunbar was run and the condition of the manager and men was amazing. When they were sober they were obviously very good managers. This was a place where any type of drama might happen at any moment.

They then took off for Mitchell River Mission, north west of Dunbar near the coast, about 200 miles up from Normanton. They landed after lunch time. As it was Sunday they had not wanted to get there during Church hours. The padre, the Rev. Norton, was an Englishman. He was known as Brother Norton because at one time he was a Bush Brother. The Mission was a native reserve, an estate of about 800 square miles which was run as a cattle station and made a profit. About 500 Aborigines lived on it; there were also two white women, a nursing sister and a schoolmistress for the children. Shute thought that Norton was a good chap. He learned that Norton was ordained in England and at one time was vicar of Pytchley, where the hunt is. He originally came out to the Gulf Country in the 1930s, then returned again in 1940 and was vicar of Cairns for a long time. Then he came to this Mission, as he was unmarried. His time was up in April and he did not know what he would do then. Shute spent the evening seeing everything and went to evening service. All the children sang Christmas carols in the great heat. He thought Norton was very good with them.

The next day they took off at about 8:30 a.m. for Cooktown, straight across the peninsula to the sea on the east coast. This was a two hour flight over very desolate country, fairly well watered to start with, and then flew down the line of the railway to Cooktown where they landed about 10:45. They intended to spend the night but received a phone call from the Flying Doctor service at Cairns. There was a six day old baby very ill at Georgetown and the ambulance plane, an old Dragon, was in for its Certificate of Airworthiness check, and no other plane was available. Would Shute go to Georgetown and take the doctor, and if necessary bring the baby back to the hospital at Cairns?

There was nothing to be done about it but to agree, especially as this was one of the babies that Marcus had delivered at Georgetown on their way out. Cooktown to Georgetown is 220 miles: they had a quick meal and refuelled and took off about 14:15 for Georgetown. They had a vile flight in the heat of the day; very bumpy and over very bad country. The rains were beginning to set in and there were many thunderstorms about. They had to leave the course altogether once and set a new course to avoid a big storm, with lightning not far away from the aircraft. After landing, Shute left Item Willie and drove in at once to the hospital. He told Marcus to make his mind up quickly if he wanted to take the baby to Cairns that night, as he had never done a night landing. He had no objection to landing at night if really necessary, as Cairns had all necessary floodlighting, but it was better to avoid it if possible. Marcus rang through after an hour and said they could take the baby in the morning. It had some kind of an obstruction in the guts and could not pass anything. The following morning they flew to Cairns first thing, with Marcus nursing the baby, who was rather better. The technique in flying newborn infants, which are frequently unable to cope with altitude, was that if the baby turned blue, you went down a bit. It had rained very heavily in the night and there were still storms about; the good flying weather was coming to an end, and heavy rains would fall till March. There was low cloud over the Atherton Tableland; and he flew under them and through the Barron Gorge and came to Cairns without trouble. On landing, Marcus and the baby went straight to hospital. Shute then went to ambulance HQ which wanted to pay him for the flight. He refused payment because it was good experience. He listened in to some of the radio schedule to the outlying stations and became familiar with the procedures used.

Shute spent the next two days resting and writing up his diary about the trip to the Gulf Country, but these rest days were marred by an upset stomach. He found the weather very trying, with alternate heavy rain and hot sun and would be very glad to fly south after Christmas. On Christmas Day he went to Communion at 9:30, followed by a merry lunch with local people at the Strand Hotel. In the evening he refused further offers of hospitality and spent the evening on his own, relaxing and preparing for the flight south on Boxing Day.

Reg was to accompany him for part of the flight south. They took off about 7 a.m. after a night of heavy rain: the weather was poor and showery. However, they followed the coast and as they flew southward the weather got better, till by the time they got to the Hinchinbroke Channel which, he remarked, was surely one of the loveliest places in the world to fly over, the weather was reasonably good.

There was a head wind, so they landed at Townsville to refuel after 1¾ hours for the 175 miles; Item Willie's fuel consumption was 12½ gallons/hour in auto weak. Shute noted that it was a universal experience that in these hot conditions performance, with all aircraft, was down in every way.

They refuelled and took off again for MacKay, still into a head wind. The weather improved but grew very rough as the heat of the day increased. MacKay had a good grass aerodrome with two paved runways and one very wide grass strip, but had no V.H.F. They landed at about noon, refuelled, and picketed down for the night. The following morning they took off from MacKay about 6 a.m. and flew through bad monsoon weather down the coast towards Rockhampton. There were almost continuous rain storms in spite of a relatively good forecast: this was a bad time of year when the rains in Queensland were just starting. Rockhampton was reached by following the railway in rather better weather, over hills that were very bumpy with a 30 mph headwind. The next stop was Brisbane where the Press was there to meet and photograph him. Afterwards he drove into town with a very pleasant young Australian, Barry Robinson, employed by the Australian Broadcasting Commission. He spent most of the afternoon being driven around Brisbane in the car. Shute gave Robinson a copy of *No Highway* and an invitation to Pond Head if he ever got back to England, as Robinson had been there in the war as part of a Lancaster bomber crew.

On 28 December Shute decided to fly down to Coffs Harbour and night stop there. Coffs Harbour is a small port between two headlands, a timber and fishing town of about 4000 inhabitants. It had a fine aerodrome with 3 runways. He landed about 12:15 and refuelled, and put Item Willie in the hangar. Next day he took off from Coffs Harbour about 9:30 and flew down the coast with a tail wind to Sydney. He found this coast very beautiful, with pastures, beaches, and woods, and a good deal of inland water in the form of sea meres and lakes. He landed at Bankstown aerodrome to the south west of Sydney. This was the principal aerodrome for light aircraft as 'A' license pilots were not allowed to use Mascot, the main airport. There he ran into trouble, which was not a good introduction to Sydney. He was told he should have flown to Mascot. He phoned the controller and said that Bankstown was his destination, that he had made forty landings in Australia and Bankstown was the forty-first: He would take the documents to the Customs house or they could come and get them, whichever they preferred. He then rang off and went to lunch.

On his return, there was a message that unless he flew to Mascot immediately, police action would be taken. He complied and flew to Mascot which he found with difficulty in poor visibility. There he was met by Jimmy and the Shell representative. Customs insisted on opening all his luggage and searching it—God knew what for, since he had been in Australia for a month. He was then allowed to take off again and fly back to Bankstown. There he arranged with de Havilland for a programme of work to be carried out on Item Willie. He thought this would take rather more than a week, owing to the New Year holidays, which would stop work for two working days. He would therefore have to stay in this unpleasant place for 10 days or so. He wished to God he had never come south in this country, but passport, visas and aircraft permits to fly home could not be secured except in Sydney or Melbourne. Sydney seemed to him to be an ugly, cheap city, full of drunks. It was already obvious that the 10 days he would have to spend here were going to be an utter waste of time.

So began a two week period in Sydney of delay and frustration. Firstly the hotel he stayed at was poor, then it rained on most days and the work on the aircraft took longer than expected, as other faults were found which needed to be put right. He was entertained by local people and visited the tourist sights. He was persuaded to take part in a sailing dinghy race in Sydney Harbour and got rather wet in the choppy waters. He went to see Laurence Olivier's film of *Henry V* but came out halfway through. His comment was that Shakespeare had been a fine story teller in his day, but that the art had improved since then! A bright spot was a visit on New Year's Day to Lee Murray's farm outside Sydney. He had not seen Murray since the early days of Airspeed in York when they had built the Shackleton-Murray aircraft. Shute also arranged for parcels of dried fruits and also hampers of food to be sent to England, one each month. Finally on 14 January work on Item Willie was finished and he flew to Mascot that evening and parked her, ready for departure the following day.

Mr Clancy of Shell called for them and drove them out to Mascot to see them off. Although they had warned Customs they would be leaving, this being Saturday morning, the one officer on duty was exceptionally rude and unpleasant, and initially would not give them a time when he could clear them. He then rang up his head office about them and evidently got a rocket, because he came back with an ingratiating attitude. He called Shute 'Sir' with every other word, and cleared them immediately.

They flew to Melbourne with a re-fuelling stop at Cootamundra. Mr James of Shell was there to meet them in his car. They arranged to hangar Item Willie and then drove into the city to the Melbourne Club, where they had rooms booked. Accommodation in Melbourne was as difficult as Sydney or worse, but Shute had an introduction to the Melbourne Club from the Oxford & Cambridge Club in London, and they were formally put up as honorary members.

To Shute the Melbourne Club was far more English than anything then left in England. There was no running water in the bedrooms. Polished copper hot water cans were brought by a valet. The furniture was incredibly Victorian but provided ugly, solid comfort. He walked out after dinner and looked at the city a little. In the shopping district it looked rather American on that Saturday night, with much neon lighting. He noted that the River Yarra on which Melbourne stands is quite narrow. Melbourne was much more to his liking than Sydney had been.

Shute spent his 50th birthday, 17 January 1949, at Shell House and saw Wright, the head of the Aviation Department for all Australia, and Penny, his assistant. He met Brayton Davies who ran Shell Aviation in Victoria, and under whom James worked. They renewed the fuel carnet, and rang the Department of Civil Aviation about permits for Item Willie to fly home. This negotiation had been initiated by Jimmy from Sydney before Christmas. The Department of Civil Aviation had done nothing about it at all, and explained that the business of obtaining these permits for British aircraft was not their affair but that of the High Commissioner in Canberra. They dealt only with Australian aircraft, and while they would be willing to oblige by handling the permits, they would have to charge the cost of all the cables and paperwork involved, which they estimated at £60. The High Commissioner would do it free. This seemed reasonable, if dilatory, so they looked for the representative of the High Commissioner in Melbourne. There wasn't one, only the Trade Commissioner and an Information Officer, neither of whom could handle a matter of this sort. Shute dictated a long letter to the High Commissioner with the Trade Commissioner's typist, and sent it off. Since he had obtained a permit to return through the Dutch East Indies at Batavia on the way out, he thought he could get to Singapore all right. And he had little doubt that he could go the whole way home without any of these permits at all.

Shute celebrated his birthday with dinner at the Melbourne Club, and Jimmy produced a bottle of Australian champagne to celebrate. A great thought for Shute was that they would start homewards the following day, 20 January, and that all courses would be north by west with the days getting longer as they passed through the different time zones.

Two days later they were on their way northwards again after a stop at Adelaide. They were flying to Oodnadatta, 590 miles by way of the railway, and far the longest hop they had attempted so far. The country at first was pasture, but later changed to pure desert and salt lakes, although homesteads were numerous all along the track. After an overnight stop at Oodnadatta they flew on towards Alice Springs. The flight to Alice Springs was delightful, sufficiently early in the day not to be very bumpy. For some of the way they flew low, at about 300 feet, to inspect the country and while doing this they overtook the Ghan train about 100 miles south of Alice and flew low over it and photographed it. The desert colours were very lovely, pink and brown and green.

Alice Springs town lies in a bowl of quite high hills, at an altitude of about 2000 feet. Connellan Airways operated all over Central Australia from there, and were most hospitable to aviators—apart from the fact that they had an introduction to Eddie Connellan. His aerodrome was in the bowl right alongside the town. They landed there, and refuelled. The Shell representative, Bob Rumble, got them rooms at the Stuart Arms Hotel, and advised them to fly the machine to the other aerodrome and put it in Connellan's hangar, as they were staying some days. Shute did so, having to land quite fast and running some distance. They put Item Willie in the hangar and drove with Bob to the hotel. They drank beer, for as usual in these parts, they were always thirsty. Mrs Connellan had invited them to swim at their pool in the afternoon. They drove round the town first with Bob and then joined Mrs Connellan. The swimming pool was at a new house that Connellan was building behind his hangar at the aerodrome, looking out over the aerodrome to the mountain range. There was a party of three or four girls and young married women plus the Flying Doctor, Steve Calder. He had been one of the Connellan pilots, but now had a cattle station. It was a pleasant party, finishing up with drinks on the lawn of Mrs Connellan's small house.

Shute thought Alice Springs a well-balanced little community. There was a good deal of small industry, with tractor and motor car companies, feed concerns, brokers and agents, the railway, civil aviation, the flying doctor centre, and hospital. All this meant that there was plenty of employment for girls, and the desperate shortage of unmarried women felt in other parts of the outback did not exist. There were almost as many young unmarried women as young unmarried men and, since wages were high, the result was plenty of small houses in pleasant suburban surroundings, and a large number of young married people with babies. It seemed to Shute to be a model town, bearing in mind the severity of the climate and the general rigours of the country. It showed what every outback place could be, if only jobs for girls could be provided.

The next day they flew to Hermannsburg, a Lutheran mission and centre of Aboriginal art. Here they met Albert Namatjira an Aboriginal artist who had developed into one of the finest watercolour painters in Australia. Others had followed his example and had created a little colony of Aboriginal artists.

With regret they left Alice Springs and flew north to Tennants Creek in just under 3 hours where they re-fuelled. It was extremely hot and they flew much of the way at 7000 feet. Another flight of over 3 hours took them to Katherine. The Shell agent met them and arranged rooms for them at the local hotel. There was a storm during the night but Item Willie, fully loaded and well picketed down, was all right. The following day, 26 January, they arrived back at Darwin, completing their tour of Australia which had lasted 63 days.

They wanted to fly from Darwin to Dilly on East Timor, a flight of some 450 miles, 400 of them over the sea. There was a Catalina aircraft scheduled to make the crossing and they arranged to fly in company with that. So on 29 January they cleared Customs for the last time in Australia. The Australian Customs had been the outstanding unpleasant feature of this journey and, Shute noted, made it difficult and unpleasant to fly a British aircraft to Australia.

They took off according to plan at 9:35 ahead of the Catalina and flew on course at 900 feet over sea through heavy monsoon rain storms. After Bathurst Island the weather improved and later cleared entirely, so that they could get up to 4000 feet. Wireless contact with the Catalina behind them was good from the start; they came in punctually every quarter of an hour, and this contact was a great comfort on the crossing of the Timor Sea. The Catalina caught up with them off East Timor and said goodbye. From there they flew along the north coast and landed at Dilly, where they were met by the Australian consul who put them up in his house.

They stayed at Dilly for some days, being entertained by the Australian consul and his wife and also by the Portuguese Administrator, Senor Mendonca. They were taken by car over a hilly road to Macobisse, which Shute thought a real Shangri-La. On the way back they had to cross a ford which had been small on the way up but was 4 feet deep on the way back. They tried towing the car across but it got stuck and the passengers had to take off their clothes and wade across. Shute's comment was that this was a type of motoring that you didn't see in England: it was great fun, but rough on the cars. They were told that they must fly to Koepang to clear Customs for the Dutch East Indies, but Shute, mindful of his bad experience at Koepang on the outward flight, decided that he would fly on to Bali by way Soembawa Besar to refuel, reckoning that the East Indies were in such chaos that probably no Customs officer would even know that they had landed at Soembawa Besar.

On 2 February they left for Bali, having fuelled the aircraft with a mixture of old Japanese 100 octane and new 73 octane petrol. They took with them 4 gallons of extra fuel in a jerrycan and 2 gallons of oil. With this overload they took off after about 550 yards, which Shute had paced out before. They arrived at Soembawa Besar, a distance of 560 miles, in improving weather and obtained fuel from a helpful KLM agent before flying on to Bali. They were both very glad to be back in that delightful place. Here they stayed for two days, meeting old friends, the Snellmans and Dronkers, and giving tools to Theo Meier which Shute had bought for him in Australia, taking one of Meier's paintings as payment. Once more they saw something of the temples and festivals of the Balinese and dancing by the village children.

On 8 February they flew on again to Batavia (Jakarta), where normal life was disrupted by the war being waged against the rebels. Their next flight was to Palembang on Sumatra. The hotel there was very crowded and, whilst waiting for rooms, they received an invitation to stay with Mr Geysel-Vonk, one of the heads of the Shell refinery there. Here they met Mrs Geysel, then aged about 27. When the Japanese invaded Sumatra in 1942, the men were taken off to prison camp. Mrs Geysel's story, as Shute recorded it, was that she, with about 80 other women and children, were marched about Sumatra. The Japanese moved them on from town to town. In 2½ years she had walked about 1200 miles, carrying her baby. Many of the other women and children died. She came out fit and well, and retained her sense of humour. Shute was fascinated by this story and, to return their hospitality, urged them to visit him at Pond Head when they came to England the following year.

It later transpired that, in reality, the women prisoners had been moved from place to place by the Japanese mostly by truck and had ended up in a women's prison camp.

On 11 February Shute and Jimmy arrived in Singapore, where they received several letters, which were welcome, including one from Captain Dennis at Songkhla, who had married Kum Chada and would be pleased for them to stay with them on their way back. Shute thought that, in the circumstances, the copy of *The Chequer Board* that Shute had given him had gone down very well. However the news from Burma, which was on their route home, was very worrying. There were reports of fighting in the streets of Rangoon and Shute thought about how he might bypass Burma carrying extra fuel or even fitting an extra fuel tank. He thought they might be able to land at Moulmein or Kyankypu, which he had visited in 1945. Either way he thought he might thus be able to avoid landing at Rangoon.

From Singapore they flew up the east coast of Malaya, landing at Kuantan and Kota Bahru where they were met by the British Advisor, Tony Churchill, a relative of Winston who accommodated them during their stay. Shute commented that it was extraordinary how much the trip had been helped by his books. Tony Churchill was a fan and Shute had signed many copies of his books along the way. He thought it helped to make everything easy as a known and popular writer.

At Songkhla they were met by Captain and Mrs Dennis, recently married, who persuaded them to stay for a day before flying on. They were happy to do this because Shute thought there would be little rest until they reached England. This proved to be only too accurate, as they were delayed in getting clearance to fly to Rangoon from Moulmein. At Rangoon they hurriedly refuelled from jerrycans and took off again for Chittagong and on 26 February they arrived in Calcutta, at Dum Dum airport. They had successfully crossed Burma with only a short delay.

Whilst Shute was refuelling at Dum Dum, armed bandits drove up and attacked the aerodrome, setting fire to a light aircraft and holding up staff in the main assembly hall, killing one policeman. Shute heard this going on only about 50 yards away. He quickly moved Item Willie 500 yards further up the tarmac away from the danger. They left Calcutta without regret after this incident and their flight across India deviated from their route on the way out. They flew via Goya, where Guatama had received the final enlightenment, and visited the Buddhist shrines. The next stop was Agra where they visited the Taj Mahal and the local bazaar. Shute thought the Taj Mahal a very wonderful place, its beauty being greatly enhanced by the garden in which it stands.

On 2 March they arrived back in Karachi, having flown there via Delhi, where they found the Civil Air Advisor very helpful in obtaining the required permits to fly onwards. At Karachi they spent two quiet days whilst Item Willie was serviced by Pakistan Aviation, the work being apparently only moderately well done, due to pressure of other work and the staff not first class. From Karachi they flew on to Sharjah with again a stop at the Jiwani staging post. At Sharjah they encountered a party of water engineers, three of them, one an elderly man, travelling to Muscat from Baghdad. Their transport had broken down at Bahrain and left them flat. The only way they could get on was to charter a dhow at Bahrain which would take them five days to reach Sharjah; from here they were to go to Muscat, 200 miles, in a hired car. They were very envious of the Proctor.

On arrival at Bahrain they stayed once again at the home of Squadron Leader Lewis and his family. They also met and dined with the Political Resident and his wife. After this rest day they flew on to Basra and Baghdad, where they had to replace a burst tyre before taking off. They flew via Rutbah Wells towards Damascus and, attempting to fly to Beirut, encountered storms over the mountains of Lebanon. They had to retrace steps and land at Damascus, although they did not have Syrian visas. The airport authorities were very pleasant about the visa, which was unexpected. The officials took the view that they had a visa for Lebanon but that the weather had obviously prohibited crossing the mountains, so they stamped the Lebanese visa as if it were theirs. They were very pleased to be back on the ground, having been in the air for nearly 6 hours and having landed just before a snowstorm.

The following morning they took off for Cyprus against a headwind which they had had all the way from Rangoon. Once more they were met by the Richards family, who were delighted to see them again and put them up. The following day they spent driving around the island and inspecting an old boat that Jim Richards wanted to buy. Shute offered to lend him *Runagate* for a week when he came to England on leave.

The following day they flew to Athens intending to go on to Brindisi but the forecast was for low cloud and fog so they stayed the night at the Rex Hotel again. They had lengthy Customs formalities at Athens where the authorities had tightened up due to an earlier episode of smuggling by a light aircraft. On March 14 they left for Brindisi with a tail wind for a change. After 3 hours they were approaching Brindisi airport but were unable to contact them on the radio; Brindisi had no VHF. The wind was from the northwest, a cross wind for landing on the longer runway but dead down the shorter runway. Italian aircraft were using the cross wind runway, so that to land on the short runway would have been dangerous. Shute made two circuits while assessing the position and trying to raise Control on the radio, to no avail. Finally he decided the only thing to do was to follow the stream and land on the long runway with about a 20 mph cross wind. Item Willie sat down nicely, well aligned with the runway. He braked sharply and held her straight, but then the brakes gradually lost power, and she swung badly into wind, and ground looped off the runway to port at about 50 mph. When finally she came to rest well off the runway, the starboard undercarriage was 20° out of vertical and the main front wing spar was obviously cracked. He could not understand why she had not responded to the brakes, till he took off the spat covering the damaged wheel. The brake cable was badly kinked in two places. The outer cover of the Bowden cable had failed, after 320 hours of hard use in many cross wind landings, and so full brake and rudder had not produced much braking force upon the wheel.

Item Willie was towed to the Civil hangar and then they cleared Customs, emptied all their belongings from the aircraft and, through various agents, began the long process of making arrangements for the repair. Shute cabled Frances with the news.

It was, he wrote, very sad that their journey should end in this way after more than 30,000 miles and many worse cross wind landings. Jimmy's thoughts were of immense sadness for Shute. This was his journey, his plan; he had had all the responsibility and it was only through his own meticulous efficiency that they had travelled this immense distance in safety. Jimmy knew that Shute had wanted like hell to get back to Portsmouth on time, with the aircraft spick and span, but had been robbed of this by sheer bad luck just 1500 miles from home.

So they packed up and flew back to England by commercial airline via Rome, Geneva and Amsterdam to London. If the six month journey had ended in bad luck, the purpose of it had been achieved. Shute now had a wealth of material which he would use in forthcoming books, and he was impatient to get home and begin writing the first of them.

Shute and Reg McAuliffe.
(Bev Clarke)

Item Willie at Normanton, December 15, 1948.
Shute is under the wing inspecting the undercarriage
after ground looping on landing.
(Bev Clarke)

Dunbar Station, December 19, 1948; Shute (in the hat). The station people
were drunk after consuming their Christmas supplies of alcohol.
(Bev Clarke)

Shute and Jimmy Riddell in front of the de Havilland hangar at Sydney.
(Ali Riddell)

11
For This You Are Directly Responsible

When Shute arrived back in England he plunged into the backlog of items that needed attention, including the mail, amongst which was a letter written in January from Sir Alan Cobham saying that he had been reading the tale about the boffins (*No Highway*) and could live every moment of it.[1] He included reports on the latest developments in flight refuelling. Frances had replied to Sir Alan saying that her husband was still in Australia. He was about to begin his flight home and she was expecting him back about the end of March. Once the backlog was cleared Shute could begin writing again, which he did within days of returning home. He had two books in mind based on the material he had gained on his journey. The first would be based on his more heroic version of the story of Mrs Geysel's experiences at the hands of the Japanese—their march on foot from place to place, suffering, illness and death. This would be combined with life in outback Australia, replete with all the details that he had picked up on his flight around the Gulf country. He had in mind a popular novel which would sell well to "pay" for a more serious novel which would follow. The first book, *A Town Like Alice*, was written in three months after his return, much faster than he usually took to write a book. Of *A Town Like Alice* he later wrote that many people regarded it as a good book, although he didn't, but it reflected his first views and experiences of Australia. As a popular novel it was highly successful and remains the one book that people tend to remember when the name of Nevil Shute is mentioned.

As he was writing this book, he and Frances attended the de Havilland Garden Party on 8 May, which was held at White Waltham airfield to the west of London. Being a former employee of de Havilland, he met many old colleagues including George Errington, chief test pilot for Airspeed. This gave him the chance to talk over old times and no doubt tell Errington of his flight to Australia. White Waltham had been bought by the de Havilland family in 1928 to house the de Havilland Flying School. In 1938 the airfield was taken over by the government, and during World War II, was the home base of the Air Transport Auxiliary.

At this time Shute wrote an article about his working week.[2] The question, he said, was which working week. He spent about 200 days a year at home on Hayling Island. He worked from nine o'clock till one every morning, seven days a week, except one Sunday in a month when he went to church. His secretary came in three mornings a week to do his correspondence, which would otherwise have taken most of every morning. He found that as time went on the correspondence accumulated more, as the scenes of the books spread more widely across the world. In Northern Queensland, for example, he had met a friendly mounted policeman in a remote district, travelled with him, and drank with him for a day or two. Back in England, if the new book required the details of alligator hunting in that part of the world, Shute wrote to ask him, and the policeman went to great pains to write a comprehensive treatise. After that, he said, he couldn't throw off the new friend he had made, and he was glad to have a letter from him every three months or so. The answers, dictated in a few minutes in his study, would mean a great deal to him in his life in the outback, and he was glad to keep the correspondence up. But when each book brought five or six new correspondents of that sort, the volume of letters was apt to grow.

Fan letters added to the correspondence. They came in a spate that lasted for about three months after the publication of each new book, perhaps at the rate of one or two a day, and then died down to one or two a week.

The correspondence over, he got on with the current book. He wrote nothing but novels, and though he had written a novel in three months, he generally found that eight or nine months was a better time. There was a time rate at which ideas occurred, so that if he wrote too quickly he was not apt to think of dialogue or situations which would have improved the book when it was too late to incorporate them. After eight or nine months, however, he had shot his bolt on the subject. He wrote directly onto a typewriter, on large quarto paper, single-spaced with a wide margin, and did corrections in pencil. Pages with many corrections were re-written, and he always re-wrote the first chapter, usually more than once. Finally the mess was re-typed for him by his secretary.

Nine till one was an invariable rule, and he usually worked for a couple of hours longer in the evening, either after tea or after dinner, making a six hour day, which was quite long enough for creative work. On top of that he read a great deal, anything and everything but novels. He read no more than two or three novels a year. Technical journals and weeklies dealing with current events were his main literary diet, to keep himself well informed.

At some time in each day he liked to do something with his hands. He could sail a boat from the end of the garden, and this was a great pleasure in the summer. He had a workshop with a small lathe, drill, and shaper, and for many years had been an enthusiastic model engineer. He knew of few more fascinating ways of wasting time than in building up a tiny steam engine or petrol motor from castings. In recent months he had tried his hand at oil painting, like many others who had been reading Winston Churchill. He had found to his own great surprise that he could do it well enough to give him a great deal of pleasure. In the school holidays, he added, his children took up any time that might be left.

This he contrasted with a week in 1948 when he had flown from Rangoon to Bangkok in the Proctor. Burma National Airways had been very helpful and had found him a contact breaker of the correct hand from a sectioned magneto in their classroom. He had flown south eastwards over the Three Pagodas Pass on the remains of the notorious Burma railway, gradually being obliterated by the jungle growth. He flew on down the east side of the Kra Isthmus to Songkhla near the frontier with Malaya, flying in bad weather which forced him down to 150 feet and he landed on a palm fringed strip. He recalled the people he had met at Songkhla, the British Consul, his gallant wife and their daughter Poon. He wrote of the lovely Ram Song dance, of the men dancing around the girl following her every move without touching.

He ended the article by saying that he sat at home picking and choosing his memories of that sort of week to find the substance of his stories, but doubted if he could say which week was most pleasurable.

He taught both daughters to sail and they kept a sailing dinghy at the jetty, which was much used to sail in Chichester harbour in the summer months. *Runagate* was also sailed on the Solent and voyages further afield, across the Channel to France and the Channel Islands.

Towards the end of May he travelled out to Brindisi to collect Item Willie and flew back to England solo. He took her to Percivals at Luton to be checked over and to have a renewed Certificate of Airworthiness. When that was completed, Item Willie returned to Portsmouth airport thereby completing the journey to Australia and back. He wrote to Sir Alan Cobham thanking him for his reports on flight refuelling and congratulating him on the feasibility of the system and battling through the prejudice that had surrounded the subject for so many years. He told him of his flight to Australia and back and that it had been a great success and that he would retain Item Willie and hope to do it again some day.[3]

Once *A Town Like Alice* was finished and sent off for publication, Shute began on the second novel he had in mind from his experiences in the Far East. It would be the story of the birth and spread of a new teaching based upon aircraft maintenance. The teacher would be a ground engineer of mixed east and western stock and the narrator was to be an English ground engineer, of humble background, who became a pilot and operator of aircraft in the Middle and Far East. Shute wanted to write that in the beginning the narrator worked for Cobham's National Aviation Day operation. In November, when the book was in its early stages, he sent the first few pages of the manuscript to Cobham since he wanted Cobham's agreement to include him in the story.[4] In the covering letter Shute wrote that he could easily place the opening in some other context if Sir Alan had any objection. He would be rather sorry to do this, since National Aviation Day represented a phase in aviation that would never be seen again, and no history of it existed. However if Sir Alan had any objection Shute said he could easily alter the opening without using the air circus at all.

On the 30 November Cobham replied that they all felt honoured that National Aviation Day was at last going down in history by being in a best seller. If Shute wanted any details or humorous anecdotes Cobham would be pleased to supply them. He ended his letter by asking when Shute was going to write a thriller about a big airliner full of women and children running low on fuel and being saved by a tanker aircraft refuelling it in the nick of time but having to ditch and swim home. He added, "Just think of the film rights!"[5]

By May 1950 the final draft of *Round the Bend* was complete and Shute again sent copies of the first few pages to Sir Alan Cobham. Again he asked for Sir Alan's approval to make the references to National Aviation Day and also asked for his comments and suggestions on this part. Shute summarised the plot of the book and added that "it is rather a curious book in many ways and is likely to be more of a prestige book than a popular one."[6] He was evidently uncertain whether it would sell well and explains why he wrote *A Town Like Alice* first, as an insurance policy against the possible failure of *Round the Bend*.

Cobham replied to Shute's letter with a number of comments. He was never aware that his staff got tips; it was always discouraged. He thought he would have offered an outsider 5 shillings for doing the Gretna Green stunt, not half a crown—say 10 shillings for two performances. A boy would have been paid £5 a week not £1. The engineers got £7 to £8 and the pilots £25 to £30 per week. Sir Alan added that a boy who worked on the aircraft would never have the job of picking up the waste paper but would do cleaning jobs on the aircraft. Picking up litter was the job of the ground staff. Also the show moved more rapidly than described in the book. They very rarely stayed more than two days in any one place.[7]

In mid June 1950 Shute wrote to Cobham that he had incorporated the changes. He was having the final manuscript of *Round the Bend* typed, adding that it was still not too late to make any alterations, but that time was getting short. He finished the letter by saying that he was packing up in England and going to live in Australia and taking his Proctor as deck cargo. His decision to leave England was prompted by several factors, not least of which was a major row over his petrol ration. In Britain in 1950 petrol rationing was still strictly enforced, five years after the end of the War. In that year Shute chose to make a major public issue over his treatment at the hands of the Ministry of Fuel and Power regarding his petrol allowance.

On 17 January 1950 he wrote to the Regional Petroleum Officer at Reading, requesting an increase in his supplementary petrol allowance of 20 E coupons that he was allowed for literary research.[8] He wrote that for many years he had earned an income of over £10,000 a year from his literary work. For the years 1938 to 1949 he had earned a total of $277,000 from royalties in the United States, the whole of which had been available to Exchange control. He was, he said, quite a considerable "invisible export" as well as being a very large tax and surtax payer. He needed to travel in connection with his writing, to collect visitors from Havant Station and to keep abreast of film developments. He mentioned that the film of *Landfall* was currently being shown and that *No Highway* was being filmed by Twentieth Century Fox. He needed to travel to follow the progress of the filming, but found that his business was becoming more and more hampered by shortage of petrol. In the past year he had only made two journeys outside a twenty mile radius of his home. He mentioned his allowance of petrol for his aeroplane of 100 gallons a month. However very little of this was used, as he did not use his aeroplane for journeys in England. Any unused coupons were surrendered at the end of the period. An allowance of 200 miles a week, or double the present issue of coupons, would permit him to carry on local journeys without waste of time. Could these coupons be issued to him?

The Ministry replied on 25 January with a standard letter regretting that, having regard to the continuing need for economy in the use of petrol, they could not grant him any additional coupons.

In his next letter of 25 January Shute wrote that their refusal to grant additional petrol "for my business" seemed to him unreasonable.[9] He lived in this country and carried on his business here because he liked to do so. As his annual dollar income for the last ten years had been $27,000, it would be perfectly possible for him to live and carry on his work in the United States, where he would pay lower taxes and be free from the continual irritation over petrol. He lived and paid heavy taxes in England because this was *his* country and for no material reason. If he came to the conclusion that his countrymen were impeding his business unreasonably, either because officials were jealous of the way of life he had built up for himself or through bureaucratic folly were unable to cater for the requirements of his business, then he would leave immediately and take up residence in another part of the world. The dollars that he earned paid for his requirements of petrol many times over and "it was impossible to resist the suspicion that jealousy of my way of life is at the bottom of this refusal to grant petrol."

Shute then offered to give up some of the petrol allowance for his aeroplane in return for an increase in the allowance for his car. In a sarcastic tone he wrote, "I realise of course that though Government is one to me this proposal may be agonising for you since it involves another Ministry." He would watch for their reaction to this proposal with interest since the ability of the Government to conduct itself with good sense in such matters would seriously affect the decision he took whether to stay in England or go. He asked the Ministry to let him know without delay whether they would increase his allowance from 20 to 40 gallons a month in return for which he would request the Civil Aviation Authority to reduce his aircraft allowance from 100 to 50 gallons a month.

Nearly a fortnight went by without a reply from the Ministry, which caused Shute to send a letter rebuking them for the delay which in business circles would be "regarded as an act of studied insolence." The reply from the Ministry was at least in the form of a personal letter stating that the supply of petrol was still limited and that petrol obtained by coupons could not be used for any journey for which public transport was reasonably practicable. He had received the maximum allowance that the rules permitted for business or professional use and this should be regarded as the greatest measure of assistance that it was possible to give at the moment. The Ministry wrote that "for obvious reasons it would not be possible under the petrol rationing scheme to exchange petrol issued for an aeroplane for use in car journeys."

In his reply of 13 February, Shute said that the Ministry's letter was totally unsatisfactory.[10] Their "obvious reasons" for rejecting his proposal for adjusting his car and aeroplane allowances were not obvious to him at all. He wrote that he had no option but to reject their rules "in toto." Unless and until his business received individual consideration in regard to its petrol requirements he would use "every means within my power to force a major public issue on this point." He then went on to put some more arguments in support of his case, which he hoped might make the Ministry reconsider. His 1938 novel *Ruined City*, the fictional town of Sharples had been based on Blyth. The book was intended to be socially useful, which perhaps it was. To research this he motored around the district that he wanted to do something useful for. He drove around 2000 miles, using perhaps 100 gallons of petrol. He would now like to write another book about the industrial north and this would be impossible to do if he had to use public transport. If he had 150 gallons at his disposal he would go to the north that summer and a useful book would probably result. Otherwise he would have to confine his stories to parts of the world where petrol was available to him.

He listed his dollar earnings for the last ten years again but thought they would "increase the ideological bias against me." He had travelled freely in South East Asia and elsewhere without trouble over petrol. Plenty about Australia, Malaya and Burma would be found in his recent novels but nothing about England north of London. For that, he said, "you [the Ministry] are directly responsible." He was bound by rules that bore no relation to the requirements of his work; in consequence he doubted he "would ever write of England again except critically." He said that he would shortly be making a trip to Cyprus flying his aircraft and that on his return would obtain petrol for his business by unconventional means, supply details to the Ministry, and challenge them to prosecute him in the courts. He would defend such a prosecution with all the resources at his command. If sentence was passed he would serve it with a good grace and an eye for copy and would then leave the country with an easy mind and no regrets, being well out of it.

He said that he was having 1500 copies of the correspondence printed and that a copy would go to every member of the new House of Commons and to the editor of every daily newspaper. He ended the letter by saying "As soon as it becomes irrevocable that I must leave this country, copies of this correspondence will go to every Senator and Congressman in the United States, the country in which I hope to establish a permanent residence."

Shute sent copies of this correspondence to the Society of Authors, and the Secretary wrote back on 15 February that he was "delighted with the cogency with which you have presented your case."[11] Woodrow Wyatt, an M.P. and member of the Society's Committee of Management, had raised the matter with Mr Gaitskell (The Minister of Fuel and Power) with particular reference to the case of the author John Moore.

Shute wrote to the Society of Authors on 15th April, saying that he had engaged a solicitor and had been prepared to make a major issue of his case and fight it up to the House of Lords if necessary. Since this matter directly affected his business and as he paid 19 shillings in the pound (95%) on the top level of his earnings, he could face the expenses of a case like this. His solicitor had had two meetings with the Ministry, the outcome of which was a reluctant increase in his petrol ration to the 40 gallons a month he had originally asked for. He had won a victory, albeit a Pyrrhic one. This was the third major row over petrol that he had had since the war, and he felt he could not go on with this sort of row every eighteen months or so. By the time he won this victory he had made up his mind to leave England and "my house was in the hands of agents and I had booked passages for myself and my family for Melbourne, Australia.... I sail on 20th July."

The row over petrol rationing, like the demise of the airship program, marked a turning point in Shute's life. The timing of the correspondence must be put into context. The post-war Labour government had been in power with a large majority since 1945; in 1950 a General

Election was called and took place on 23 February, just at the time of the row. Was Shute somehow attempting to influence the election by his threat to publish 1500 copies of the correspondence? He seems to have been sure enough of his position as a major novelist to take the risk, and electoral interference features in *Lonely Road*. The outcome of the election was that a Labour government was returned but with a single-figure majority. It was this result probably more than the rationing issue which finally made up Shute's mind to leave England. In fact petrol rationing in Britain ended completely on 26 May 1950, well before Shute departed in July.

Bureaucracy, always Shute's bête noir, had raised its obstructionist head and inflamed his anger, vented in the letters to the Ministry. He chose to make a major issue of it and it was a factor, but not the sole reason, in his decision to leave England. He did not leave for the United States as he told the Ministry, but Australia. It is said that he wanted to live in a country which was part of the Commonwealth, with the Monarch as Head of State. He had been impressed with Australia during his visit there, more so with Melbourne than Sydney. In his letter to the Society he said he reckoned he could get three good books out of there which would probably take him five years to research and write, and five years was as far ahead as anybody could see in those times.

A Town Like Alice was on sale and *Round the Bend* was at the publishers, but Shute asked them to delay publication until he moved to Australia, so that there would not be a gap in his one novel a year output. So the household was packed up, *Runagate* sold, and Pond Head House put on the market. The destination came as something of a shock to Heather. When she was told that the family was moving, she assumed it would be to somewhere else in Hampshire, but was told no, Australia. In 1948, having passed her School Certificate, she left Sidcot and went to a "cram school" in Oxford. Her intention was to try and get into Oxford University at Lady Margaret Hall. So when the family sailed for Australia, Heather, aged 18, remained in England to try for Oxford.

Shirley was not happy about the move and later recalled that she went to Australia "kicking and screaming". She had recently moved to Sidcot from Bedale's school in Petersfield, where she had not done well. At Sidcot, she had settled in happily and was just beginning to enjoy learning and was making new friends. Now she was to be uprooted again.

Shute, Frances, Shirley together with his secretary Mrs Bessant, boarded the P&O ship *Strathnaver* on 20 July bound for Melbourne. Although he would visit England several times in the coming years, he would never again live there.

12
This Exceedingly Attractive Country

When Shute arrived in Melbourne there was quite a crowd of reporters waiting to question him at the foot of the gangway. They wanted to know if it was true that he had ducked out of England to avoid high taxes. Shute replied that taxes in England were unpleasant and so was the current government's experiment in socialism. He added that he had also decided to come to Australia because everything about the country fascinated him—even the climate.[1]

Finding a home was a first priority, and the family moved into a house called Harfield in Mount Eliza south of Frankston and close to the sea in Port Phillip bay. This accords with his dislike of living in cities, preferring to be out in the rural areas and he chose a location some thirty miles from Melbourne. Heather did not gain a place at Oxford and sailed from England on 21 December to rejoin her family. The following year she enrolled at Melbourne University to study Law. Because she was, as she put it, a rather argumentative teenager, her father thought she would be well suited to be a lawyer. A contemporary recalled that Heather was very proud of her father, yet wanted to establish herself as her own person. She found her fellow students perhaps rather more irreverent than she had been used to in England, but settled in and made new friends.

One of the things that struck Shute once he had settled in was the prospects for young authors in Australia. *A Town Like Alice* had been serialised in the *Australian Women's Weekly* with a circulation of over 700,000 copies. He had received £150 for this, which he had accepted at the time because Australia was a long way away and he didn't know about local conditions. He imagined that other authors accepted the same small payments through ignorance of Australia. He discussed this with the Secretary of the Melbourne PEN, an international association of writers.[2] He found that 30 shillings per thousand words was about the norm and that young authors got very much less than that. Writing to the Society of Authors in England, he said that he was taking an interest in this because he was struck by the lack of knowledge of Australia in the outside world. Remarkably few good stories of life in this exceedingly attractive country had got to England or America. If a young man worked for a couple of months to turn out a first class short story, only to be offered a small sum, it would be a disincentive to him to take up writing as a career, when he could do another job more profitably. One of the chief complaints of PEN was the dumping of syndicated stories from America and England at rates as low as 6 shillings per thousand words. PEN were collecting information about this, in the hope that the general rate of remuneration could be raised.

It became clear to Shute that the interests of authors would have to be protected in some way. There were no literary agents working in Australia, so he suggested that the Society of Authors might want to establish a branch in the country, as some sort of assistance to young authors was urgently needed.

Shute liked what he found in Australia. The country was prosperous and he reckoned that its expansion in the next few years would be one of the wonders of the world. In a letter to Sir Alan Cobham in April 1951[3] he said that things were going well; Australia was booming but there was a good deal of inflation. Everyone seemed to be making money and "everyone has a smile on his face." He told Cobham that he had bought a small farm of 30 acres and the one next to it of 22 acres and was proceeding to build a house in the middle of the lot and to start raising beef cattle. He added that he did not think he would ever be likely to regret the change—the move to Australia. His purpose in writing to Cobham was to send him a copy of *Round The Bend*. He said it was "rather an odd book" but had been quite well-received in America. It would not be published in England until June. He hoped Sir Alan would like it.

The land that Shute bought was at Langwarrin, inland from Frankston, and about thirty miles from Melbourne. The plot was at the corner of Robinson Road and the Hastings-to-Dandenong road, on the Mornington peninsula. At that time you got to it on unmetalled dirt roads, and apparently on the dust-choked trip from Frankston you were likely to run into anything from kangaroos to deadly diamond snakes.

Here he could at last build a house to his own requirements, and what he built was a long single storey house set on a slight rise in the ground with excellent views. Shute made sketches of the type of house he wanted and engaged a local firm of architects to do the plans. As work progressed he was on site almost daily, checking what had been done and making alterations as required. To many of the questions he asked of the builders, the stock reply was generally "She'll be right, mate." In addition to the living rooms there was also a roomy garage and workshop. For his daughters there was a separate "cottage" to give them their own living space. In his study Shute had his roll top desk, given to him by his parents many years ago and at which all his novels were written.

Being out in the wilderness, the house had its own water storage tanks, a generator for electricity and sewage system. Gradually the land was cleared and made ready for livestock. Pasture was sown for the cattle and fenced paddocks made. Charlie Wilson, a farm manager in England, emigrated to join the family. When he retired, his daughter Ruth and her husband Fred Greenwood took over with Fred managing the farm.

Fred found Shute an excellent employer. He always knew where he stood and Shute was "as square as they come, as straight as a gun barrel. He was very decisive in what he wanted. If he wanted a bit of metal cut 6 inches, he didn't want 6 and a quarter. And if it was wrong, well, you knew all about it."[4]

One thing Shute always said to him was that if you've got a job to do and you haven't got the tools to do it, then don't do it. There was another thing that the Greenwoods liked about Shute and Frances. If they brought people round to look at the pigs, for example, they wouldn't just walk around and show them. They would find Fred or Ruth, introduce the visitors, and say that they would like to show them around the piggery.

So he assembled his household in this location and became a farmer as well as a writer, because to him no man could live in the country and not do something with the land. That year, 1951, he made a trip to Queensland to meet his old friend Jimmy Edwards on whom he had based the character of Joe Harman in *A Town Like Alice*. Jimmy was managing a cattle station, and Shute no doubt got his advice on stocking his farm and raising beef cattle. Pigs were also kept, eventually quite a herd and a far cry from the one or two pigs that had been kept at Pond Head to supplement the wartime meat ration. According to his daughter he loved to go and see how the pigs were doing in the afternoon break from his writing. For in Australia, as in England, he established the same daily routine: working in the morning from nine o'clock to lunchtime, the afternoons for the farm or other activities and working in the workshop on the latest model in the evenings after dinner. Sailing was another activity. The family kept a sailing dinghy *Nicolette* at the yacht club on Port Phillip Bay.

He got on well with his neighbours and fitted in well with their society. One neighbour later said of him "He's a dinkum bloke. Nothing uppish about him like other Pommies around here. Fights the bushfires and comes to the agricultural shows just like the other fellows. Besides you can tell from his books he really knows what Australia is all about."[5] He would, though, have betrayed his Englishness by using in conversation expressions such as "How extraordinary" and "You don't say".

Soon after he arrived in Australia, Shute was planning his next novel. It would be a contrast between the thriving enterprise he found in his newly adopted country, and England in whose bombed cities he had smelt a whiff of decay. Early in 1951 he visited the Mount Buller area and stayed for about 10 days at the pub in Merrijig, sitting on the veranda and making notes. On that trip he visited and fished in the Howqua river and stayed in the hut of Fred Fry who was a ranger for the area. He would have learned about the sheep stations in the area and the prosperity due to the high prices of wool. He also found a prototype for Jack Dorman, a main character, a sheep farmer who had struggled through the depression of the thirties to achieve prosperity through his own hard work.

Although Shute was himself an immigrant he was by no means a "ten pound Pom", one of the large number of immigrants from England who received an assisted passage for a payment of ten pounds, although there were probably a large number of them on the ship that had brought him and his family to Australia. He would also have known of the large numbers of displaced persons who emigrated to Australia from war-torn Europe—many of them highly qualified in their own country but who were required to work where directed by the Government for two years.

In his correspondence with the Ministry over his petrol ration he had written that he "did not think he would write of England again except critically" and that was certainly true in the novel that emerged with the title of *The Far Country*. He contrasted the life of Jennifer Morton in drab, rationed, Socialist England in winter, with the rural, prosperous life of the sheep farmer and his community in the sunny Australian summer. In the book Jennifer's English grandmother dies in penury because the pension of her late civil servant husband has run out. For good measure the electricity board cuts off her supply because the account is unpaid and the manager is unwilling or unable to use his own discretion in a hardship case.

All this went into the book, including small details such as the Dormans sending food parcels to England, something which Shute had arranged during his visit in Item Willie in 1948–49. Another character is Carl Zlinter, a qualified doctor in his native Czechoslovakia, whose medical qualifications were not recognised in Australia. He is a displaced person, an immigrant who is working out his two years in a lumber camp but like Shute is delighted with his newly adopted country.

If Shute had intended to write a book advertising the benefits of life in Australia he could hardly have done better. By the middle of 1951 he had finished *The Far Country*[6] and sent it off to the pub-lishers.

Another immigrant from England was Shute's old friend and wartime colleague Ian Hassall. Hassall had served with him in the DMWD, working on the arming of merchant ships with rockets, but he was in fact an artist, the son of John Hassall a well-known cartoonist and he had illustrated some of Shute's unpublished wartime articles. After the war Hassall had resumed his career doing freelance work and teaching art. In 1949 he came to Australia and in 1951 staged an exhibition of his work in Melbourne, which Shute was invited to open. In notes[7] for his opening speech Shute wrote that he greatly admired Hassall's work because he was an artist who created his art to please others and not just himself, which was something he tried to do with his writing. He said that Hassall was a disciple of the old school, where drawing was regarded as at least as important as the painting. He was a disciple of the likes of Holbein and Burne-Jones, men who strove to make their art an opening of the horizons and a source of pleasure to people who did not know very much about it.

On 6 February 1952 King George VI died. He had planned a tour to Australia and New Zealand but was too ill to travel, his place being taken by his daughter Princess Elizabeth and Prince Phillip. They were in Kenya when news of the King's death reached them and they returned to England at once, the Princess to be proclaimed Queen. The news of the King's death would have saddened Shute, for he would have had great respect for him, not only as a loyal subject, but as a fellow stam-merer who had struggled with the affliction all his life. He would have remembered how Airspeed had achieved the honour of designing and building a special Envoy for the King's flight in 1937, and being told of the need to accommodate a steward to see to the King's requirements aboard after the rigours of public engagements. Like millions of others, Shute would also have venerated the King and Queen for their example of steadfastness and courage throughout the war. He would recall that he had once sat down and written to the King in blazing indignation on behalf of an old lady who had suffered an injustice from officialdom. Within three days action had been taken and within two weeks the injustice had been righted.

Given the continuation of the Labour Government in England, and what he fully expected to be the economic emergence of Commonwealth countries like Australia, he began to wonder what life might be like for the new Queen in thirty years time. For it was the Monarch who formed the link between the old and new Commonwealth countries. Even before he finished *The Far Country* he began making notes for a new book and was thinking about it as he joined Alan Moorehead for a trip to north Australia in June 1952. Moorehead was a correspondent, writing articles for the American and Australian press. He put his car on the rail up to Alice Springs, where Shute flew to join him. They drove up to Darwin and then back through the Barkley Tableland to Camooweal and Mount Isa, where they put the car back on the train and flew to Townsville and then back home. This trip would have refreshed Shute's memories of these places, including a visit to a local horse race meeting which he said was a lot of fun.

In a speech[8] he gave shortly after this trip he said that he had visited Alice Springs and the Northern Territory recently after a lapse of four years and was surprised to see the changes since his previous visit. Alice itself had grown by thirty percent in population. The radio service, which four years ago had been principally concerned with accidents to stockmen now spent sixty percent of its time transmitting from the outback stations telegrams which were largely of an amenity nature. He was impressed by these developments brought about by the rising price of commodities such as beef. He predicted that in thirty years time the population of Australia would have grown to about 23 million, whilst that of England would have decreased to a point where the country could feed its population, which he guessed would be about 40 million or less.

Here then were the elements for the next book—the position of the Queen in a Commonwealth where countries such as Canada and Australia would have greatly developed economically. Advances in aviation, which he was well placed to envisage, would allow the Queen to travel between Commonwealth countries much more easily and quickly. He would include political stagnation in England under successive Labour administrations and contrast it with a new multiple vote electoral system, of his own devising, which gave the newer countries a superior type of politician.

All this he turned into *In the Wet*, which he finished writing by the middle of 1952. Like *What Happened to the Corbetts* before it, the novel looked ahead, this time many years into the future, to warn people what they might face. In the Author's Note at the end he wrote "No man can see into the future, but unless somebody makes a guess from time to time it seems to me that we are drifting in the dark, not knowing where we want to go or how to get there."[9]

As a member of the Society of Authors he received their quarterly magazine *The Author*. An item in the summer issue of 1951 caught his attention and he wrote a letter entitled "Replying to Critics" which was subsequently published in the next issue.[10] The item he noticed was by Arthur Calder-Marshall who wrote "The best seller gives an idea of what is on the periphery of literacy, the literature of those who have graduated from the lavatory wall to the printed word." Shute replied that he took a different view. In 1938, 1945 and 1949 he had found himself with a large public for his books and enough money saved to keep him for ten years. On each occasion he had cashed in on his popularity to "slam down on my public with a book that would have real social value, accepting that sales would decline heavily in consequence" because it seemed to him a good thing to do. On each occasion he had written the book as a work of fiction to reach the widest possible audience. In each case the book had sold in larger numbers than anything else he had written before. He said readers were far more intelligent than unsuccessful writers believed. Readers were experts in detecting, and merciless to, the conceited and the insincere author and the author who, with all the tools of his trade, had nothing to say worth saying. He took a swipe at reviewers, saying that they misunderstood the intelligence of the reading public. He thought most reviewers were unsuccessful writers, or else why would they take the meagre fees they got for their reviews. He said that young authors should accept the embittered fulminations of reviewers with great reserve since these people were unlikely to know what they were talking about.

At this time Shute made some notes about writing novels, which

give some interesting insights into his thoughts.[11] He began by analys-
ing who wrote fiction and why they wrote it. He estimated that about
5000 new titles in the English language were written each year and of
these one in twenty was published. It was a delusion that writing was
an easy way to earn money. He categorised the motives for writing; self
expression in adolescents was a good motive but exhibitionism in adults
was a bad reason to write. Again he said that the public were far more
intelligent than this type of writer assumed and were merciless to him.
Another good reason to write was, in the guise of entertainment, to tell
the public things they ought to know. This was a very good approach,
for the novelist was responsible to nobody and so was freer to say what
he thought was right. However the writer should not preach sermons; it
was his duty to entertain and he should work entirely by the example of
a good story. Many people, he thought, were not imaginative enough to
realise that if they did certain things, certain results would follow. The
craft of the novelist was to work by example and if he was clever enough
the message would be absorbed in the "hypnosis of a good story".

Books, he thought, were sold to people mostly over 40, possibly to
give to a young person. These were people who were past the first flip-
pancies and extravagancies of youth and were beginning to think and to
wonder what life was all about. What did they want for their entertainment? Firstly he thought they wanted information. He also warned that
extreme sex did not pay. They knew all about it and it was not novel to
them. Everyone liked a love story because people in love were normally
seen at their best and the love story could be combined with stories of
heroism and self-sacrifice.

He ended the note with how much a first class author was paid, and
his answer was about the same as a small grazier in Victoria. The income
came from book sales in England and America, from serials, book club
selections, translation rights and film sales. He ended the note by saying
that of the 5000 or so books written each year probably about 20 authors
made over £20,000 from novels and of these, 5 made over £30,000. Judging by his literary income at that time Shute was certainly one of those 5
authors. An author, he said, was paid by the world according to the job
he did for the world.

1953 was a significant year for Shute. It began peacefully enough
with a voyage in February on board the yacht *Saona* to the Port Davey
area of Tasmania where he met the King family who became friends. By

early May he was in London to coincide with the publication of *In The Wet*, staying at his Club and doing a book signing at Harrods, an event he shared with the ballerina Moira Shearer. He also attended the First Reunion dinner of the DMWD at Simpson's-in-the Strand on 8 May. Goodeve, then Director of the Iron and Steel Institute, and recently knighted, was in the chair, and many of his old wartime colleagues were there, including Jock Davies, Richardson, Alec Menhinick and Gerald Pawle. It was an evening for yarning, swapping stories of wartime exploits, an evening Shute would have greatly enjoyed.

At the time of the Queen's Coronation on 2 June, Shute was in New York on his way back home. He watched the Coronation on TV there, and the broadcast was apparently sponsored by a soap company, which he did not think appropriate for so solemn an occasion. Everyone in America, he noted, seemed to be as excited about the Coronation as if it were taking place there rather than in England. He later remarked, too, that perhaps the Queen would not be pleased at his portrayal of her in his book as a plump middle-aged woman. Writing to his publisher[12] he said that reviews of *In The Wet* in the USA were mixed, some very good and others very bad and also that the multiple voting idea had attracted a lot of attention.

1953 was notable for Shute in another respect—he gave up flying and sold his much loved Proctor that he had flown for many thousands of miles. He gave up flying following a heart attack the previous year, this time a serious one that struck while he was driving to a friend's house to return an unwanted kitten. He was in the local bush hospital for three weeks whilst tests were made and cardiographs taken, all of which produced negative results. Then they sent him home to rest and recuperate. But whilst in the hospital his practical nature could not be repressed. The sister in charge told him that the autoclave was not working and Shute promptly repaired it. He found that the system used by patients to call for assistance was antiquated, so he designed, installed and paid for an improved bell and light system.

The decision to give up flying must have been a difficult one. The medical tests had shown no positive results and he admitted that he could probably have bluffed his way through a medical and retained his pilot's license. He would have been willing to take the risk if flying solo, for to him to lose his life whilst flying might have been a fitting end. Flying with passengers was a different matter; he could not take that risk and he enjoyed flying with friends and sharing the experience with them.

In hospital, and then at home resting in bed, was not a hardship, he said, for a man who could use a typewriter on his knees in the morning and do oil painting in the afternoon. He had time to reflect on his life and to think about writing his autobiography. His reflections centred around his time in the aviation industry, mainly his work on the *R.100* and setting up Airspeed. What emerged was an unconventional autobiography. True, he did write about his childhood, schooling, and Oxford, but the majority of *Slide Rule* deals with the *R.100* and with Airspeed up to the time he left in 1938. What seemed to matter to Shute, and what he thought his readers would be interested in, was his work. There is only a passing reference to his marriage and to his children, probably because he was essentially a private person.

He dealt at length with the airship programme and the rivalry between the *R.100* and *R.101* and placed the blame for the *R.101* disaster squarely on the civil servants and Lord Thomson in particular. Reflecting his experience of that time and also probably his treatment at the hands of the Ministry of Fuel and Power, he wrote that "a civil servant or politician is still to me an arrogant fool until he is proved otherwise."[13] Certainly his account of the airship episode, written 25 years after the events, cannot be said to be an unbiased or unprejudiced account, as is evident from the correspondence between Shute and Wallis when he sent him a copy of *Slide Rule*. In his covering letter Shute wrote "although I cannot expect everyone to agree with all that I have said since everyone is entitled to his own opinions, I hope you will not find that the account is very much in error."[14]

Wallis replied on the 9 August 1954. He said that he had read the copy with "a great deal of interest and enjoyment, though I must admit that I started with an unfortunate bias due to my having been shown some extracts from it in the less reputable English Press."[15] Wallis basically objected to Shute's treatment of the *R.101* tragedy. Wallis stated that he had re-read the original enquiry report and admitted that clearly they were intent on exonerating the actions of those involved. He then said that if he seemed to endorse Shute's conclusions, he did not agree with his actions because "you are not sufficiently acquainted with the unwritten history of the whole airship adventure to make a right judgement" and "it is too early for a full and impartial account to be published, since relatives of the principal actors are still living."

In a letter dated 19 August 1954 Shute replied to Wallis, explaining himself. At the beginning of the letter he explained his response: "As we are such very old friends and associates, I want to put before you something of my motives for writing this book and for the general tone of my recent novels."[16]

He explained that a successful writer can either "play safe, avoid all controversial issues, and devote himself to the role of the entertainer. or he can use his command of a large public to say the things that he thinks should be said." He then went on to recognise that this could cause many problems for him, but "His one reward is that of having used the power that he possesses in what he conceives to be the right way." He suggested that the details of the *R.101* accident and the report of the enquiry would not be accessible to the "young thinkers in the British Commonwealth today," and suggested that Wallis himself had to refresh his memory of the report. Shute felt that a study of the accident could "provide data to rectify many of the ills that plague our democracy today." He suggested that this justified his writing about it even though he might not be the best qualified. He then went on to say that he believed the enquiry was right to "whitewash" the incident. He still laid the blame at Lord Thomson, but that because he was effectively an appointee of Ramsay MacDonald (the Prime Minister of the day) and had not been elected, a critical report would have reflected badly on MacDonald. He stated that as the country was just entering the Depression and needed a strong political coalition, the enquiry took "the proper course for England and the Commonwealth."

This exchange shows something of the relationship between Shute and Wallis. Shute clearly still had regard for Wallis and deferred to Wallis as more capable of writing the story of the *R.101*. He seemed in his second letter to be seeking to justify himself to Wallis, something he would probably have not bothered to do with others. Wallis on the other hand seemed to have little regard for Shute's capabilities, albeit he seems to acknowledge at one point that the book was well written and entertaining. However in a marginal comment Wallis wrote "I think Norway was quite unjust to Thomson on this [the *R.101* disaster]—he, Lord Thomson, must have been entirely misled by the powerful senior staff at Cardington. —Norway did not know enough of the previous history of Airships and their designers to pass competent opinion."

Sir Peter Masefield was another who felt that Shute's account of the airship venture was biased. In an aide memoir[17] he wrote: "The part of Norway's autobiographical book 'Slide Rule' about his five airship years, is marred by a bitter, and in many ways, inaccurate tirade against the Royal Airship Works and its personnel at Cardington." Sir Peter visited Shute at Langwarrin late in 1953 and later said that Shute told him he regretted the biased account of the *R.101* episode that he had given in *Slide Rule*. According to Sir Peter, Shute had applied to Richmond at Cardington for a job there but had been turned down as being of insufficient experience. However there seems to be no documentary evidence of such a job application by Shute.

Shute also sent Hessell Tiltman a copy of *Slide Rule*. In the covering letter he wrote of the part of the book that covered the formation of Airspeed: "I hope you find this to be accurate. Inevitably since we devoted ourselves principally to different parts of the business it is a different account to the one you would have written since I placed more emphasis on the business side whereas you would have placed more emphasis on design . . . I have the advantage of access to all the Director's minutes of the old Company, so that I think the main facts can be taken as correct."[18] Tiltman's reaction to the book is unknown because, apparently, they had remained estranged after Shute left Airspeed.

Being probably read by a wider audience than other accounts of the airship venture, Shute's account in *Slide Rule* is the one that is best remembered by many people. Subsequently people asked him if he intended to write another volume of autobiography, to cover his wartime work, the post-war years and his move to Australia. Shute's reply was that there might be such a book one day but not yet. He felt that no-one should write about his life until at least ten years had passed, for no autobiography could be of value unless it was objective, since it took many years before you could see your life in true perspective. He added that when he finally did turn to writing another volume of his life it might well deal more comprehensively with what little he had learned about the art of writing.

At about this time Shute wrote a lengthy memoir of his days at DMWD and sent it to Gerald Pawle, who was writing a book about the Department. Shute said Pawle could make whatever use of the material he wished. The book, entitled *The Secret War* was published in 1956 and Shute wrote the foreword to it. In it he said that, looking back, it was the people and personalities rather than their exploits that most interested him. He did not think that such an organisation would ever be likely to be created again.[19] It was Goodeve's brainchild and he had the luck to bring together a collection of civilian scientists and Naval personnel who came from many different walks of life. Through imagination and persistence, coupled with a knowledge of industry, they achieved remarkable results.

In 1953 Shirley, aged 18, left the school at Mount Eliza which she had attended since arriving in Australia. Like her sister, she enrolled at Melbourne University, choosing to study Arts. University life suited her, not the academic work, but the social life—she was intent on having a good time. At a weekend event she met Barbara Norris, who was then in her second year at University. For that weekend they were assigned to share a room, only to find that it contained just one bed. They found this hilarious, working out who would sleep in the bed and who on the floor. They became firm friends, but at the end of her first year Shirley passed in just one subject—Russian—and so could not continue to the second year. Her father then intervened and made arrangements for her to join the Navy, which Shirley rather reluctantly agreed to. Perhaps, he reasoned, that as she was a good swimmer and enjoyed sailing boats, she might enjoy life in the Navy. He probably also thought that the discipline of the Navy would be good for her. Shirley enrolled at the Point Cook base but discovered, after initial induction, that she could either leave then or sign up for three years. She could not face the three years, so she left, but without telling her father what she was doing. Not for the first, or last, time Shute was angry with his younger daughter's behaviour. Shirley lived away from home for about two years, but came to an understanding with her father and later took a business course.

Shute's review of his life whilst writing *Slide Rule* also probably included his wartime work, the Wrens on the river Beaulieu and the shooting down of the Junkers at Exbury. He had made, and put aside, two attempts to write a story based on these stored up memories and the effects of war of the subsequent lives of young service people. Thinking them over again, he finally saw a way to write the story to the satisfaction that had eluded him previously. He added an Australian dimension by making the narrator, Alan Duncan, the son of a prosperous sheep farmer in Victoria who joins the RAF as a fighter pilot and whose brother falls in love with Janet Prentice, a Wren at HMS Mastodon. Shute tells Janet's story through her diaries, of her shooting down the Junkers and her guilt at causing the deaths of seven men. To her this becomes a crime that can be atoned for only by the deaths, one by one, of those she loves until she, the last of seven, commits suicide. Like all his other novels, *Requiem for a Wren* is skilfully crafted and also extremely poignant.[20]

In 1954 he was travelling again, once more in search of material for his books. In that year he made a six-week journey by road through Western Australia, visiting oilfields that were being opened up there. This strenuous trip of over 5,000 miles included driving across the Nullabor Plain from Adelaide to Perth in a station wagon, most likely with an overnight stop at Eucla, which was to feature in a later story. They drove in rainy weather and more than once got bogged down and had to dig themselves out. On this trip he met the Anderson family running a sheep station in Western Australia. Originally from Ireland, the two Anderson brothers had exchanged a wife for a race horse and had had children by Aboriginal women. Both hard drinking men, one had a knack of being able to tame wild animals, such as the goanna, a small Australian monitor lizard. The Anderson household was also home to a defrocked Anglican clergyman. This was another example of the colourful characters to be encountered in outback stations such as he had come across at Dunbar station in the Gulf during his fly about in that region—men who were good managers when they were sober.

All this was grist to Shute's mill, and in September he made another visit to what had once been a frontier country—the Pacific Northwest of the United States. He visited friends in this area, including Sydney `Hansel and his family. Hansel had moved to the States after the war and set up a company which made machines for stripping the bark off trees by high pressure water jets—the Hansel debarker. His daughter remembers his visit vividly. She recalled that he was an impressive man, gentle in manner but with a stammer about which her mother had warned her. She remembered looking down at her dinner plate to avoid embarrassment when he became rather red in the face from stammering. Despite this, she found, as others were to experience, that Shute could keep a dinner audience thoroughly entertained with his stories. During his stay her uncle took him out on his fishing boat on Puget Sound and her elder sister drove him all round Seattle. He told them about the trip he had recently taken on pack horses on the trails of the Northwest.

This trip was made with another friend in the area, Dr Gilstrap and his wife, following trails in the mountains of the Northwest, camping overnight and included a visit to an Indian settlement. He would no doubt have met friends of both the Gilstraps and Hansels and absorbed details of their domestic lives in this part of the United States.

Back home, Shute compared his experiences from these two trips, to Western Australia and to the American Northwest and realised that the real frontier way of life was now in the former. The American Northwest, a frontier region in the nineteenth century, now had all the trappings of civilisation, including motor cars, television and convenience stores in neat, well-ordered towns. Riding the trails on horseback and hunting were now essentially recreational activities.

From these thoughts, and the details he had absorbed, he began making notes and then writing his next book. He combined life on a Western Australian station, where the heroine, daughter of an Irish station owner based on the Andersons he had met, meets and falls in love with the hero, a young American geologist who comes to drill test bores on the station. Shute gives the contrast between life in the Australian outback and life in the American Northwest.

The working title for the book was "The Kindest Goanna" which Shute thought best reflected the sentiment of the story. However the publishers objected to this title believing that the public would not know what a Goanna was and might be mystified by the title. Shute was well known for insisting on his choice of book title. This time he lost his battle with the publishers and the published title became *Beyond the Black Stump*, a favourite old Aussie saying, meaning far off in the back country, far from civilization. There was also a more serious matter to be resolved before the book went to print. In the manuscript Shute had modelled the Regan family in the book on the real life Andersons, including details of the swapping of the wife for a race horse, the defrocked Anglican Canon and the fathering of half caste children by Aboriginal women. A legal advisor warned that, as it was drafted, the Andersons could be identified in the book and possibly sue the author for libel. Ronald Watt, Shute's literary agent, forwarded this warning to Shute and asked what changes he proposed to make. In the published version the wife was swapped, not for a race horse but for a Mauser pistol used in the Irish Rebellion. The defrocked Canon became a disgraced English judge; however the fathering of children by Aboriginal women was kept, as it was apparently not uncommon on remote stations in those parts. The legal advisor hoped that the Americans in the book were entirely fictitious. In fact by including stereotypical American families, Shute had made sure that the

Gilstrap family could not consider themselves portrayed in the book.

Shute worked steadily on the book during 1955 but the re-writing required, as mentioned above, probably delayed its completion. Shute liked to visit his literary agent and publishers every two years or so and in November 1955 he travelled to London. This time Heather went with him. Due to sickness, she had not completed her University Law studies and had taken a course in shorthand and typing at Stott's College, Melbourne. She was also developing an interest in her father's literary work. On this visit to England Shute certainly met Ronald Watt and, no doubt, they discussed *Beyond the Black Stump* and the changes that were needed to avoid any potential libel action. One of the things that Watt wanted his opinion on was a proposed change to the copyright law as embodied in a Bill then going through the House of Commons. The main change would be to reduce the copyright period for films to 25 years and to include this for television and broadcast rights. Watt pointed out that his firm preferred to sell the rights for a period of years rather than outright and in this way they had been able to sell the copyright to a film more than once. Shute also discussed this with the Society of Authors, whose Secretary asked him to add his signature, along with other well known authors, to a letter to the *Times*.

On this visit to London Shute suffered another minor heart attack, which confined him to hospital for a few days. By the end of November he was well enough to travel and arrived back in Australia on 1 December. Early in 1956 *Beyond the Black Stump* was published with the alterations[21,] which included a long list from the American publishers suggesting changes to dialogue to give accurate American idiom.

Yet even as he was writing it another idea for a novel had been forming in his mind and was to result in a book that would have a far greater and more lasting impact than anything he had written before. This book, and the film that followed it, would affect both him personally, and his readers, to an extent that he could never have foreseen when he started on the road to writing it. That book was *On the Beach*.

Shute at Kota Bahru 15 February 1949. On Shute's left is the Resident,
Tony Churchill.
(*Flight of Fancy*/James Riddell)

8 May 1949, Frances and Nevil at the de Havilland garden party at White
Waltham. Second from right is George Errington, an Airspeed test pilot.
(BAE Systems)

The house at Longwarrin.
(Fred Greenwood)

Family sailing the dinghy *Nicolette*.
(Heather Mayfield)

13
This Is the Way the World Ends

The atomic bombs dropped on Hiroshima and Nagasaki in 1945 hastened the end of World War II but also ushered in the atomic age with the threat of destruction on an unprecedented scale. After the end of the war and into the 1950s, nations developed, manufactured and tested these weapons. The age of nuclear proliferation had begun, and by the middle of the decade there was growing public anxiety that these weapons, available in increasing numbers, would be used. The anxiety also extended to the fallout and radiation effects from the above ground tests that were being carried out, principally by the United States and Soviet Union, but also by Britain.

Britain had been one of the pioneers in assessing the feasibility of building atomic weapons. In fact, Professor G.P. Thomson, who had served with Shute on the Toraplane and Doravane Committee, had been struck by the possibilities when the fission of uranium by neutrons was discovered at the beginning of 1939. He was interested in its military and other possibilities, and had persuaded the British Air Ministry to procure a ton of uranium oxide for experiments. However these experiments were incomplete at the outbreak of war.[1]

In 1940 Thomson was appointed Chairman of the top secret MAUD Committee to consider Britain's actions regarding the "uranium problem". A research programme concerning isotope separation and fast fission was agreed upon. During June 1940 Franz Simon was commissioned to research on isotope separation through gaseous diffusion. Ralph H. Fowler was also asked to send the progress reports to Lyman Briggs in America from that date. The Committee concluded, after Franz Simon had completed his work in December 1940, that isotopic separation was possible. James Chadwick, discoverer of the neutron, wrote later that he then "realised that a nuclear bomb was not only possible, it was inevitable."[2]

Another of Shute's wartime colleagues at the DMWD was Dr William Penney, whom he mentioned in his foreword to Gerald Pawle's book *The Secret War* saying that "Pure scientists such as Guggenheim, Penney and Purcell were invaluable to the department." At the DMWD, Penney worked on the Mulberry harbour with Lochner and others, and Shute, as Head of Engineering, had no doubt met him in connection with this project. In 1943, Penney was released from his duties at Imperial College London to work on the Tube Alloys project, the code name for the British development of the atomic bomb. Shortly before D-Day in 1944 he went to America to work at Los Alamos as part of the British delegation to the Manhattan Project. On the Manhattan Project, Penney worked on the use of the atomic bomb, its effects and in particular the height at which it should be detonated. He quickly gained recognition for his varied talents, his technical and policy skills, his leadership qualities, and for his ability to work in harmony with others. Within a few weeks of his arrival he was added to the core group of scientists who made all key decisions in the direction of the program. Other members of that team included J. Robert Oppenheimer, Captain William Parsons (U.S. Navy), John von Neumann and Norman F. Ramsey.

However the passing of the McMahon Act (Atomic Energy Act) by the U.S. Congress in August 1946 made it clear that Britain would no longer be allowed access to U.S. atomic research. So Penney left the United States and returned to England, where he initiated his plans for an Atomic Weapons Section, submitting them to the Lord Portal (Marshal of the Royal Air Force) in November 1946. During the winter of 1946–1947, Penney returned once again to the United States, where he served as a scientific adviser to the British representative at the American Atomic Energy Commission. With almost all other aspects of atomic co-operation between the countries at an end, Penney's personal role was seen as keeping the contact alive between the parties. Attlee's Labour government decided that Britain required the atomic bomb to maintain its position in world politics.

Officially, the decision to proceed with the British atomic bomb project was made in January 1947—however arrangements were already under way. The necessary plutonium was on order from Harwell, and in the Armaments Research Department of the Ministry of Supply, an Atomic Weapons Section was being organised. The project was based at the Royal Arsenal, Woolwich and was code-named High Explosive Research (H.E.R.).

In May 1947, Penney was officially named to head the H.E.R. project. The following month he began assembling teams of scientists and engineers to work on the new technologies that had to be developed. In June 1947, Penney gathered his fledgling team in the library at the Royal Arsenal and gave a two-hour talk on the principles of the atomic bomb. Centred at Fort Halstead, the work proceeded on schedule and, in 1950, it was realised that arrangements had to be made to test the first bomb, since it would be ready within two years.[3]

On 3 October 1952, under the code-name "Operation Hurricane", the first British nuclear device was successfully detonated off the west coast of Australia in the Monte Bello Islands. This was a remarkable achievement and confirmed Penney's qualities of scientific ability and leadership skills. On his return to England, Penney received a knighthood for this work.

He was also aware of the public relations issues associated with the tests, and made clear-speaking presentations to the Australian press. Before one series of tests the Australian High Commissioner commented: "Sir William Penney has established in Australia a reputation which is quite unique: his appearance, his obvious sincerity and honesty, and the general impression he gives that he would rather be digging his garden—and would be, but for the essential nature of his work—have made him a public figure of some magnitude in Australian eyes."

A year after the Monte Bello test, the first nuclear test on the Australian mainland was Totem 1 (9.1 kilotons) at Emu Field in the Great Victoria Desert, South Australia, on 15 October 1953. Totem 2 (7.1 kilotons) followed two weeks later on 27 October.

In October 1953 the British government formally requested a permanent test facility in Australia. Due to concerns about nuclear fallout from the previous tests at Emu Field, the recently-surveyed Maralinga site was selected for this purpose. The new site was announced in May 1955. It was developed as a joint, co-funded facility between the British and Australian governments. Prior to selection, the Maralinga site was inhabited by the Pitjantjatjara and Yankunytjatjara Aboriginal peoples, for whom it had a "great spiritual significance". Many were relocated to a new settlement at Yulata, and attempts were made to curtail access to the Maralinga site. These attempts were often unsuccessful.

British nuclear tests took place between 1955 and 1963 at the Maralinga site, which was part of the Woomera Range, in South Australia. A total of seven major nuclear tests were performed, with approximate yields ranging from 1 to 27 kilotons of TNT equivalent. The site was also used for hundreds of minor trials, many of which were intended to investigate the effects of fire or non-nuclear explosions on atomic weapons.

The first fusion bomb was tested by the United States in Operation Ivy on November 1, 1952, on Elugelab Island in the Enewetak Atoll of the Marshall Islands. The test was code-named "Mike". Its explosion yielded 10.4 megatons of energy—over 450 times the power of the bomb dropped onto Nagasaki—and obliterated the atoll, leaving a huge underwater crater where the island had once been. Truman had initially tried to create a media blackout about the test—hoping it would not become an issue in the upcoming presidential election—but on January 7, 1953 Truman announced the development of the hydrogen bomb to the world, as hints and speculations of it were already beginning to emerge in the press.[4]

The "Castle Bravo" test of 31 October 1954 was the first test of a deployable thermonuclear weapon at Bikini Atoll in the Pacific Marshall Islands, and also the largest weapon ever tested by the United States (15 megatons). In terms of TNT tonnage equivalence, Castle Bravo was about 1,200 times more powerful than the atomic bombs which were dropped on Hiroshima and Nagasaki during World War II. Fallout from the detonation, which was intended to be a secret test, poisoned the islanders who inhabited the test site, as well as the crew of a Japanese fishing boat, and created international concern about atmospheric thermonuclear testing.

The Soviet Union tested its first atomic bomb in August 1949, which was similar to the first American plutonium bomb. Several more tests followed, and the first Soviet hydrogen bomb was tested in August 1953 which gave a yield equivalent to 400 kilotons of TNT.

This, then, was the situation when, some time in 1955, Shute began planning the book that was to become *On the Beach*. It has been suggested that the idea may even have begun as a joke when Shute wrote to his friends in America that "Now that I was living in Australia, I kidded my friends in the Northern Hemisphere, telling them that if they weren't careful with atomic explosions they'd destroy themselves and we Australians would inherit the world."[5] The question that grew in his mind was, if the Northern Hemisphere had been wiped out by cataclysmic nuclear warfare, and the radiation fallout was gradually encircling the world, how might ordinary Australians behave in such circumstances whilst awaiting their inevitable fate?

Since for a novel about such a topic he could not draw upon any past experience of his own, as he had done in most of his previous novels, he had to begin from scratch. He had, as it were, metaphorically to pin a clean sheet of paper on his drawing board, and begin researching and then creating the scenario of the story. The characters in the book piece together the events of a nuclear war that lasted 37 days and was born out of an Israeli-Arab war.

The Israeli-Arab conflict was something of which Shute had knowledge. In 1948 on his flight to Australia he had met Dr Ralph Bunche on Rhodes. He was one of the United Nations diplomats concerned with Palestine and Shute talked to him about the Palestine situation over dinner. On the return from Australia, when flying from Baghdad to Damascus, Shute mentions keeping north, being afraid of getting "down into Palestine where . . . they shoot people down."

In the story, the Israeli-Arab conflict had led to a Russian-NATO war, with Russian aircraft, manned by Egyptian crews, bombing Washington and London. Colonel Nasser, who was in power in Egypt at the time Shute was writing, had an independent and anti-imperialist policy which earned him enthusiastic support from the Communist government of the USSR. At that time, and later, the Russians supplied aircraft and other military hardware to the Egyptians. In 1956, just as Shute was writing *On the Beach*, Nasser closed the Straits of Tiran to Israeli shipping, and blockaded the Gulf of Aqaba, in contravention of the Constantinople Convention of 1888. On July 26, 1956 Egypt nationalized the Suez Canal Company, and closed the canal to Israeli shipping. Israel responded on October 29, 1956 by invading the Sinai Peninsula with British and French support, which led to the Suez crisis that same month.

Shute has the war escalating to the point where, with the statesmen and leaders dead, the war became unstoppable with over 4000 nuclear weapons used, most of them hydrogen bombs, and many of them with "a cobalt element." This is the way Shute envisaged the nuclear holocaust that had engulfed the northern hemisphere, together with the proliferation factor, in that many countries had nuclear weapons. As one character says "The trouble is, the damn things got too cheap. The original uranium bomb only cost about fifty thousand quid towards the end. Every little pipsqueak country . . . could have a stockpile of them, and every little country that had that, thought it could defeat the major countries in a surprise attack, That was the real trouble."[6]

Shute's notes for *On the Beach* are numerous and detailed. He mooted the use of cobalt bombs, for radioactive cobalt with a half life of just over 5 years was considered a possibility to destroy life in a particular area whilst giving the prospect that it might be re-inhabited in 20 to 25 years once the radioactivity had decayed sufficiently. The radioactive fallout from cobalt bombs, dropped in sufficient numbers, would spread across the earth, resulting in the elimination of all life.

Shute's source for much of the data on radiation effects and fallout was derived from a 1956 book *Facing the Atomic Future* by the scientist Ernest Titterton.[7] Titterton was Professor of Nuclear Physics at the Australian National University, Canberra. In April 1952, the British had asked Prime Minister Menzies if he would agree to Titterton assisting in the forthcoming test, code-named 'Hurricane', in view of his experience with tests in the USA. They also requested that Menzies ask the Vice-Chancellor of the A.N.U. to release him for this purpose, which they did. Shortly after being approached, Titterton had a personal meeting with Menzies, who explained his views and asked him to act as an observer, looking after Australia's interests, and to give the British team under Dr Penney every possible help.

In his notes for the book, Shute wrote that 5000 cobalt bombs could raise the background activity over the whole world to 30 R per week. Here the symbol R stands for Roentgen Absorbed Dose, an established unit for absorbed radiation dose. Assuming that doses were cumulative, he lists, from Titterton's book, the levels at which man and other animals die. A dose of 600 R causes 100% of death. He noted that for man, 50% die at 400 R. For other animals the doses at which 50% die were: mice, 650 R; dogs, 550 R; rabbits, 750 R. These were chilling statistics, but were adapted for the dialogue when the characters discuss their fate.

Shute also consulted Frank Kingsley-Norris, a Major-General in the Australian army and a specialist on the effects of radiation on the human body.[8] He was then Director-General of Medical Services for the Australian Military Forces and a member, like Shute, of the Melbourne Club. On 5 October 1956 he sent Kingsley-Norris a draft of the unedited manuscript and asked him to read and comment on specific pages and on the first and last chapters. Kingsley-Norris replied with comments on specific pages. One of his comments was that death "was from infection because blood-forming tissues are knocked out (by radiation) and we are deprived of these blood cells which assist to overcome infection or else they run riot as leukaemia and kill us."

Shute began writing the book in March and concentrated exclusively on it over the following months. According to his daughter Shirley it was "*On the Beach* for breakfast, lunch and dinner." If he was obsessive about writing it, his research was meticulous. For example the nuclear powered submarine, captained by Dwight Towers, is described as having a liquid sodium-cooled reactor with turbines using helium gas. The technically astute reader may dismiss that description as incorrect, since pressurised water reactors were, and are, the norm in submarines. Yet in fact the Americans did have a submarine, *USS Seawolf*, which initially had a liquid sodium cooled reactor and which was under construction at the time Shute was writing.[9]

Shute set the events in the book forward in time. The nuclear war had happened in August 1961 but the first chapter begins in the New Year of 1962–63 and the events unfold over the next nine months, during which time the radiation slowly works its way down over the southern hemisphere.

On the Beach was to feature a motor race towards the end and, early in 1956, Shute ordered a Jaguar XK140 sports car. This was so that, he claimed, he could obtain first hand experience of racing a high performance car, for the Jaguar was an open top, two seater, with a 3.4 litre engine and a top speed of well over 120 miles per hour. At the time, he wrote to a friend "I suddenly went crazy the other day and ordered an open two-seater Jaguar XK140 so you will probably see my obituary before long."[10] He took delivery on 11th May. So began another career as an amateur racing driver. As he wrote in *Slide Rule* "it is very good for the character to engage in sports which put your life in danger from time to time. It breeds a saneness in dealing with day to day trivialities which cannot be got in any other way, and a habit of quick decisions."[11]

Soon after taking delivery of the Jaguar, he and a friend were returning home after a visit to Albert Park, south of Melbourne, when it came on to rain and the hood was down. Shute struggled to put the hood up but could only succeed in getting it half way up. They drove home holding onto the hood to stop it blowing down and got thoroughly wet in the process. Frances was highly amused when they got home, saying that she thought her husband was an engineer and that sort of thing should have been no trouble to him. He muttered a remark about Jaguar engineering, but the following day fathomed out precisely how it worked so that there would not be the same problem again.

Although he might have taken up motor racing as research for *On the Beach*, he continued racing long after he had finished writing the book, for the manuscript was completed by the end of September 1956.

Since he was so pre-occupied with writing *On the Beach*, he seems to have had little time for other engagements. However he was in Alice Springs in July for the Australian premiere of the film of *A Town Like Alice* which starred Virginia McKenna as Jean Paget and Peter Finch as Joe Harman. The film was made by the Rank Organisation and directed by Jack Lee. Afterwards Shute expressed himself "a little dismayed" at the truncation of the story in the film. The film concentrated on the first part of the book—the plight of the women under the Japanese in Malaya and ends when Joe and Jean are reunited in Australia.

On the domestic front, life continued at Langwarrin in the same vein. Over the years Shute purchased adjacent land for the farm, which now ran to around two hundred acres. The number of cattle had been increased and the quality of stock improved, thanks to the advice of Jimmy Edwards, whom Shute continued to consult on this matter, and the hard work of Fred Greenwood. Each morning at 8 o'clock on the dot Shute expected the generator to be running to provide electricity and would want to know what was the matter with it if it wasn't running. More than once the generator broke down or failed to run properly and Shute and Fred had to strip down the diesel engine to repair it. Normally the generator was shut down when the household went to bed but on the night of Shirley's 21st birthday party the generator was kept running into the small hours. Not only the noise of the generator kept Shute awake that night, but also the rowdy nature of the party with, apparently, a trumpet being played at 3 a.m.

Shute expected high standards of behaviour from both his daughters and that arrangements, once made, would be adhered to. Shirley's failure to do so, as, for example, leaving the Navy without telling him, incurred his anger from time to time. His view of his daughters is, perhaps, exemplified by his comment to his aunt, Grace Gadsden. In drawing up her will she planned to divide part of her estate into two portions, leaving one portion to each of the daughters. Shute told her that he thought Heather would look after the money so that its value would increase over the years. On the other hand, he said Shirley would probably spend the money in six months. In fact Shirley inherited the money at around this time and took off to study in Europe.

Shute sent the manuscript of *On the Beach* to the publishers, with the firm expectation that they might well ask to be excused from publishing it, for it was a novel quite unlike anything he had written before. It was the one book, above all others, written with a purpose to show what might happen if nuclear proliferation remained unchecked, with the message wrapped in the "hypnosis" of the story.

His publishers did not refuse it, publishing it in 1957. Far from being the financial disaster he had expected, it turned out to be his greatest financial and critical success; eventually it sold over 4 million copies. It was welcomed as "evangelical" by some and was admired and used by Billy Graham in his rallies. It has also been credited with helping to start anti-nuclear movements, such as the Campaign for Nuclear Disarmament in Britain and the National Committee for a Sane Nuclear Policy in the United States.

Yet its reception was is some cases hostile, being dismissed as "Communist sedition" by some on the right wing, with its "tiresome descriptions of vast atomic destruction." However it remained at the top of the bestseller lists for longer than any of his other books.

It changed the life of Helen Caldicott when she read it at the age of 19. She later wrote[12] that the story haunted her because, although much literature had been written about nuclear war since *On the Beach*, much of it more horrific and emotive, the novel was set in Melbourne, where she grew up, and described places she knew, devastated by nuclear catastrophe. She felt so alone, that nowhere was safe and she felt unprotected by adults who seemed to be unaware of the danger. She originally trained as a doctor, but subsequently devoted her life to the cause of nuclear disarmament. Shute's American publishers, William Morrow, sent a copy to Senator John Kennedy and there is a letter in their files from him thanking them for the copy. It is perhaps ironic that the Cuban Missile Crisis occurred in October 1962 when he was President and just at the time that *On the Beach* was set.

At the time he wrote it, Shute believed that the scientific data on which he based the book was correct, in particular the spread of nuclear fallout around the world. After publication, eminent scientists refuted his premise on this. But the book achieved its purpose—to show the world that mankind now possessed the capability of destroying itself completely.

The eminent scientist Freeman Dyson wrote[13] that: "On the Beach . . . is technically flawed in many ways. Almost all the details are wrong. . . . Nevertheless, the myth did what Shute intended it to do. On the fundamental human level, in spite of the technical inaccuracies, it spoke truth. It told the world, in language that everyone could understand, that nuclear war means death. And the world listened."

Of the impact that *On the Beach* had, Shute remained silent. It was a time for reviews of the book rather than interviews with the author. However he was asked in an interview in 1959 if he believed the world would end up like *On the Beach*. He replied that it was difficult to say. He felt that there would always be a definite possibility of war, but that if World War Three was fought in the northern hemisphere, it would end long before the 4000 bombs he had written about in *On the Beach* were dumped. He doubted whether enough bombs would be dropped for the southern hemisphere to be contaminated. He had changed his mind about that. The world would go on.

Shute had worked intensively on the book during 1956, then, having said his piece, it was time to move on to other things. Yet *On the Beach* was not to be put aside quite so easily. Soon after publication, Stanley Kramer, the film producer, read the book and was so impressed that he bought the film rights.

11 May 1953, Shute at a book signing at Harrod's, an occasion he shared with the ballerina Moira Shearer.

I. A/A.W.& D. D.A.A.W. D.M.W.D.

ADMIRALTY 1939/46

FIRST REUNION at SIMPSON'S-IN-THE-STRAND

Friday, May 8, 1953

In the Chair

Commander Sir Charles Goodeve, O.B.E., F.R.S., R.N.V.R.

Whilst on his visit to London, Shute also attended the first reunion dinner of DMWD.

Shute driving his Jaguar XK140 at a Rob Roy hill climb meeting.
(Autopics.com.au/Peter D'Abbs)

Start of a race on Boxing Day, 1957 at Phillip Island.
Shute's Jaguar No. 8 is on the second row of the grid.
(Autopics.com.au/Peter D'Abbs)

14
Still an Engineer at Heart

Delivery of his Jaguar XK140 opened up for Shute a new interest, that of motor sport as an amateur racing driver. He competed in several meetings on the circuit at Phillip Island, but his first venture seems to have been on hill climbs. In hill climbs competitors compete, not against each other, but against the clock. The object is to complete the uphill climb in the shortest possible time. In November 1956, shortly after he got his Jaguar, he competed in the Rob Roy hill climb in the mountains north of Melbourne. The competition was held on a specially designed and constructed bitumen track about half a mile long with curves and sloping steeply upwards in places at a gradient of one in three. Shute's time was 32.9 seconds, a reasonable one for a novice entrant. He competed here in later events but never significantly improved on this time.

Peter D'Abbs, a teacher at Geelong Grammar School met Shute and got talking to him and told him that, as he had bought a number of Shute's books, he thought it was only fair that Shute should buy some of his photographs. Shute agreed and asked, next time they met, where his photographs were. D'Abbs had forgotten all about them and apologised. Shute remarked: "Oh, I know, this change of life business catches up with everybody."[1] D'Abbs was then only in his late thirties. From then on he got to know Shute reasonably well and they would meet at clubs and events.

In addition to Rob Roy, Shute also competed at the Templestowe hill climb. The 969 metre long track was designed and constructed in 1951 by members of the Victorian Sporting Car Club, and multi-club hill climbs at the venue were enormously popular in their day. It is recorded that at one of the early events there were an estimated 20,000 spectators in attendance.

For circuit racing against other competitors, there was the Phillip Island track, about an hour's drive from Langwarrin. Shute competed here from early 1957. His name appears on the programme for the Easter Monday meeting on 22nd April. From the first he enjoyed the competition and was a careful driver, not aiming to be the fastest, just the oldest. At this meeting he competed in the Mobilgas trophy but was not placed. The final event of the day was an open handicap, with cars of all sizes and shapes intermingling around the circuit. In this race Shute went into the lead and held it until entering the straight on his run to the finish when he was caught and passed and finished in second place. He took part at Phillip Island events in October and Boxing Day 1957 but was never able to better his second place, finishing third and fourth in races at that meeting.

For Shute and his friends it was a good day out, with the thrill and risk of taking part in an amateur sport. For Peter D'Abbs, who went along as photographer, it was a long drive from Geelong to Phillip Island and Shute invited him to stay over for the weekend at Langwarrin and D'Abbs remembers that they chatted about aircraft and World War II. Frances also seems to have been keen. She certainly drove the Jaguar, though whether she actually competed in races is not certain. Peter remembered driving her to Phillip Island in the American Ford station wagon, which was known as the "Yank Tank". On his American trip in 1955 Shute had liked the Ford station wagon and decided he would import one to Australia for his own use. For some reason he was unable to import one. He got around this by importing the parts and having them assembled into the complete vehicle. It was certainly a talking point, being left hand drive and a rather large vehicle.

One youngster who went with Shute to race meetings was Jeremy Lee, the teenage son of neighbours. Being keen on racing cars, he went to many of the meetings, as also did other friends, such as Alec Menhinick, Shute's wartime colleague from the DMWD. According to Jeremy, Shute was as fast as anyone on the straights but never took risks in overtaking. Menhinick and other friends would act as the pit crew.[2] Shute came to know how keen Jeremy was on cars and on one occasion got him out of trouble. Jeremy had borrowed his father's car whilst his parents were away. He took a corner too fast and clipped the back end of the car. To avoid Jeremy getting into trouble from his father, Shute got the car repaired before his parents got back from holiday. He said that Jeremy could pay him back for the repair when he had some money. In the end he paid two pounds, which Shute thought was enough.

On 15 July 1957 Shute and Frances set off on what was described as a "writing holiday" to Fiji. At Sydney airport they happened to meet George Errington, the Airspeed test pilot and an old friend, who had flown an Elizabethan airliner to Australia. The press recorded the meeting[3] and quoted Shute as saying that George was "one of the cleverest people that ever flew a plane." He recalled that George had started at Airspeed as a ground engineer and had repaired a badly crashed aircraft that had been returned in several crates. To everyone's amazement it flew, and George kept it flying for several years. George recalled seeing a Courier with its retractable undercarriage. He thought that a very clever idea and decided he wanted to work for the company that invented it. That was how he got started with Airspeed.

Shortly before this meeting, Harry Worrall had visited Shute at Langwarrin and not long after that meeting Harry died at the age of 69. Shute had a great regard for Harry from his time as instructor at Sherburn and his test flying of the Ferry. From his meeting with these two old friends, both pilots, came the idea for his next book. He combined contemporary aviation in the airline service on which he had flown to Fiji, with memories from 30 years before of the instructors at Sherburn and even further back to pilots of the First World War. He remembered Geoffrey Beck, Harry Worrall's predecessor at the Yorkshire Aero Club, and Beck's involvement with a married woman awaiting a divorce. From these memories he began to weave a story of the life of a pilot from his time in the Royal Flying Corps to his flying the Pacific route in a modern airliner. As ever his research was detailed and thorough. He remembered sitting in the cockpit of a Sopwith Camel at Dover in 1918 just before his demobilisation and how he had studied its controls. For the book he needed first hand information on what it was like to fly the Camel. He got in touch with Harry Rigby, an Australian First World War pilot who lived in Canterbury near Melbourne. In a letter Harry provided many details from his own notes of the Camel with a Clerget engine. It was, he said, very manoeuvrable and a nice plane to fly. It was very light on the controls and could be flown with two fingers on the stick. Its main drawback was lack of diving speed when trying to shoot German planes diving away in their heavier machines with water-cooled engines.

All this detail, together with Shute's memories of his flying experiences over more than thirty years, went into the writing of *The Rainbow and the Rose*. The main character is Johnnie Pascoe, a name borrowed from his grandmother's first published book *The Adventures of Johnnie Pascoe*. Brenda Marshall, the woman Johnnie has an affair with, might possibly have been modelled on Amy Johnson. Brenda's death in her Tiger Moth was perhaps evoked by his memory of the fatal crash of a Moth at Sherburn in Elmet, which happened when he was a Director of the Yorkshire Aero Club.

The book is set in Tasmania, which Shute had visited in 1953 when he had met and become friends with the King family in the Port Davey area. The fictional town of Buxton, where Johnnie Pascoe flew from, might have been based on the town of Sheffield in northern Tasmania. However Smithton on the north coast is a more likely candidate, having an airstrip, which Sheffield did not.

If *On the Beach* had been a book with a purpose, *The Rainbow and the Rose* was firmly in the entertainment category and he found it fun to write. It was also Shute's tribute to pilots like Harry Worrall and his successors. In this book Shute uses a "flashback technique that I am developing more and more."[4] This refers to his use of dream sequences to shift the narrative back and forth in time, a technique he had begun to use as far back as *Lonely Road* written in 1931.

In November 1957 Shute attended a writers convention in Seaford, just north of Frankston. He gave a talk about his own approach to writing novels[5] and began by saying that nobody could help with the quality of writing—that came from the author himself. What he believed was required was leisure and freedom from anxiety, which gave time to think. Money to travel helped, as did the freedom to write something that would be profitable. The development of the writer might not, he said, be very impressive and he gave the example of the novels of Edith M. Dell. She had been a writer of popular romance novels, which her readers loved, but the critics hated with a passion. The reviews of her books got worse and worse and in the end became devastating. But her novels sold well and she earned a considerable income from them. It was not, Shute said, an uncommon experience and perhaps he had in mind his letter to "The Author" of a few years earlier where he dismissed literary critics.

Australian writers, he said, should accept the fact that Australia was only 4 per cent of the English speaking world and it was too small a country, in those terms, to support an author in the style which would give him leisure for full development. Authors should get to know the other 96 per cent, and so write about Australia in a way that non-Australians would understand. They should try to build bridges to America and England. They would do well to travel there, perhaps work there, to lay the foundations for bridges to the other side. However he said they should come back to Australia when the work became more profitable, because Australia had the lowest maximum tax rate and the most generous deductions. The author must retain enough income to invest in himself. He told his audience that they should concentrate on book sales to provide for their pensions. Serialisations of books and films from books were of a transient nature. He thought that good authors developed a faithful readership who, as they aged with the author, would have more money to buy books, more time to read them and tended to become less receptive to new authors. He stressed the importance of having an efficient agent in England which gave him access to publishing in the rest of the English-speaking world.

He was encouraged by developments in Heinemann, the company that published his books. They had put Theo Sambell in charge of the Australian end of their business, and Shute thought this was a good choice. He ran the business as a good book salesman would, and as a result they had a successful business in Australia. Sambell seemed to be operating independently of London. His books were now printed and bound in Australia, which reduced the delays in publishing, although delays in getting the proofs from London could hold things up. The advantage of printing in Australia was that, if a book sold well, it could be reprinted, or another edition put out quickly. If books were shipped out to Australia from England there would be a delay of a couple of months.

Early in 1958, as he was writing *The Rainbow and the Rose*, Shute suffered another heart attack. Although minor, it was sufficient to remind him of his mortality, and at this time he made his Will. He had a firm of Melbourne solicitors, Messrs Hedderwick, Fookes and Alston, who had acted for him before. The previous year he had helped out his friend Jimmy Edwards by providing him with funds for a mortgage to buy a property and the mortgage contract had been handled by this firm. However he drew up the terms of his Will himself without, it seems, taking legal advice. He felt that solicitors would not be able to understand his thinking and would wrap everything up in legalese, which he felt to be unnecessary in what he believed was a simple Will.

He appointed Heather and the Union Trust Company of Melbourne to be executors and trustees of his estate. He directed them to use A.P.

Watt, his literary agents, in all dealings relating to his literary property, unless there was strong reason not to use them. Watt had been his agents from the time of publishing *Marazan* back in 1926. They had come to his rescue when his own efforts at dealing with Cassell's had failed, so he had great faith in them as literary agents. He then made several bequests. The first was to Mrs Bessant, his secretary. She was to receive £1,000 and the price of a first class sea passage to England, to which she was entitled in her contract of employment. He also directed his Executors to acquaint themselves with her situation in old age and to make provision for her as seemed necessary to prevent her falling into penury. Fred Greenwood, his farm manager, was to receive £500 and would be entitled to a proportion of the profits from the farm (although it never really paid its way). If Fred continued to manage the farm successfully for a period of five years after Shute's death, he was to receive a further legacy of £1,000. All other employees were to receive bequests of £100 each.

He bequeathed his godchildren, Angela Menhinick and David Gadsden, £500 each. In Angela's case he expressed the wish that the money be used for a visit to England; in David's case that the money be used to visit Australia.

Frances was to receive an allowance of £1,200 a year from his estate for the rest of her life. He directed that the estate should maintain the Langwarrin house and garden and pay the wages of a gardener. If at any time his wife should want to move to a smaller and cheaper house, that such a house should be provided for her from the estate, with the house and furniture remaining the property of the estate. The clause went on to say that it was Shute's wish that the trustees should make further provision for his wife, either in the form of payments to her, or payments for her benefit, as they might consider reasonable "after balancing the interests of all parties and I put the matter in this form because it is impossible for me to estimate the value of my estate."

The estate would pay all probate, death and other duties, funeral and testamentary expenses. After setting aside the money to pay Frances, the trustees were to maintain a reserve for the money that would flow into the estate. At six monthly intervals, monies in the account were to be divided into five parts, three of which would go to Heather and two to Shirley. On the death of Frances, the funds would be paid to Heather and Shirley in the same proportion. On the death of his daughters, Balliol College and Shrewsbury School would benefit in equal parts. He requested the trustees to consider the various benefactions that he had already entered into with relatives and friends. The will was signed by Shute and two witnesses and dated 24 April 1958.

Shortly before that, Shute had competed in his Jaguar for the last time. This was at the Templestowe hill climb on 20 April. His active racing career had been short but enjoyable.[6] What might have begun as research for *On The Beach* became an enjoyable recreation for its own sake, providing a new challenge and exciting excursions with friends. It seems that after his heart attack he gave up competing and was content to do so. However at this time he took an interest in the development of the Repco Record, a sports car based on the Australian Holden chassis and engine. Designed to be used as a test bed for Repco components, it was painted bright yellow and apparently caused a sensation whenever it was driven in public. Shute was photographed sitting in the car, but he did not drive it competitively.

On his visit to the Pacific North West, a few years earlier, Shute had had some spare time in Vancouver and went down to the yacht harbour to see what sort of sailing boats the Canadians used. Here he found the yacht *Tzu Hang* and met the owner Miles Smeeton. He was invited on board, they got talking and he learned that the Smeetons were English. Miles and his wife Beryl had tried farming in Canada after World War II, but because of currency restrictions, had been unable to transfer money from England. They returned to England, bought *Tzu Hang*, and taught themselves to sail on the way to Spain. They then set sail for the Canary Islands and crossed the Atlantic, passed through the Panama Canal and out into the Pacific before setting course for Vancouver. It was the sort of story that appealed to Shute and he wanted to know what problems they had encountered. He was told that they had had to heave-to on account of a gale on more than one occasion and also that they had made the voyage with their daughter Clio on board and ensured that she did three hours of school work every day during the passage.

The Smeetons kept in touch and Shute visited them in Melbourne just before they set sail across the Pacific en route for Cape Horn. By then their daughter was back at school in England. On that voyage the boat was overturned and dismasted in high seas not once but twice. Both times they had recovered and sailed to a Chilean port under jury rig. Miles wrote the story of this voyage in a book entitled *Once is Enough* and Shute, with evident pleasure, wrote a foreword to the book.[7] He described Beryl

Smeeton as a remarkable wife helping to repair the damaged boat despite having a broken bone and a deep scalp wound. She was able to take a sextant sight under very difficult conditions, work out the position with accuracy and plot it on the chart. To Shute this was a remarkable skill, but he may have been unaware that Beryl had been an explorer before the war and had attempted to climb a mountain in the Hindu Kush with Tenzing Norgay, who later climbed Everest with Edmund Hillary.

In July 1957 Stanley Kramer bought the film rights to *On the Beach*. Kramer had a reputation for making thought-provoking films and at once saw the potential for a film based on the book. The following September Shute wrote to Kramer that he was delighted that a film of the book was going to be made and that, with Kramer's production, it would make a magnificent film. Shortly after that, Shute said in a letter that he had never taken an active role in the scripting or production of films made from his novels and that "I do not expect to do so this time. Changes are inevitably made when a story is transferred from the book market to the cinema seat market, and these changes are usually distasteful to the author of the book so that he does better to keep out of it and occupy his time in writing another story."[8] On previous occasions with *Lonely Road*, *Pied Piper*, *Landfall*, *No Highway* and *A Town Like Alice* he had let the scriptwriters get on with it and if he had any concerns about their adaptations of novels for the screen he seems to have kept them to himself. The only time he had made an adaptation for a film was for *Pastoral* and then the film had not been made.

On the Beach was different. He had written it with a purpose. The dramatic impact of the book was heightened because his characters behaved well right to the end. John Paxton, Kramer's scriptwriter, sent him the first draft of the script in June 1958. When he received it, Shute was about to set out on an extended trip with Frances to the United States and Europe. He took Paxton's script with him to mull over during the trip and, no doubt, to discuss with A.P. Watt when he got to London. He had a number of reasons for making the trip. He wanted to go to America again, to visit friends there and also in England. In England they would meet Shirley, who was then travelling in Europe and provide for Frances' elderly parents, who lived in Cambridge. Frances had not been to England for some time, so she too had a lot of catching up to do. Also, *The Rainbow and The Rose*, his twenty-first book, was about to be published. He also wanted to visit the Model

Engineer Exhibition in London and to attend the Farnborough Air Show.

They flew via Honolulu and on to Seattle and then spent a weekend in Hollywood where, reportedly, they had a grand time. In Colorado it seems they panned for gold, the small quantity of gold dust being noted in a press interview when they arrived in New York in July. Whilst he was in London, perhaps having consulted A.P. Watt, Shute wrote to Kramer about Paxton's script. His first reaction was that the script was a good start but seemed to fall apart towards the end. He followed this up later by totally dismissing the script and setting out his detailed objections to it. His main objection was Paxton's "hotting up" of the love interest between Dwight Towers and Moira Davidson and the implication that their love affair had been consummated. In the book Dwight had remained faithful to his wife, even though he knew that she and his family would have been killed in the nuclear war. He created characters who behaved calmly under threat, a characteristic he had noted during his time in the London blitz during the war. He objected to Paxton's injection of "realism" into the script and wrote:[9] "What Paxton didn't realise was that by 'improving' the story by making the characters more realistic he was destroying the essential dramatic impact of the story as a whole. That intense dramatic impact depends upon a set of characters who are 'too good to be true'." If Towers and Moira did consummate their relationship, then, Shute wrote, it would produce in the audience a feeling that these weren't very good people. If they got killed by radiation, they had it coming to them. As Paxton had written the script, one couldn't care less what happens to any of these people.

The more he read Paxton's script the less he liked it. He objected to the use of alcoholism as a source of drama. Towers, the submarine captain on assignment to a foreign navy, would have behaved very correctly at all times. He could not envisage Towers, talking to Peter Holmes, referring to the Australian Admiral as "Your old man". He took these and other examples as evidence of Paxton's "Americanisation" of the script and he urged Kramer to engage another scriptwriter, preferably a younger English one, who would obey orders and do exactly what he was told. In another letter he remarked that "I have written twenty-one books, all of them first class stories. Believe me, I know more about storytelling than Paxton, or you, or anybody else in your organisation. And I'm flat out to help you."[10]

Having got this reaction off his chest, Shute could get on with the other business of his visit to England. They visited Frances' parents and Shute arranged for alterations to be put in hand to their house in Cambridge. They had their reunion with Shirley who had bought a Lambretta scooter in Italy and, apparently, driven it all the way to England. She had plans to visit Vienna to study German. Shirley was with her parents at a party given by Heinemann to celebrate the publication of *The Rainbow and the Rose*, his twenty-first book.

That August, Shute happened to meet Frances Phillips, his editor at William Morrow in New York. Shute told her about his intense dislike of the script for *On the Beach*. He was livid and Miss Phillips wrote that "I warned him that he would have a heart attack if he kept on."[11]

In late August he visited the Model Engineer Exhibition. He had subscribed to the Model Engineer magazine since 1947 and had occasionally contributed to it. At the Exhibition he was seen to be deep in conversation with Edgar Westbury, a writer for the magazine whose clear and lucid articles on model-making Shute greatly admired. They chatted about model-making and found that they shared a profound admiration for the work of craftsmen in every branch of skilled work. They deplored the fact that such craftsmen were often taken for granted and rarely received either the credit or remuneration they deserved. Westbury recalled Shute saying he had an ambition to build a Seal model petrol engine to Westbury's design—if he was clever enough.[12]

The Farnborough Air Show took place in the first week of September. Here Shute could see the latest in aircraft developments, including the English Electric Lightning Jet Fighter and the Avro Vulcan bomber. There was also an Airspeed Ambassador fitted as a test bed for Rolls Royce jet engines. Here he could marvel at the enormous strides made in aircraft development in the twenty years since he had left Airspeed. Such developments were also far beyond any he could possibly have imagined when he wrote the chapter for Burney's book in 1929.

Also in September Shute met Mr Oldham who presented him with a signed copy of his book *Blind Panels of English Binders*.[13] Oldham was an renowned expert on English book binding, dating from his custody of the Ancient Library at Shrewsbury School. Shute, with typical generosity, had paid for the publication of this specialized book noting that "it seems only fit that entertainment books should be brought in to assist more serious scholarship."

Given the publicity surrounding publication of *The Rainbow and the*

Rose, Shute did talk to the press.[14] Inevitably he was asked whether he still took the same view about England that he had depicted in *In The Wet*. He said he did not. The atmosphere had changed and Labour Parties all over the world were now much more concerned with the facts of industrial life. They were more tolerant and there was more sense in politics. In the same interview he remarked that no one seemed to have pointed out that *Requiem for a Wren* and *A Town Like Alice* were the same story; one had a happy ending and one a tragic ending. When asked which he regarded at his best novel he said he doubted if any of his books would still be read in fifty years, but if one did live that long it would be *Round the Bend*. He told the interviewer that he read very little fiction but kept up to date with current affairs, adding that if anyone had influenced him in his early days he would say it was the poet John Masefield. He also said that many literary people tended to forget that business was the key to everything—to arts, the good life and civilisation itself. The artist, like the civil servant, was living at second-hand on trade. One of his books could be bought only because someone had made a saucepan or something else to create the wealth.

So the visit came to an end and Shute and Frances flew back to Australia, arriving at Sydney on 14 September. They were very glad to be home. A few days later he wrote to a friend:[15] "Frances and I are back, somewhat the worse for wear but not too bad; these long journeys to the other side of the world certainly take it out of you as you get older! However we have got back this time without either of us being sick which is something of an achievement and are very glad to be home again."

Having seen *The Rainbow and the Rose* published, he had in his mind the elements for his next book. Earlier that year he had drawn up his Will and appointed trustees to his estate. He had supplied the foreword to Miles Smeeton's book and perhaps wondered what might have happened to the Smeeton's young daughter if they had not survived the overturning and dismasting of their boat. Fresh in his mind was his visit to the Model Engineer Exhibition, his meeting with Edgar Westbury, and that the magazine had an avid readership all over the world. He began making notes for the plot of the book with the main character a tool room engineer and model maker, who had a gift for writing clear descriptions of his models for a magazine.

As he was making his plans for the book, Stanley Kramer and his pre-production crew arrived in Melbourne to set up for the filming of *On*

The Beach. In his dealings with Shute, Kramer had used a great deal of tact and diplomacy, writing that he had taken on board many of Shute's criticisms of the script and that a large number of changes had been made. He wrote to Shute that he agreed with him on many things but that there were others where they completely disagreed. Kramer hoped to be able to orient the script to a point which would satisfy him while giving Shute reasonable pride in his association with the transition from the book to the film. However the differences between Kramer and Shute were seemingly irreconcilable. On 17 November Shute wrote to a friend "this week the Kramer business is all coming to a head over the movie."[16] Kramer had wanted to discuss the film face to face with Shute; indeed he had written to Shute that he was looking forward to seeing him when he arrived in Australia. In November Kramer and some of his senior production staff went to Langwarrin for dinner. Shute and Kramer had a heated argument, "a hell of a blue", as Kramer's driver later recalled. Kramer, angered at the way Shute spoke to him, stormed out. Fred and Ruth Greenwood remembered Frances, rather ashen faced, telling them that the meeting had not gone at all well.[17]

There was to be no reconciliation between them, and Shute took no further part in the filming. He probably thought it better to take his own advice and get on with writing the next book. He must also have realised that, having sold the film rights, he could in reality exercise no control over the script nor influence the outcome of the film. However the debasing of the book's message continued to rankle with Shute, and his pent up anger might well have contributed to the stroke he suffered on 22 December, about a month after his row with Kramer. The press reported that he had suffered another heart attack, but it was in fact a stroke. Although he later made light of it, referring to it as minor, it was serious enough for him to be in the Royal Melbourne hospital over the Christmas and New Year period. Shirley flew back from Europe to be with her father. That is a measure of how serious the stroke was.

Shute was lucky, in that the damage was not more severe. His arms and legs were not affected, but it did affect his eyesight and speech. For a period he wore an eye patch to counter his blurred vision. He spent January convalescing at home and, writing to Jimmy Edwards, said that he didn't expect to leave home for the next couple of months except for very short excursions in the car. In that letter he told Jimmy[18] "I always thought a stroke was something that happened to business tycoons who controlled ten or fifteen thousand men and drank a bottle of whisky a day, but I assure you now that it is not. One always thinks that it is something that happens to somebody else and could not possibly happen to you, but it can and it does." He said that the only thing wrong with him was that he looked as if his face had been kicked by one of Jimmy's horses. However as he wasn't an oil painting to begin with, perhaps that was an improvement.

In late January Shute had been due to attend the 10th Annual Citizenship Convention in Canberra to be opened by the Governor General Sir William Slim. This was a major event with Government and Opposition representatives present as well as High Commissioners from Commonwealth countries.[19]

As one of Australia's most famous immigrants, Shute was scheduled to present a paper on the future population of Australia. This, and other papers, were to be discussed by a panel chaired by the Minister for Immigration. Shute could not attend, due to his state of health, and he was represented by Sir Richard Boyer, a landowner and grazier, ex-soldier, and former Chairman of the Australian Broadcasting Commission. No text of his paper has survived, but it would, no doubt, have been based on what he had said at the time he wrote *In The Wet*. He expected the population of Australia to rise to over twenty million in the coming decades due to immigration combined with natural growth; that there would be an expansion of Australian food production, exports and domestic manufacturing.

By the end of January 1959 he was back at work on his book, which would later be titled *Trustee from the Toolroom*. An acquaintance who visited him at this time saw a large navigation chart on his wall, with Shute plotting the voyages of his characters John and Jo Dermott, in their sailing boat. As ever his preparation and research were meticulous as the extensive notes with the manuscript testify. Keith Stewart, the main character, describes how to build a Congreve clock in the *Miniature Mechanic* magazine. Shute knew that such a clock had been described in the Model Engineer, but, looking through his back issues, realised that it must have been in an issue before he began subscribing in 1947.

In May he wrote to his friend Ron East, a fellow member of the Melbourne Society of Model and Experimental Engineers. He said that he was writing a book that had a model engineer as its main character, based to some extent on Edgar Westbury. One of the points he wanted to make concerned a Congreve clock.[20] The theme of the book was that the *Model Engineer* magazine spread all over the world and that the author of a serial in it therefore had friends all over the world, even in the most unlikely places. He asked Ron East, whose collection went back further than Shute's, if he would look through issues for 1946, as he recollected that a series on the clock had been published that year. He added, "I hope that a popular novel on our mutual interest may do it some good and the loan of these copies would be a material help in making the technical side of the book authentic."

Ron East provided Shute with the copies he wanted. In the 1946 issues of *Model Engineer*, Dr Bradbury Winter had written a series of articles on how to build a Congreve clock. Shute then had the material he needed for authenticity.

In February he gave a rare interview at home to a journalist, Betty Lee of the Canadian *Globe* magazine.[21] He normally shunned publicity, because he claimed that interviews with authors "never sold one damned book." One of the subjects they discussed was the making of films from his books. He told her how he had heard, whilst on holiday in France, that the film rights for *Ruined City* had been bought, but that the film was never made. According to Betty Lee's article, Shute insisted that "he worries very little about his stories once a movie company mails the cheque." He told her he usually saw the script and he usually approved of it, which was a remarkable statement given his views of the script for *On the Beach* and his recent row with Kramer. Betty Lee wrote that Shute received $100,000 for the film rights to *On the Beach*. In fact the sum he received was never officially disclosed, but another source says that the film rights contract indicated a "compensation" to Shute of $78,000 plus 3% of the gross takings.

At this time Kramer and his team were busy shooting *On the Beach* at locations around Melbourne. Gregory Peck, Ava Gardner, Anthony Perkins and Fred Astaire were the main stars, all top names in Hollywood. Given his feelings on the script, it is not surprising that Shute never seems to have visited the filming locations or taken an active interest in the film's production. Moreover, whilst filming was going on, he was recovering from his stroke. His eyesight was affected and he was taking things easy.

He told Betty Lee that he would probably invite the stars to dinner at some time. Fred Astaire did visit and they found him really charming. Gregory Peck was asked several times if he would come to lunch. His "people" replied that such and such a day was not convenient, or, no, he was busy on another day. Eventually they said that Mr Peck could come to lunch on a particular day. By that time Frances was so fed up with it that she replied that lunch on that day was not convenient for them. They never got to meet him.

The Grand Prix scenes were filmed at the Phillip Island circuit. If there is a cameo appearance of Shute's white Jaguar in the film, it was driven by Alec Menhinick who took an active part in the motor racing part of filming.

In March Shute replied to a letter from Flora Twort.[22] He told her about his stroke and that his eyesight and face had been affected. He added that he had been working steadily on the current book since the end of January, that he hadn't much to complain about except that he got tired fairly quickly and would have to take things easy for some months. He said that driving a car was the main problem. He could drive on quiet country roads without a problem but definitely would not feel safe in heavy traffic. Shirley had been home since he had the stroke and had been doing a lot of chauffeuring for him. Flora must have written that she now had television and Shute replied that they hadn't got as far as that yet, possibly because the Australian television programmes weren't as good as the English ones. He thought it was only a matter of time before they got it too. If he had still been living in England they would have got television long ago, but he was not quite sure if they would think it worthwhile just yet. In another letter to Flora at the end of May he said that he had suffered another stroke about a fortnight before, due to an ill-advised cutting off of certain drugs. As a result he was still "cross-eyed". Though there was little evidence of the stroke in his face, his signature was affected. He said that most of his writing now took place through a tape recorder, with Heather's assistance. She had now taken over as his secretary. She had always been interested in her father's literary work and, as she was his trustee and executrix, Shute wanted her to gain practical experience of handling his literary affairs.

As an artist, Flora, who had made sketches of Shute, would have been interested to know that in 1959 Shute sat for his portrait to be painted by Graham Thorley. The portrait shows Shute, almost full length, in a duffle coat and with his pipe in hand; the painting was entered for the Archibald prize for 1960. This prize was awarded annually for the best portrait painting, preferentially of some man or woman 'distinguished in art, letters, science or politics'. It gave artists the opportunity to have their work shown in the prestigious Art Gallery of New South Wales. The portrait did not win the prize that year and is now privately owned.

Early in August Shute returned the borrowed copies of *Model Engineer* to Ron East. He had studied the articles on the Congreve clock and said that he would send him a copy of the new book when it was finally published, which he expected to be in February or March of the following year. Shute added that he might ask to borrow the articles again some day as, having written about the Congreve clock, it would be rather fascinating to make one! At the moment, he said, he was busy with the Seal petrol engine. So far, he had made many of the parts. He was machining the crankshaft which would be followed by the camshaft. He wanted to get all the parts finished before he began assembly so that he could do the assembly in one go with everything to hand.[23]

The following month Shirley returned to Vienna to take up her studies of German. En route she planned to visit her grandparents in Cambridge to see how they were getting on in their house, which had been altered thanks to the generosity of her father. That was the last time she saw him. Their relationship had been, at times, a stormy one with Shute often being enraged with what he thought was her thoughtless or self-centred behaviour.

From his earliest days in Australia, Shute had taken an interest in the fortunes of young Australian writers. Shortly after his arrival he had worked with the Melbourne PEN to collect information about what writers were paid for their work. He also felt a duty to pass on what he had learned in his 40 or so years as an author, which he had tried to do in his talk to the Seaford Writers Convention in 1957. He had also hinted that this would be the main theme of the next part of his autobiography, which he never got round to writing. He was on friendly terms with Robert Menzies, the Prime Minister, and also with Richard (Dick) Casey, then Minister of External Affairs, whom he met from time to time at the Melbourne Club. With *Trustee from the Toolroom* finished and sent off for publication, he wrote a memorandum to Menzies.[24] The purpose of the memorandum was to set out his thoughts, not only on creative writers, but also on artists and composers in Australia. The memorandum would also include his recommendations, both legislative and financial.

He began by saying that the uncommitted countries of Asia might see Australia as fundamentally irreligious compared with their standards, where places of worship were poorly attended and religious people seldom engaged in prayer either in private or in public. Australia might be seen as a materialistic country with little or no devotion to the arts of peace.

Australia was a country in which few writers, if any, made a living by creative writing, despite the fact that they wrote in the English language and therefore had a large public for their books.

It was the purpose of the memorandum to show how Australian prowess in the creative arts of peace might be nurtured and displayed to the world. He would set out how this might be achieved for creative writers and also for artists and composers. His recommendations would fall upon the Department for External Affairs, since diplomacy would be the beneficiary.

At the outset he said that he did not believe it was wise to assist writers with any form of subsidy so that they could write a book. He reiterated what he had said before—that it was best for the young man or woman who wanted to write to take a job in a commercial occupation and write in the evenings until the writing became more profitable. That way the writer would get to know the characters of men and women during his or her formative years. They were the raw material for the stories, and also the readers who would buy the books in years to come. The writer would learn more about, say, women, from the typist at the next desk when she had a tray full of work, a cold in the head, at the conclusion of a very hot day than in weeks of meeting her socially outside work. Commercial employment bred the discipline of regular working hours, which writers should apply when writing in the evenings.

Recalling his own experience at Stag Lane, he said that writers should minimise the travelling time between work and home. He had written eight or nine published books in the evenings but had always contrived to live within a short distance of the office. On the other hand, practically every Australian author who had achieved international recognition had spent a portion of his life in England. He listed Alan Moorehead, Paul Brickhill and Russell Braddon as examples.

There were two factors that affected creative writers in Australia. One was the lack of literary agents. The literary agent took a lot of work off the shoulders of the writer in securing good contracts for publication. The best agents had contacts in many countries and also in the film industry around the world.

As a young writer Shute had received considerable help from the

Society of Authors. Although he had encouraged them to start a branch of the Society in Australia, apparently they had not done so.

A certain degree of success was of course necessary or the young writer would stop writing. But too much encouragement from literary authorities, without corresponding support from the public, might induce in the writer an illusion that he was a superior person to the common man and a belief that, if the public would not read the pearls of wisdom he laid before them, they should be made to do so in their own interest.

The Commonwealth Literary Fund had been established for many years and was the main body which assisted authors and subsidised publications. Shute wrote that subsidies from the Fund to magazines such as *Meanjin* and *Southerly* should continue. Such magazines gave useful encouragement to young writers. Pensions paid to a writer or his widow should also continue, but all subsidies to writers from the Fund should be abandoned. To his way of thinking there was no point in subsidising writers to produce what the public did not want to read.

Shute suggested that the Australian High Commissioner in London should discuss with the Society of Authors the possibility of setting up a branch in Australia, offering initial financial assistance, if necessary.

His prescription for young writers was that they should follow the path he had taken in his writing career. They should begin by writing in the evenings whilst doing a commercial job in the daytime. They should travel as widely as possible to refresh their ideas and pick up material for stories. They would need the services of a first rate literary agent to handle the commercial side of publication.

Turning to the creative artist, he wrote that the difference here was that, unlike books, there could be no mass production means to increase the income of the artist. If he was to make a living he must do so by producing a succession of unique works and selling them for a high price. This was a drain on his creative ability, much greater than for the creative writer. If the writer fell sick and stopped writing that might not affect his income for some time. This was not so with the artist.

Many new buildings—for the government, schools, hospitals and factories—were going up all over Australia, mostly devoid of any artistic embellishment. Shute's idea was that it should be a statutory requirement that one percent of the cost of any new building over £100,000 should be spent on artwork to enhance the appearance of the building, both external and internal. Shute well knew, from his experience at Airspeed, that business owners would resent the imposing of such a regulation by the State. But he thought that no real case against such regulation could be made, given that only 1% was involved. The artwork, for example a painting or sculpture, could be chosen by the work force who would use the building and might or might not reflect the business that used the building. He thought that having such art works in the office which people passed by every day might slowly have an influence on the taste of those who worked there.

Shute recommended that one mature and experienced artist each year should be selected by a committee to visit six countries in which Australia was diplomatically represented. The artist should be required to paint two pictures of subjects chosen by the diplomatic representative and that the pictures should remain in the country visited. By this means Shute hoped that Australian art would become appreciated more widely around the world.

Shute knew that composers and musicians spent a great deal of time in copying out scores for instruments, in particular for full orchestral pieces. He cited one case in which copying out the score for a ballet of thirty minutes took over two hundred hours of the composer's time and during this time the composer would not be composing new pieces. He thought that the federal government could relieve composers of this drudgery, and the cost of copying could be charged to the Commonwealth Literary Fund, perhaps renamed as a Literary and Musical Fund.

Australian composers, Shute wrote, existed in conditions of poverty. The most that he had heard one composer of front rank earn was £300 a year. In most cases it was far less, and so all composers wrote their music as a hobby whilst earning their living in other ways. The only full-time composers in Australia were those who had private means. One reason for this state of affairs was the Australian Copyright Acts 1912–50, where the statutory royalty payable to the composer was 5% of the retail price of the recording. Under the Act it was quite legal for anybody to re-record the work and sell it without permission, by paying the same royalty to the composer and so creating an internal price war between recording companies, which prevented any expenditure on advertising or sales promotion.

All in all, Shute believed the Australian composer got a raw deal and went on to show how this could be greatly improved. The Australian Copyright Act should be repealed and a new Act passed which was much more favourable to the composer, giving him a larger royalty and neutral to the interests of business houses that at present it protected. He recommended that copies of suitable works by Australian composers should be made and deposited in the Embassies or High Commissions in every country in which Australia was diplomatically represented. The choice of works to be provided would again be made by Selection Committee, as for works by artists.

In conclusion Shute wrote that a person who was gifted with creative powers could usually exercise those powers in many fields of the world's creative activities. In his early years, his work on new aircraft designs was very satisfying to the creative side of his character and those years were followed by creating a new aircraft company and working it up from zero until it employed a thousand men in time of peace. He went on to say that, compared with creative work of that magnitude, the writing of fiction stories seemed to him at the time to be "a pansy occupation" and still did. If the aircraft industry had continued as it was when he was a young man, when aircraft could fly within six months of first conception, then he might still be an engineer. As it was, he was a novelist and the novel created still took about six months to produce and he could work on a new one each year, as he had done with aeroplanes.

Shute carefully costed all of his recommendations and they added up to nearly £35,000. His income tax to 31 March 1959 was £39,037, which, he said, was paid within six weeks and the income on which this tax was charged came entirely from creative writing in Australia. 95% of this income had been earned in overseas countries and had been collected for him by his literary agent. So the cost of his proposals could easily be met from the income of one individual writer provided with the organisation he recommended in this memorandum. The legislative and financial proposals would pay for themselves and would, in due course, yield a handsome profit, for Australia was by no means devoid of artistic talent.

He finished the memorandum and sent it off to the Prime Minister on the 20 October, with the expectation that he would probably never find time to read it. He did receive acknowledgement of its receipt from Menzies on 3 November.

His workshop had always been his relaxation in the evenings. After writing the Memorandum, he wrote a letter to the *Model Engineer* about an adaptation that he thought might interest readers.[25] Because of his stroke he may well have found using a hand-held hacksaw to cut metal too physically demanding. He found a simple and effective method to adapt one of his machine tools to make a powered hacksaw. His main machine tool was his Myford lathe, but he also had an Adept No. 2 powered shaper, which was used to remove metal. Unlike a milling machine, the shaper had a single point cutter that moved back and forth in a reciprocating motion, cutting metal in each forward stroke. What he described was his means of attaching a hacksaw to the shaper head, which gave a powered hacksaw, capable of sawing as straight as he could, which, he wrote, wasn't saying much. The article also had photographs of his machine shop, which was fairly crowded with his lathe, bench drill and shaper.

After writing his memorandum, Shute began planning his next novel. His working notes show that he originally had a play in mind with the title "Nativity at Eucla".[26] It was to be set in the rainy season at Eucla, a place he had visited during his trip to Western Australia in 1955. He had in mind a nativity with a cast of characters and a date of 20 December 1954. If he planned a modern re-telling of the Christian nativity, his notes indicate that throughout the play "the parallel is never drawn". The characters would gather for shelter from the rain, and the cast was to include a white girl with a half caste brother, a white English boy, a grazier's manager and two scientists, one an American oil geologist, the second a French physicist, an expert on the design of H-bomb explosions. The notes contain details about the effect of H-bombs, raising the level of radiation, throwing up billions of tons of dust which may float for years, cutting the strength of sunlight and possibly acting to promote condensation, stimulating rainfall. This was no doubt all information that Shute had gathered in his research for *On the Beach* and subsequently when his depiction of radiation slowly spreading into the Southern hemisphere had been criticised by experts.

After five pages of notes for a play, and seemingly unable to develop the play further, he began notes for a novel, with the working title of "Incident at Eucla". Again it would have a nativity theme with three wise men who brought gifts. The first was to be the gift to Australia of producing oil from brown coal. The second was the gift of water by "magnetic distillation" a rather improbable concept, and the third was the gift of a defence against radioactivity. The three wise men were to be scientists. The first was to be a scientist from Cambridge attached to Melbourne University, the second an American scientist from Boulder University in Colorado and the third an Australian scientist from Sydney.

The notes also indicate that there were to be "miracles", the feeding of the assembled people from five tins of bully beef and two of salmon with plenty for everyone. A second miracle was to be an old unroadworthy Ford coupé carrying "Joe and Mary" over bad potholes, to the amazement of the police.

With these notes, Shute began typing the novel on 15th November and the writing progressed throughout that month and into December. The film of *On the Beach* had been completed and was due for world-wide release on the 17th of that month. A week before its release Shute attended a private preview of the film and his worst fears about it were realised. He declared that it was "the worst film that has ever been made of one of my books, without exception." He announced that he would not be attending its premiere.[27]

Shute concentrated on writing "Incident at Eucla" and working on the parts for the Seal petrol engine. Both progressed well. Christmas and New Year came and went, ushering in the new decade of the Sixties. Shute carried on with his usual regime, dealing with corre-spondence and writing in the mornings, working on the farm in the afternoons and on workshop activities in the evenings. He received a letter from Clem Christensen, editor of the literary magazine *Meanjin*, asking if he would send some of his books to David Martin who wanted to write an article about him for the magazine. On 11th January Shute sent a selection of his books to David Martin with a covering letter.[28] In the letter he explained that his books fell into two clearly defined categories—those written with a purpose and those written as pure entertainment. He sent copies of *The Chequer Board, Round the Bend,* and *On the Beach* as examples of those written with a purpose, which, when he was writing them, he had not expected to make much money. It the case of *On the Beach,* when he was writing it, he said he genuinely expected his publisher to ask to be excused from publishing it. He said that the popular author could act as an *enfant terrible* in raising subjects which ought to be discussed in public but which no statesman cared to raise. In this way, he said, an entertainer could serve a useful purpose. He noted that his books written with a purpose tended to be more financially successful than the purely entertainment books, because they were invariably sincere, and sincerity was the first attribute for making money in the writing of novels.

Examples of the entertainment books he sent were *Pastoral, Most Se-*

cret, A Town Like Alice, and *The Rainbow and the Rose.* His entertainment books outnumbered the books written with a purpose by about three to one. Of these he thought that, from a strictly technical point of view, *Most Secret* was the best formed book he ever wrote. He included *A Town Like Alice* because many people thought it was a good book although he didn't, but it reflected his first views and experience of Australia. He ended the letter by saying how much he admired their courage in tackling so much reading matter.

By that time he was well on with writing "Incident at Eucla". He had drafted the first two chapters and was writing the third where the characters were gathering at the old Telegraph station at Eucla. On 12 January 1960 he was at his typewriter and had just typed "There was a fluffy haired young girl with them, helping somewhat ineffectually and she was weeping, the tears running quietly down her cheeks." when he was taken ill. An ambulance was called at about noon. As it sped him to the Freemasons Hospital in Melbourne, some thirty miles away, he lost consciousness. A neighbour, Alan "Bush" Bandidt, drove Frances to the hospital. Shute had suffered a cerebral haemorrhage and died in hospital at about 8 p.m. that evening without regaining consciousness. He was just five days short of his sixty-first birthday.

Shute's funeral service was held on 15 January. Frances and Heather were the chief mourners; Shirley was in Europe and so unable to attend. As well as family and friends, there were other authors and literary representatives present, and there were floral tributes from friends and colleagues in England. Dick Casey, Minister for External Affairs, was also there to pay his respects. The service was conducted by J.D. McKie, the Bishop of Melbourne, who described Shute as a man of reason and a man of faith. He had, he said, a desire for truth and a restless inquisi-tiveness.[29] The service was followed by a private cremation at Springvale crematorium. In accordance with his wishes, Shute's ashes were later taken to England and scattered in the Solent, a stretch of water dear to his heart, where he had spent many happy times sailing and which featured in so many of his novels.

Tributes flowed in from many authors. Among the first was one from Eric Linklater on behalf of the Society of Authors. "Story telling was his genius and, like Kipling, he had a profound faith in the abilities of the dedicated man. But his sympathy was kindlier than Kipling's and his generosity was as wide as it was unpublished. He had the gift of enormous popularity which he earned by the genuine myth-making quality of his writing."[30] J.B. Priestley said that "He was one of the best story-tellers of our age. He had a curious prophetic element in his writing—so many of his stories seemed to be borne out by subsequent events. I only hope "On the Beach"—the destruction of humanity from radio-active clouds—is not going to follow that pattern."[31] Sir Compton Mackenzie envied the gift he had of producing the sustained narrative. Shute had worked with the Melbourne PEN since his first arrival in Australia. Alan Pryce-Jones, speaking on their behalf, said that "Nevil Shute was a rare conjunction of scientist, administrator and novelist. And he was an idealist as well. I believe he gave more pleasure to more people than any other person writing his kind of fiction in the past 20 years."

The obituary in the *London Times*[32] recorded his career both as an engineer and an author, adding that "as a novelist his virtues are in the first place those of a storyteller. He had a narrative ease and liveliness that made him never less than readable, a fund of sympathy, especially with the young, that warmed the reader and a quiet air of veracity that enabled him to communicate excitement and danger without ever shocking the reader's sense of probability. Nevil Shute was, in brief, the sort of novelist who genuinely touches the imagination and feeling of the book-borrowing public."

A more personal letter to the *Times* was from Basil Oldham, his housemaster at Shrewsbury.[33] He wrote that Shute was a generous man but always took the trouble to think out how best his generosity could be used. In an oblique reference to an arrangement that Shute had made to supplement Mr Oldham's pension, he wrote that "he [Shute] thought that a 'friend' ought in his old age to have comforts that he could not afford" and opened a special bank account to provide for these comforts. On another occasion he had made possible, by an outright gift, the publication of an expensive specialist book, a reference to Shute's financial assistance in the publication of Oldham's book on bookbindings.

Arthur Dowling, writing to the *Times*, was surprised to find no reference in the obituary to Shute's novel *Round the Bend*. He recalled a conversation when Shute had told him that he had put more into that book than any other and thought that, if any of his books survived into posterity, it would be *Round the Bend*.[34]

Shute was mentioned in a debate in the House of Commons in June by the Conservative M.P. Charles Curran who was taunting the Labour opposition about their failure in the General Election of 1951 and the possible effect that writers such as George Orwell and Nevil Shute might have had on that election defeat. He said that "Mr Nevil Shute, in 30 years of writing, had achieved an almost unique ascendancy over a new section of society, the non-professional middle class. Mr Shute could almost have been called the Dickens of red brick. And Mr Shute had hated Socialism so bitterly that in the late 1940s he had moved to the other side of the world to avoid living under a Labour Government in Britain."[35]

This prompted a letter to *The Times* from A.S. Freare, Chairman of Heinemann, and a personal friend of Shute. He wrote[36] that "Mr Curran is reported to have told the House of Commons that the late Nevil Shute 'hated Socialism so bitterly that in the late 1940s he had moved to the other side of the world to avoid living under a Labour Government.' What Nevil Shute fled from was the repressive and penalizing taxation imposed upon authors in this country, initiated in the first place by a Tory Chancellor and ruthlessly maintained ever since by successive Tory Governments".

In March 1960 *Trustee from the Toolroom* was published. It received mixed reviews. Some, whilst liking the story, thought that the convenient instances of those who help Keith Stewart along the way were a little too contrived at times. Not surprisingly the book was enthusiastically received by *Model Engineer* magazine. They published a full length article about it[37] with the title "Did we inspire this story of a model engineer?". The answer was yes, for wasn't it the case that Shute made his last journey to England in part to visit the Model Engineer Exhibition when he was seen in conversation with Edgar Westbury? The writer of the article thought that "every reader of this review should get the book and keep it as a model engineer's gesture of love for his hobby." Getting rather carried away, the reviewer wrote that "When I think of the hundreds of thousands who will read the book, of the millions who will see the film (and I hope the film people will consult *MODEL ENGINEER*), I do not hesitate to say that Nevil Shute's last book will do more for the prestige of model engineering than anything done since *Model Engineer* was founded." The reviewer ended his piece: "There is a land of the living and a land of the dead, and the bridge is love. If this is true then the bridge built by Nevil Shute Norway will not crumble so long as there is a model engineer to read *Trustee from the Toolroom.*"

At the time of his death Shute had published twenty-one books and the twenty-second was in the press. Six of his books had been turned into successful movies and the latest—*On the Beach*—was showing to packed cinemas around the world. In the book that he thought was his best, *Round the Bend*, Connie Shak Lin, the dying teacher and first class ground engineer, had stripped down the engine of the Proctor, but had not re-assembled it before his death. In parallel Shute, who claimed to be "still an engineer at heart", had not lived to assemble the parts he had lovingly machined for his model engine.

A de Havilland DH51 aircraft of 1924.
Shute did many of the stress calculations for this aeroplane.
(Author)

An Avro Vulcan. Shute would have seen this fly on his visit
to the Farnborough Air Show in September, 1958.
(Flightglobal archive)

Shute's Myford Super 7 lathe.
(Dr G.E. Thomas)

Engine block and liners for a Seal model engine of the type Shute
was working on at the time of his death.
(Duncan Munro)

15
Nevil Shute's Legacy

After Shute's death, whilst much of his routine correspondence was cleared out, the manuscripts for his novels were acquired by the National Library of Australia. This was only fitting for a major author and undoubtedly the best selling author who had lived and worked in Australia. In his methodical way all the manuscripts of his published novels were filed together with the extensive notes and correspondence and reference papers for each one. Amongst his papers were the manuscripts for the two earliest novels, *Stephen Morris* and *Pilotage* that had been rejected early in his career. The manuscript of *Stephen Morris* had remained on the shelf since, when writing *Slide Rule*, he had read, or rather skimmed, through it and commented that he did not think anyone would have the patience to read through the whole thing. He had also doubted whether much, if any, of it was written twice—the appearance of the typeface was against it. In *Slide Rule* he had dismissed *Pilotage* as equally bad.

In 1961 Heinemann published these two stories in one book with the title of *Stephen Morris*. The publishers felt that, not only were they good stories in themselves, but that they also contained "strongly personal elements" which readers would find interesting as a supplement to *Slide Rule*.[1] Some editing of the manuscripts was done chiefly to "cut out the juvenile philosophising and lengthy opening sections which had postponed the main action." The publishers were right in saying that there were strongly personal elements, particularly in *Stephen Morris*. In the story Stephen Morris breaks off his engagement to Helen Riley, a fellow undergraduate at Oxford, whose character he might well have based on his real life fiancée there.

The manuscripts contain both unpublished as well as published works. There are the Second Front articles, his despatches to the Ministry of Information sent from India and Burma, as well as several short stories, none of which was ever published, with the exception of "Air Circus" and "Airship Venture", both of which appeared in *Blackwood's* magazine during the 1930s at the time he was starting and working up Airspeed. There are two treatments that he did of *Farewell Miss Julie Logan*, a story written by J.M. Barrie of Peter Pan fame. One is a dialogue treatment and the second a script for a film or play.[2] Neither manuscript is dated but it may be assumed that he wrote these in 1945 whilst waiting for his passage to the Far East. At this time he also wrote the film treatment of *Pastoral* and the play *Vinland the Good*, so he had film and play scripts as a working theme at that time.

Barrie wrote *Farewell Miss Julie Logan* in 1932 and it is a Scottish tale of a young minister's enchantment under the spell of the amorphous Julie Logan, thought to be the ghost of a Jacobite heroine believed to have sheltered the Young Pretender.[3] Such a tale of the supernatural would have appealed to Shute. His short story "Tudor Windows" is a ghost story and there are elements of psychic phenomena in many of his books such as *No Highway* and *In the Wet* to name but two. Shute's comment in 1958[4] was "I am very interested in the mind and think that we have a good deal to learn about such things as extra-sensory perception and related matters."

For Frances, now a widow, this was a time for settling Shute's affairs. Shute had loved his adopted country, but Frances did not wholly share his enthusiasm. Hers had rather been the role of supporting wife and mother, although she had taken a great interest in the management of the farm, even doing veterinary work as necessary from time to time. She had not practised as a doctor for many years, her medical expertise being provided as required for Shute's novels. She enjoyed the motor racing and driving the Jaguar and had flown with Shute in the Proctor until he gave up flying after his heart attack. In fact at the time of his death she was herself learning to fly at the Victoria Aero Club, where Item Willie had been kept. Her instructor at the Club was Beth Garret, the first woman in Australia to hold a first class airline pilot's license.[5] She had taken the job of Club instructor after the air transport company that she worked for ceased operations. Frances was issued with a student pilot's license in July 1960 but did not go on to qualify for a full license.

There was another project on which Frances was consulted—the building of a new church in Langwarrin. A weatherboard building, a relic of the First World War, had served as a church at Langwarrin for many years. As the community grew, it became quite unsuitable and by the end of the 1950s the parish was in need of something better. Shortly before his death Shute made a donation of £8,000 towards the cost of a new church, which enabled plans to be drawn up. In June 1960 the local architect, David Caldwell, had a discussion with the Minister, the Rev. Peter Kissick, about the design of the church. The architect had a subsequent meeting with Frances who wanted to know what other work he had to his credit. She was impressed when he told her that he had been involved in the design of the John Flynn Church at Alice Springs.

The design brief for the church was that it should seat a congregation of 120 with a vestry for the Vicar and one for the Choir, and that the total cost should not exceed £12,000. The architect produced a modern design with steeply sloping roofs and walls faced with local granite. Much of the church furniture was to be designed by the architects but Frances said she wanted to donate a font for the church in memory of her husband. She commissioned the painter and sculptor, Ian Hassall, a DMWD colleague and long time friend of Shute's, to design and create the font.

After approval of the plans, work began on the building in early 1963, with a Foundation stone laid that September.[6] Work progressed well over the following months and by August 1964 the completed Church of St Thomas Langwarrin, to give it its full name, was consecrated in a service conducted by the Archbishop of Melbourne, Dr Frank Woods. The font, of an unusual design, bears the inscription:

IN LOVING MEMORY OF

NEVIL SHUTE NORWAY

17TH JANUARY 1899 – 12TH JANUARY 1960

FROM HIS WIDOW

FRANCES

HIS ASHES WERE COMMITTED TO THE SEA

IN THE ENGLISH CHANNEL

David Caldwell sent photographs of the church to Frances, who was by then back in England. In her letter of thanks she congratulated all concerned on the finished building and was sure that her husband would have been very happy with this achievement. In this she was correct for Shute once said that he would much rather look at modern buildings such as the Rockefeller Plaza in New York than the Parthenon in Athens.

The final cost of the church was nearly £16,000 and the congregation worked hard over the years to clear the debt. But without Shute's donation the project could not have been attempted. The parishioners are justifiably proud of this striking building with its steeply pitched roofs and large windows which give the interior a light and airy feel.

With the immediate tidying up of Shute's effects taken care of, the publication of *Stephen Morris*, and with Heather shouldering the work of trustee, there was little to keep Frances in Langwarrin or even in Australia. Shirley was in Europe and not likely to return to Australia. In 1962 Heather became engaged to be married to an American, Don Mayfield, and would subsequently make her life in the United States. Frances' father had died in England in 1959 shortly after her visit the previous year; her mother, now in her eighties, was living in Cambridge. Although Frances had many acquaintances in the area and kept in regular contact with Australian friends such as Jimmy Edwards and his family, she had no family or other ties to keep her in Australia. For her, Langwarrin was something of a cultural backwater. She loved music but the distance to Melbourne for concerts tended to preclude regular visits, but she did cherish the occasions when she could go in for concerts.

Shute had anticipated in his will that Frances might want to move to a smaller and cheaper house and had stipulated that his estate should buy such a house for her, with the property to belong to the estate. He had probably never expected that his wife would want to leave Australia but this is exactly what Frances decided to do in 1962. In May that year the Langwarrin farm, comprising 183 acres, was sold for £34,000. Frances packed up and left Australia shortly afterwards. She had always been keen on travelling and seeing new places. Her route back to England was by way of Kathmandu, Kabul, Tashkent, Samarkand and Moscow, places she had always wanted to see but had never had the opportunity to visit.

On arrival back in England, Frances at first lived in a hotel in London and then rented a flat. In 1964 she bought a property of her own, Oak Barn at Walberswick on the Suffolk coast. After Shute's death, the value of his estate, after payment of taxes and estate duties, had amounted to £80,261. Yet in the ten months following his death £180,588 in royalties had been received from sales of his novels, notably *Trustee from the Toolroom* and also from his percentage of box office receipts from the film of *On the Beach*. In the space of 12 months the value of Shute's estate doubled. Accordingly Frances received a further legacy from the estate. Her annuity was increased and she was to receive a further fifteen percent share of royalties received by the estate in the future.

Frances was thus financially secure and settled into a comfortable, if rather lonely, life in her new home. She attended painting classes given by Cavendish Morton, who was living and working in Suffolk at that time. Cavvy was an old friend from the Airspeed days, who, besides doing commercial artwork, was a very accomplished painter of land and seascapes and had kept in touch with the Norway family even after they had moved to Australia. He recalled Frances coming to some of his classes and that she seemed to have a latent talent for painting. She coped on her own at Oak Barn but in 1969 suffered a fall, breaking her wrist and injuring her back. At that time she decided that the house was too big for her, and that she would move into an old folks home not, as she put it, to "turn her face to the wall but to be relieved of chores and gardening." From April 1970 she lived in the home at Castle Hedingham in the grounds of the castle. She died quite suddenly in January 1971. She was a remarkable woman, a doctor who qualified at a time when female doctors were something of a rarity, a talented pianist with a love of music. She had shared Shute's love of travel but had subsumed some of her own interests to support her husband in his life and work and raise their two daughters. In return for her sacrifices, her marriage to Shute exposed her to a way of life which she could never have contemplated, and to which she was admirably suited, as she was a charming and gracious hostess. She also travelled much more widely than would have been possible had she married an engineer who remained just that.

~

Throughout the succeeding decades, Shute's novels, certainly the popular ones, remained in print, chiefly as paperbacks. There were a few omnibus editions, with three of the novels contained in one volume. The Windmill Press published abridged editions suitable for younger readers. In the 1960s the BBC adapted several of the books as radio plays for their *Saturday Night Theatre* series. Most of these adaptations were done by Stephen Grenfell, who, mostly successfully, captured the essence of the stories in this form with well-known radio actors of the time taking the major roles. More recently the BBC made a two-part radio adaptation of *On the Beach* as part of their Classic Serial series. Once again this was a very faithful rendering of the story as a radio play.

There were, too, other films. In 1986 *The Far Country* was made into a film starring Michael York and Sigrid Thornton. Considerable licence was taken by the makers in translating the story into film and the result is a distortion of Shute's portrayal of life in Australia compared with that in post-war Britain. By contrast the mini series of *A Town Like Alice* in 1980 faithfully and powerfully reproduces the full story, unlike the original 1956 film which omitted the second part of the book. If Shute had been angered over the 1959 film of *On the Beach*, he would have been apoplectic about the re-make of the film in 2000. The original film may have distorted Shute's message in the book, but this re-make completely destroyed it. One reviewer went so far as to suggest a trip to the dentist as an alternative evening's entertainment!

Since his death, remarkably little has been published about his life and work, with the notable exception of the biography written by Julian Smith, which was first published in 1976.[7] This monograph tells the story of Shute's life but is mainly concerned with a literary analysis of his novels, his writing style and development as a novelist.

So far as research into his life and work were concerned, one reporter in the Melbourne *Sunday Age* in 1993 wrote[8] that the "Shute trail has gone cold." Apparently his Australian publishers had no record of their dealings with him. Nor did they have any contracts or manuscripts or even scraps of paper with his signature on them. The phone book had no trace of his faithful secretary or her descendents. On enquiry the reporter said that Shute's British publishers could provide little information about whether any of the original manuscripts still existed. Tracing people who knew Shute or worked with him "is virtually impossible, for most of them are long dead." The reporter was reflecting the view that, whilst Shute had been a marvellous storyteller and a best-selling novelist in his day, he was now history, perhaps read in isolation by devotees of his work.

The growth and spread of the Internet from the mid 1990s began to change all that. Book groups developed where people could read the books and then exchange views online. In the late 1990s John Henry, in the United States, began posting pages about Nevil Shute on his company website and issued electronic newsletters. One member of a reading group in the United States noted that 17 January 1999 would be the centenary of Shute's birth and suggested the possibility of a get-together of Shute enthusiasts to mark the occasion. This idea was taken up by Dan Telfair, a long time Shute enthusiast living in Albuquerque, New Mexico. What was conceived as a modest affair blossomed into a major gathering, so that on the weekend of 16–17 January 1999 over 120 people from all over the world attended the event, at which both Shute's daughters, his grandchildren and great-grandchildren were present. Over the two days there were talks on his life and work, discussion of the novels, showing of films and a display of Shute memorabilia. The guest speaker at the dinner was David Stephens the Director of the mini series of *A Town Like Alice* who spoke eloquently about the making of the series and his view of Shute as a wonderful author.

Shortly after the Centennial gathering, as it was known, the Nevil Shute Norway Foundation was established to further public awareness of the writings and philosophy of Nevil Shute Norway. The Foundation established its own website, which has extensive coverage of virtually all aspects of his life and work and is constantly updated and refreshed.[9] A monthly electronic Newsletter was first issued in 2001 and continues to this day. There was a second gathering in 2001 in Frankston, Victoria close to Shute's home at Langwarrin and this set the trend of major biennial Conferences, which have rotated between the United States, Australia and England.

In Shute's papers were two versions of *The Seafarers*, written in 1945–46 which Shute abandoned, but had thought well enough of, to write a full text. It is a story of the effects of post-war peace on young people who had dedicated their youth to World War II. It was a theme he returned to in *Blind Understanding* in 1948, which he was unable to finish to his satisfaction, and which he published in *Requiem for a Wren* in 1955. Closer reading of *The Seafarers* by Dan Telfair and others showed that it was more than just a prelude to the later reworking of a similar theme. It was a good story in its own right. The complete text was transcribed with very minor re-writes, and Fred Weiss of Paper Tiger was interested in publishing it. *The Seafarers* was published in 2002, the first new Shute novel to be published since 1961.[10]

Since Shute was both a pilot and a pioneer in aviation, the Foundation has awarded annual aviation scholarships of $1500 to help those who wish to make a career in aviation. At the time of this writing 11 such Scholarships have been awarded to aspiring commercial pilots who have private pilot's license and also to one ground engineer. All the recipients have had a Shute connection either by way of location such as at the Royal Victoria Aero Club in Moorabin or the Sherburn Aero Club in Yorkshire. In 2007 Annabelle Coppin, the granddaughter of Shute's friend Jimmy Edwards, was awarded a Scholarship to enable her to pursue helicopter training, helicopters being a necessary part of running a large outback cattle station.

Two other memorials to Nevil Shute deserve a mention. The public library in Alice Springs has a complete set of his novels thanks to the Foundation. In addition it has the Nevil Shute Memorial Garden, which was formally dedicated at ceremony performed during the Nevil Shute Conference at Alice Springs in April 2007. Most recently the Yorkshire Air Museum opened their Pioneers of Aviation Exhibition at Elvington near York. This permanent exhibition celebrates the lives and work of local pioneers Sir George Cayley, Robert Blackburn, Amy Johnson, Sir Barnes Wallis and Nevil Shute Norway. In Shute's case the displays tell the story of his achievements both in the field of aviation, wartime work and literary career.

As a full time writer after Word War II, Shute averaged about one book a year. He doubted that his books would still be read 50 years after his death but thought perhaps that *Round the Bend* might be. It is a tribute to his skill that, more than 50 years after his death, all his books are still in print and are still enjoyed by so many people around the world. He left 23 published novels, which have the power to entertain, to move and to inspire his readers, even after many readings.

That is Nevil Shute's enduring legacy.

Shute, Heather and Frances, 1950s.
(Fred Greenwood)

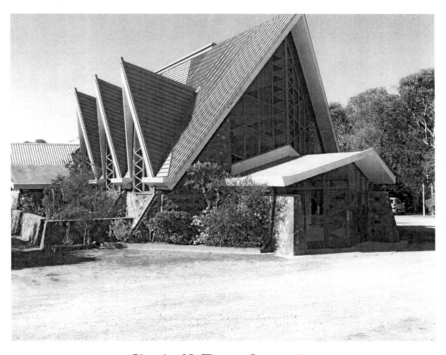

Church of St Thomas, Langwarrin.
(Author)

Notes and References

MS 2199 refers to The Papers of Nevil Shute Norway held at the National Library of Australia, Canberra.

Chapter 1
1. Nevil Shute, *Trustee from the Toolroom*, Heinemann, 1960.
2. True Crime Library see www.truecrimelibrary.com/crime_series_show.php?id=277&series_number. See also John Rowland, *The Death of Nevill Norway*, Herbert Jenkins, 1942.
3. A.H. Norway, *Highways and Byways of Yorkshire*, MacMillan, 1899.
4. Nevil Shute, *Slide Rule*, p. 5 (Stratus Edition).
5. I am grateful to Miss Gay Sturt for providing this information.
6. Quoted in *The Times* obituary of Michael Grover, *The Times*, June 8, 2005.
7. *Slide Rule*, p. 9 (Stratus Edition).
8. *Slide Rule*, p. 7 (Stratus Edition).

Chapter 2
1. See the Wikipedia entry for Cyril Alington http://en.wikipedia.org/wiki/Cyril_Alington.
2. M.L. Charlesworth, *J.B. Oldham of Oldham's Hall*, 1986.
3. *Slide Rule*, p. 14 (Stratus Edition).
4. Cyril Alington, *Shrewsbury Fables*, Longmans Green , 1917.
5. John Betjeman, *Summoned by Bells*, John Smith, 1960.
6. Keith Jeffrey (Ed) *The Sinn Fein Rebellion as They Saw It*, Irish Academic Press, 1999.
7. *Slide Rule*, p. 17 (Stratus Edition).
8. Mary Norway, *The Sinn Fein Rebellion as I Saw It*, Smith Elder & Co, 1916.
9. The Salopian, *Easter Week in Dublin*, May 1916.
10. I am indebted to Dr Mike Morrogh of Shrewsbury School for

providing copies of the Study Fasti (records) from Oldham's House for the period.

11. Letter from Arthur Hamilton Norway to A.L. Smith October 1918. Balliol Archives.

Chapter 3

1. Letter from Arthur Hamilton Norway to A.L. Smith October 1918. Balliol Archives.
2. Letter from C.A. Alington to Dr Pickard Cambridge 1918. Balliol Archives.
3. Letter from J.B. Oldham to Dr Pickard Cambridge 1918. Balliol Archives.
4. Letter from A.L. Smith to A.H. Norway 1918. Balliol Archives.
5. Letter from N.S. Norway to A.H. Norway 1918 Balliol Archives.
6. Letter from A.L. Smith to N.S. Norway 1918 Balliol Archives.
7. Letter from N.S. Norway to A.L. Smith 1918 Balliol Archives.
8. Ibid.
9. Ibid.
10. Geoffrey de Havilland, *Sky Fever*, Hamish Hamilton, London, 1961.
11. N.S. Norway, "The Case for the Revival of the Water Channel", *Journal of the Royal Aeronautical Society*, No 167, November 1924 Vol. XXVIII pp. 647–652.
12. British Library Additional Manuscript 56763 Society of Authors Archive. Vol. CLXXXIX ff. 157.
13. Ibid. ff. 159.
14. *East Hampshire Post*, Thursday, February 26 1981, p. 27.

Chapter 4

1. Minute Book of Director's Meetings, Airship Guarantee Company, Vickers Archives, Cambridge University Library.
2. *Flight*, April 12, 1928, p. 252.
3. *East Hampshire Post*, Thursday February 26 1981, p. 27.
4. Letter Nevil Shute to Flora Twort 28 September 1925, Petersfield Museum Collection.
5. Letter Nevil Shute to Flora Twort 30 September 1925, Petersfield Museum Collection.
6. *Slide Rule* p. 53 (Stratus Edition).

7. British Library Additional Manuscript 56763 Society of Authors Archive. Vol. CLXXXIX ff. 157.

8. *The Times*, August 22, 1966, p. 8.

9. *East Hampshire Post*, February 26, 1981, p. 27.

10. Cambridge University Library, Vickers Archives, Microfilm L49.

11. *Flight*, July 1926, p. 468.

12. *Flight*, September 30th 1926, p. 635.

13. P.L. Teed, *The Chemistry and Manufacture of Hydrogen*, Edward Arnold, 1919.

14. J.E. Morpurgo, *Barnes Wallis*, Longman, 1972.

15. *House of Commons Debate*, 4th May 1927, Hansard vol. 205, pp. 1615–8.

16. BT31/32708/208402 No. of Company: 208402; *Yorkshire Aeroplane Club Limited*, National Archives.

17. *Flight*, December 8, 1927, p. 836.

18. The accident report is contained in AVIA 5/9 Type: DH 60 Moth (G-EBRZ); Location: Sherburn in Elmet; Report No.: C109, National Archives.

19. *Flight*, April 10 1931, p. 313.

20. Letter, Nevil Shute to Flora Twort, 17 June 1927, Petersfield Museum Collection.

21. Quoted by Mary Stopes-Roe in an after dinner speech, York, 2009.

22. Nevil Shute, "The Airship Venture", *Blackwoods Magazine*, May, 1933, p. 627.

23. Vickers Archives, Microfilm L49, Cambridge University Library.

24. Nevil Shute, "The Airship Venture", *Blackwoods Magazine*, May, 1933, p. 627.

25. Dennis Burney, *The World, The Air and The Future*, Alfred A. Knopf, 1929.

26. Cambridge University Library, Vickers Archives, Microfilm L49.

27. Ibid.

28. From Movietone newsreel of the arrival of *R.100* in Canada.

29. *Slide Rule*, p. 85 53 (Stratus Edition).

30. *Slide Rule*, p. 86 53 (Stratus Edition).

31. Quoted in Sir Peter G. Masefield, *To Ride The Storm*, William Kimber, 1982.

32. Cambridge University Library, Vickers Archives, Microfilm L49, Frames 82–83.

33. Cambridge University Library, Vickers Archives, Microfilm L49.
34. See www.cranfield.ac.uk/library/cranfield/about/archive/airships/
    page28838.html.
35. Cambridge University Library, Vickers Archives, Microfilm L49,
    Frame 37.
36. Cambridge University Library, Vickers Archives, Microfilm L49,
    Frame 32.
37. Cambridge University Library, Vickers Archives, Microfilm L49,
    Frame 44.
38. Cambridge University Library, Vickers Archives, Microfilm L49,
    Frame 41.
39. *Slide Rule*, p. 103 (Stratus Edition).

Chapter 5

1. Correspondence, Sir Alan Cobham, *Airspeed and Ferry*, Cobham
    Archives.
2. D.H. Middleton, *Airspeed, The Company and its Aeroplanes*, Ter-
    rence Dalton, 1982, p. 5.
3. BT 31/33245/254813 No. of Company: 254813; *Airspeed Limited*.
    National Archives.
4. Correspondence, Sir Alan Cobham, *Airspeed and Ferry*, Cobham
    Archives.
5. Ibid.
6. Nevil Shute, "Down the Humber in a Motor Cruiser", unpub-
    lished manuscript, MS 2119.
7. British Patent 397,964, *Improvements in or relating to Aeroplanes*,
    November, 1932, Airspeed Ltd and Alfred Hessell Tiltman.
8. British Patent 483,583, *Improvements in or relating to indicating
    or recording instruments for use on aircraft*, April, 1938, Airspeed
    (1934) Ltd and Nevil Shute Norway.
9. BT 217/865, Air Navigation Directions 1930: Waiving of regula-
    tions Section IX on fitting of W/T apparatus for Airspeed Ferry
    aircraft for pleasure flights, National Archives.
10. These figures are quoted in D.H. Middleton, *Airspeed, The Com-
    pany and its Aeroplanes*.
11. Research by Phillip Nixon, presented at the 6th Nevil Shute Con-
    ference, York, July 25–29, 2009.

12. D.H. Middleton, *Airspeed, The Company and its Aeroplanes*, Terrence Dalton, 1982, p. 29.

13. Nevil Shute, "Down the Humber in a Motor Cruiser", unpublished manuscript, MS 2199.

14. Nevil Shute, "Knightly Vigil", unpublished manuscript, MS 2199.

15. Nevil Shute, "Tudor Windows", unpublished manuscript, MS 2199.

16. Nevil Shute, "The Uttermost Parts of the Sea", unpublished manuscript, MS 2199.

17. Letter Nevil Shute to Sir Alan Cobham, 8 May 1932, in Correspondence, Sir Alan Cobham, *Courier*, Cobham Archives.

18. An account of this is given in a note in Ref. 17.

19. D.H. Middleton, *Airspeed, The Company and its Aeroplanes*, Terrence Dalton, 1982, p. 38.

20. Ibid, p. 37.

21. *Slide Rule*, p. 129.

22. *The Times*, July 24,1934, p. 19.

23. *The Times*, September 5, 1934, p. 17.

24. Airspeed Aeronautical College Brochure 1934, BAE Systems Heritage, Farnborough.

25. The case of Stack and Turner vs. Airspeed was fully reported in *The Times*. See *The Times*, Law Report, December 11, 1935.

26. D.H. Middleton, *Airspeed, The Company and its Aeroplanes*, Terrence Dalton, 1982, p. 42.

27. Chairman's Report, Airspeed (1934) Ltd, BAE Systems Heritage, Farnborough.

28. D.H. Middleton, *Airspeed, The Company and its Aeroplanes*, Terrence Dalton, 1982, p. 49.

29. *Slide Rule*, p. 163 (Stratus Edition).

30. N.S. Norway, *R.100 Canadian Flight, 1930, Journal of the Royal Aeronautical Society*, May, 1931, p. 401–414.

31. Nevil Shute, "The Airship Venture", *Blackwoods Magazine*, May, 1933, p. 627.

32. D.H. Middleton, *Airspeed, The Company and its Aeroplanes*, Terrence Dalton, 1982, p. 102.

33. Ibid. p. 107.

34. *Slide Rule*, p. 168 (Stratus Edition).

Chapter 6
1. *New York Times*, April 25th 1939.
2. *The Times,* January 3rd 1939, p. 12.
3. Andre Maurois, *Splendide Isolement, Les Annales Politiques et Literaires*, 114, September 25 1939, p. 308–9.
4. ADM 179/137, Combined naval and air staff requirements for gliding torpedoes; reference to Toraplane invented by Sir Dennis Burney; Doravane development and trials minutes of meetings. National Archives.
5. Letter from Admiral James to Prof. Lindemann (Lord Cherwell) 4/10/1939, Cherwell papers, G446/1, Cherwell Archives, Nuffield College, Oxford.
6. The letter from Churchill is contained in Ref. 4.
7. See Ref. 4.
8. AVIA 13/723, Gliding torpedo, Pt I, National Archives.
9. Minutes of this meeting are contained in Ref. 4.
10. Minutes of this meeting are contained in Ref. 4.
11. AVIA 13/724, Gliding torpedo, Pt II, National Archives.
12. See Ref. 4.
13. Cherwell papers, G447, Cherwell Archives, Nuffield College, Oxford.
14. AVIA 13/730, Gliding torpedo, Pt VIII, National Archives.
15. George Orwell, *New Statesman and Nation*, December 7, 1940, p. 574.
16. Nevil Shute, Foreword to Gerald Pawle, *The Secret War*, Harrap, 1956.
17. *Slide Rule,* p. 2 (Stratus Edition).
18. Nevil Shute, "Journey into Normandy", unpublished manuscript, MS 2199.

Chapter 7
1. Edward Terrell, *Admiralty Brief,* George Harrap, 1958.
2. ADM 271/6, *Acoustic Warning Device*, National Archives.
3. ADM 271/1, *History of the department, a survey of its projects and a key to its technical history*, National Archives.
4. Nevil Shute, "Second Front II", unpublished manuscript, MS 2199.

5. *East Hampshire Post*, Thursday, February 26 1981, p. 27.

6. Flora Twort, Diaries 1940–1944, Petersfield Museum.

7. Nevil Shute, Foreword to Gerald Pawle, *The Secret War*, Harrap, 1956.

8. Nevil Shute, *Second Front III*, unpublished manuscript, MS 2199.

9. Letter Nevil Shute to A.D.Evans January 13 1943, Heinemann files.

10. James Close in a letter to the author, 2004.

11. ADM 271/16, *Fresh water*, National Archives.

12. ADM 271/11, *Gliders*, National Archives.

13. ADM 271/11, *D.M.W.D Technical history No. XII*, National Archives. See also John Anderson, *Swallows on the Beaulieu.*

14. Nevil Shute, "Second Front IV", unpublished manuscript, MS 2199.

15. Nevil Shute, "Second Front I", unpublished manuscript, MS 2199.

16. ADM 271/27, *Beach obstacle demolition*, National Archives.

17. John Anderson, *Nevil Shute and Exercise Trousers.*

18. Nevil Shute, "Second Front III", unpublished manuscript, MS 2199.

19. Howard Margolian, *Conduct Unbecoming: The Story of the Murder of Canadian Prisoners*, Toronto University Press, 1998.

20. Nevil Shute, "Second Front III", unpublished manuscript, MS 2199. See also John Stanley, *The Exbury Junkers a World war II Mystery*, Woodfield Publishing, 2004.

21. Nevil Shute, "Journey into Normandy", unpublished manuscript, MS 2199.

22. Nevil Shute, "Second Front IV", unpublished manuscript, MS 2199.

23. ADM 271/37, *Landing Craft Tank (Rocket) (LCT(R)) GRASS-HOPPER*, National Archives.

24. Quoted in Julian Smith, *Nevil Shute, a Biography*, p. 57, The Paper Tiger, 2002.

Chapter 8

1. Nevil Shute, "Pastoral Film Script", unpublished manuscript, MS 2199.

2. Nevil Shute, *Vinland the Good*, Heinemann, 1945.

3. Nevil Shute, *Vinland the Good*, The Paper Tiger, 1998.
4. Nevil Shute, unpublished article for the Ministry of Information, MS 2199.
5. Nevil Shute, second unpublished article for the Ministry of Information, MS 2199.
6. Nevil Shute, third unpublished article for the Ministry of Information, MS 2199.
7. Nevil Shute, fourth unpublished article for the Ministry of Information, MS 2199.
8. Nevil Shute, fifth unpublished article for the Ministry of Information, MS 2199.
9. Nevil Shute, sixth unpublished article for the Ministry of Information, MS 2199.

Chapter 9
1. Walter White, *A Rising Wind*, Doubleday & Co., New York, 1945.
2. Nevil Shute, *The Chequer Board*, Heinemann, 1946.
3. Nevil Shute, *The Seafarers*, The Paper Tiger, 2002.
4. Nevil Shute, Letter to *The Times*, June 29, 1949.
5. Nevil Shute, "Anglo-American Relations", *New Statesman and Nation*, July 26, 1947.
6. *Flight*, April 10, 1947.
7. Nevil Shute, "Blind Understanding", unpublished manuscript, 1948.
8. Donald Stevenson, "Models and Fiction", *The Model Engineer*, January 27, 1949.
9. Sir Peter Masefield, unpublished aide memoir.
10. Discussion of P.B. Walker, "Fatigue of Aircraft Structures", Journal of the Royal Aeronautical Society, Vol. 53 (1949), pp. 763–778.
11. Nevil Shute, *No Highway*, Heinemann, 1948.
12. Betty Lee, "Nevil Shute: He Believes the World Will Survive After All", *The Globe Magazine*, February 21, 1959.
13. Letter from A.S. Freare to B.O.A.C., September 21, 1948, Heinemann files.
14. James Riddell, *Flight of Fancy*, Robert Hale, 1950.
15. Nevil Shute, Foreword to *Fight of Fancy*.
16. Letter from Nevil Shute to A.D. Evans, July 14, 1948, Heinemann files.

Chapter 10

1. This chapter is based on "Flight Log", an account of his flight to Australia compiled from notes and letters sent home during the trip (MS 2199) and also from James Riddell's book *Flight of Fancy*.
2. See Richarda Morrow-Tait, *Thursday's Child*, Cirrus, 2001.

Chapter 11

1. Letter, Sir Alan Cobham to Nevil Shute, January 26, 1949, Cobham archives.
2. Nevil Shute, "My Week", unpublished article c. 1949, MS 2199.
3. Letter, Nevil Shute to Sir Alan Cobham, May 23, 1949, Cobham archives.
4. Letter Nevil Shute to Sir Alan Cobham, November 25, 1949, Cobham archives.
5. Letter Sir Alan Cobham to Nevil Shute, November 30, 1949, Cobham archives.
6. Letter Nevil Shute to Sir Alan Cobham, May 8, 1950, Cobham archives.
7. Letter Nevil Shute to Sir Alan Cobham, June 19, 1950, Cobham archives.
8. British Library Additional Manuscript 56763, Society of Authors Archive, Vol. CLXXXIX, folio 186–188.
9. Ibid. folio 190–192.
10. Ibid. folio 195–199.
11. Ibid. folio 198.

Chapter 12

1. Betty Lee, "Nevil Shute: He Believes the World Will Survive After All", *The Globe Magazine*, February 21, 1959.
2. British Library Additional Manuscript 56763, Society of Authors Archive, Vol. CLXXXIX, folio 189.
3. Letter Nevil Shute to Sir Alan Cobham, April 23, 1951, Cobham archives.
4. Telfair Interview with Fred & Ruth Greenwood, 2003.
5. Quoted in the Betty Lee article.
6. Nevil Shute, *The Far Country*, Heinemann, 1951.
7. Nevil Shute, Notes for the opening of Ian Hassall exhibition, MS 2199.

8. Nevil Shute, Speech to the Royal Empire Society ,c.1952, MS 2199.
9. Nevil Shute, *In the Wet*, Heinemann, 1953, Author's note.
10. Nevil Shute, *Replying to Critics*, The Author, Autumn issue, 1951.
11. Nevil Shute, Notes on Writing, MS 2199.
12. Nevil Shute letter to A.D. Evans, June 2, 1953, Heinemann files.
13. *Slide Rule*, p. 100.
14. Letter, Nevil Shute to Barnes Wallis, Vickers Archive.
15. Letter, Barnes Wallis to Nevil Shute, Vickers Archive.
16. Letter, Nevil Shute to Barnes Wallis, Vickers Archive.
17. Sir Peter Masefield, unpublished Aide Memoir.
18. Letter, Nevil Shute to Hessell Tiltman, June 1954, Portsmouth Library.
19. Foreword to *The Secret War*.
20. Nevil Shute, *Requiem for a Wren*, Heinemann, 1955.
21. Nevil Shute, *Beyond the Black Stump*, Heinemann, 1956.

Chapter 13
1. Richard Rhodes, *The Making of the Atomic Bomb*, Simon and Schuster, 1986.
2. See Wikipedia article on the History of Nuclear Weapons.
3. See Wikipedia article on William Penney, Baron Penney.
4. Richard Rhodes, *Dark Sun, the Making of the Hydrogen Bomb*, Simon and Schuster, 1995.
5. Quoted in Julian Smith, *Nevil Shute, a Biography*, The Paper Tiger, 2002.
6. Nevil Shute, *On The Beach*, Heinemann, 1957, p. 45.
7. Ernest Titterton, *Facing the Atomic Future*, MacMillan, 1956.
8. F. Kingsley-Norris, "Over the Hills and Not So Far Away", *The Medical Journal of Australia*, August 13, 1955.
9. See Wikipedia article on USS Seawolf.
10. Quoted in Julian Smith, *Nevil Shute, a Biography*, The Paper Tiger, 2002.
11. *Slide Rule*, p. 8 (Stratus Edition).
12. Helen Caldicott, *A Desperate Passion. An Autobiography*, W.W. Norton, 1996.
13. Freeman Dyson, *The New York Review of Books*, February 13, 2003.

Chapter 14

1. Telfair Interview with Peter D'Abbs, 2003.
2. Telfair Interview with Jeremy Lee, 2003.
3. "Novelist Nevil Shute Meets an Old Friend", *Sydney Morning Herald*, July 16, 1957.
4. Letter, Nevil Shute to David Martin, January 11, 1960.
5. Notes for a talk to the Writers Convention, Seaford, November 1957, in MS 2199.
6. For more information on Shute's motor racing career see Keith de La Rue web pages: http://delarue.net/racing.htm.
7. Nevil Shute, Foreword to Miles Smeeton, *Once is Enough*, Rupert Hart-Davis, London, 1959.
8. Quoted in Phillip Davey, *When Hollywood Came to Melbourne*, Chapter 2.
9. Ibid.
10. Ibid.
11. Quoted in Julian Smith, *Nevil Shute, a Biography*, The Paper Tiger, 2002.
12. Model Engineer, Vol. 124, Jan 5, 1961.
13. J.B. Oldham, *Blind Panels of English Binders*, Cambridge University Press, 1958.
14. "Shute Shoots Back", *Books and Bookmen*, September 1958, p. 11.
15. Letter, Nevil Shute to Jimmy Edwards, September 18, 1958.
16. Letter, Nevil Shute to Jimmy Edwards, November 17, 1958.
17. Phillip Davey, *When Hollywood Came to Melbourne*, Chapter 2.
18. Letter, Nevil Shute to Jimmy Edwards, November 17, 1958.
19. "Citizenship Talks to Open Today", *Sydney Morning Herald*, January 20, 1959.
20. *Model Engineer*, December 22, 1960, p. 774.
21. Betty Lee, "Nevil Shute: He Believes the World Will Survive After All", *The Globe Magazine*, February 21, 1959.
22. Letter, Nevil Shute to Flora Twort, March 2, 1959, Petersfield Museum collection.
23. *Model Engineer*, December 22, 1960, p. 775.
24. "A memorandum about creative writers, artists, and composers in Australia with legislative and financial recommendations", MS 2199.

25. N. Shute, "Converting Shaper", *Model Engineer*, October 1, 1959.
26. Nevil Shute, "Incident at Eucla", unpublished notes and manuscript, MS 2199.
27. *Sydney Morning Herald*, December 17, 1959.
28. Letter, Nevil Shute to David Martin, January 11, 1960.
29. *Sydney Morning Herald*, January 15, 1960.
30. British Library Additional Manuscript 56763, Society of Authors Archive, Vol. CLXXXIX ff. 217.
31. *The Times*, January 20, 1960.
32. *The Times*, January 16, 1960
33. *The Times*, January 28, 1960, p. 16, col. 7.
34. *The Times*, January 16, 1960, p. 10, col. 6.
35. Charles Curran, M.P. House of Commons Debate, July 21, 1960.
36. *The Times*, July 23, 1960.
37. Joseph Martin, "Did we inspire this story of a model engineer?", *Model Engineer*, April 28, 1960.

Chapter 15

1. Publisher's Note in Nevil Shute, *Stephen Morris*, Heinemann, 1961.
2. *Farewell, Miss Julie Logan: a Wintry Tale* by J.M. Barrie, dialogue treatment by Nevil Shute. Also *Farewell, Miss Julie Logan,* adapted for film script by Nevil Shute, MS 2199.
3. J. M. Barrie, *Farewell, Miss Julie Logan: A Wintry Tale*, Charles Scribner & Sons, 1932.
4. "Shute Shoots Back", *Books and Bookmen*, September 1958, p. 11.
5. "She's a pilot without an Airline", *Sydney Morning Herald*, November 17, 1960, p. 35.
6. David Caldwell, *The Church of St Thomas Langwarrin: A Potted Construction History*, David Caldwell Publications, 1999.
7. Julian Smith, *Nevil Shute, a Biography*, The Paper Tiger, 2002.
8. "A Man Called Nevil", *The Sunday Age*, January 10, 1993.
9. See www.nevilshute.org.
10. Nevil Shute, *The Seafarers*, The Paper Tiger, 2002.

Selected Bibliography

Nevil Shute, Slide Rule, Heinemann, 1954.

N.S. Norway, Heavier than Air Craft, Chapter VI in Dennis Burney, The World, The Air and The Future, Alfred A. Knopf, 1929.

Gerald Pawle, The Secret War, Harrap, 1956.

Sir Peter Masefield, To Ride the Storm, William Kimber, 1982.

James Riddell, Flight of Fancy, Robert Hale, 1950.

George Meager, My Airship Flights 1915-1930, William Kimber, 1970.

Julian Smith, Nevil Shute: A Biography, Paper Tiger, 2002.

E.A. Johnston, Airship Navigator, Skyline Publishing, 1994.

D.H. Middleton, Airspeed, The Company and its Aeroplanes, Terrence Dalton, 1982.

Acknowledgements

In writing this book I have received help from very many people, both in the research and the preparation of the text.

My grateful thanks go to Heather Mayfield, Nevil Shute's elder daughter, for her support, for patiently answering my questions about her father's life and writing the foreword. Dan Telfair made many helpful comments on the text and very generously made available transcripts of interviews that he and his wife Zia conducted with those in Australia who knew Shute when he lived there. My friend and co-researcher Laura Schneider shared with me the findings of her researches, both in the National Library of Australia, where Shute's papers reside, and also from the University of Syracuse Library. She has also been extremely helpful and encouraging throughout the preparation of the book.

My thanks also go to Andy Burgess, with whom Mike Meehan and I made visits to the National Archives and to BAE Systems Heritage at Farnborough. At Farnborough we were given great assistance by Barry Guess and Mike Fielding. With their help we found many of the original files of calculations done by Shute during his time at de Havilland and a wealth of information on Airspeed and its aircraft. Andy and I visited Cambridge University Library, where we scanned through microfilm records of Shute's correspondence from the Airship Guarantee Company records which form part of the extensive Vickers archive. John Wells and Godfrey Waller of the Manuscripts Department kindly made this archive material available to us.

On the aviation side my thanks go to Phil Nixon, who originally got in contact with Colin Cruddas, archivist at Cobham PLC. Colin kindly made available the archive correspondence of Sir Alan Cobham relating to the formation of Airspeed and the contract for the *Ferry* and *Courier* aircraft. Also in these archives was a file of letters between Shute and Sir Alan relating to *Round the Bend*.

Oxford featured large in Shute's life. Gay Sturt, archivist at the Dragon School, not only laid on a most informative guided tour of the school, but also provided copies of articles Shute wrote for *The Draconian*, the school magazine. She is the grand-daughter of Mr and Mrs Sturt, with whom Shute lived whilst attending the school, and niece of Oliver Sturt, Shute's school friend. Without Gay's family connection we would never have known the precise location of their house, 55 Park Town. At Balliol College, Anna Sander, Lonsdale Curator of Archives and Manuscripts, provided Shute's admission correspondence. Dr Penelope Bulloch, Librarian, was most helpful in providing copies of contemporary records, as were Rebecca Staples, Librarian at Lady Margaret Hall, and Kirsty Walker, Librarian at Nuffield College which houses the papers of Lord Cherwell (Professor Lindemann).

At the British Library Steve van Dulken, Curator of Patents and a Shute enthusiast, pointed the way to the Society of Authors manuscripts which contain his letters to the Society and provide a valuable insight into, in particular, his row with the Ministry of Fuel and Power over his petrol ration. Steve also introduced me to the wonders of the Times Digital Archive and also provided other newspaper articles as well as, naturally, researching Shute's patents.

Dr Mike Morrogh, Head of History at Shrewsbury School, researched the School records to provide details of Shute's time there. During a visit by Shutists in June 2010 he gave a fascinating account of what life at Shrewsbury was like in Shute's time there, including an insight into the character of Basil Oldham, Shute's Housemaster who became a lifelong friend.

I am most grateful to Phillip Davey from Australia for providing source material that he used in his book *When Hollywood Came to Melbourne*, a detailed account of the filming of *On the Beach*.

On two occasions I have had the pleasure of talking to people who knew and worked with Shute. Bert Judge, who worked at International Model Aircraft during the War, provided a glimpse of Commander Norway during his time at the DMWD and reminisced on his work on the Target Glider and Swallow pilotless aircraft. Cavendish (Cavvy) Morton, who with his brother Concord, did much publicity for Airspeed, made me very welcome during a visit to his home on the Isle of Wight. He reminisced about his friendship with Shute and sailing together. He showed me wonderful examples, not only of his artwork for Airspeed, but his superb paintings of aircraft, land and seascapes. I am most grateful to both Bert and Cavvy for their generous hospitality.

Others who have kindly provided documents or information include the Rev. John Wilcox, who began researching Shute's life and work many years ago. He provided me with a copy of Shute's Will. In Australia, Richard Michalak and William Laing kindly shared their findings from their visit with Jimmy Edwards' daughter Pauline. Rebekah Hamilton generously shared her findings from her search of the correspondence archives of Heinemann, Shute's publishers. Richard Morris kindly provided the photograph of the group at Sherburn-in-Elmet.

I am indebted to the late Professor Donald Cardwell of Manchester University. As my postgraduate tutor in the History of Science and Technology, he was an inspirational mentor who emphasised the vital importance of consulting, and where possible cross-checking, primary sources and of interpreting findings in the context of the time and place in which they occurred.

My thanks go to my daughter Claire and also to Laura Schneider, Alison Jenner and David Dawson-Taylor for proofreading the manuscript. Keith Minton did a thorough editorial review and provided valuable advice along the way.

In the transition from manuscript to print I express my thanks to the following: Dr. Michael S. Berliner who did a painstaking, thorough and detailed final proof read; Mark Van Horne for his expert book design, layout and indexing; Linda Robinson for her excellent cover design, and Fred Weiss of The Paper Tiger for undertaking the publication with enthusiasm.

Despite the input of so many people, any errors or omissions are entirely mine.

Finally, my thanks go to my wife Janice for her patience, tolerance and encouragement throughout the writing of this book.

Permissions

I express my thanks to the Trustees of Nevil Shute's literary estate, who have, through A.P. Watt Ltd, granted permission to quote from both his published and unpublished works and letters.

The lines from John Betjeman's poem Summoned by Bells are quoted by kind permission of Messrs John Murray (Publishers).

Extracts from Flora Twort's diaries and letters are quoted by permission of Sara Sadler, Curator of the Petersfield Museum.

Extracts from D.H. Middleton's book Airspeed, the Company and its Aeroplanes are quoted by permission of The Lavenham Group.

I acknowledge the permission of the Syndics of Cambridge University Library to quote extracts from the Vickers archive material.

I am most grateful to Pauline Edwards for permission to quote from letters Shute wrote to her father.

Nevil Shute's Published Novels

Title (American titles in brackets)	Written	Published	Original Publisher
Stephen Morris	1923	1961	Heinemann
Pilotage	1924	1961	Heinemann
Marazan	1926	1926	Cassell
So Disdained (The Mysterious Aviator)	1928	1928	Cassell
Lonely Road	1931	1932	Cassell
Ruined City (Kindling)	1937	1938	Cassell
What Happened to the Corbetts (Ordeal)	1938	1938	Heinemann
An Old Captivity	1939	1940	Heinemann
Landfall	1939-40	1940	Heinemann
Pied Piper	1941	1941	Heinemann
Most Secret	1943	1945	Heinemann
Pastoral	1944	1944	Heinemann
Vinland the Good	1945	1945	Heinemann
The Chequer Board	1945-46	1946	Heinemann
The Seafarers	1946	2002	Paper Tiger
No Highway	1948	1948	Heinemann
A Town Like Alice (The Legacy)	1949	1949	Heinemann
Round the Bend	1950	1951	Heinemann
The Far Country	1951	1952	Heinemann
In The Wet	1952	1953	Heinemann
Slide Rule	1953	1954	Heinemann
Requiem for a Wren (The Breaking Wave)	1954	1955	Heinemann
Beyond the Black Stump	1955	1956	Heinemann
On The Beach	1956	1957	Heinemann
The Rainbow and the Rose	1957	1958	Heinemann
Trustee from the Toolroom	1959	1960	Heinemann

Nevil Shute's Non-Fiction Publications

N.S. Norway, "The Case for the Revival of the Water Channel", *Journal of the Royal Aeronautical Society*, No. 167, November 1924 Vol. XXVIII, pp. 647–652.

N.S. Norway, "Heavier-Than-Air-Craft", Chapter VI in C.D. Burney, *The World, The Air and The Future*, Alfred Knopf, 1929.

N.S. Norway, "R.100 Canadian Flight, 1930", *Journal of the Royal Aeronautical Society*, May 1931, p. 401–414.

Films of Nevil Shute's Books

Title	Year
Lonely Road Scotland Yard Commands (USA)	1936
The Pied Piper	1942
Landfall	1949
No Highway No Highway in the Sky (USA)	1951
A Town Like Alice	1956
On the Beach	1959
A Town Like Alice (TV mini series)	1981
The Far Country	1986
The Pied Piper Crossing to Freedom (UK)	1990
On the Beach	2000

Index

About the Author

John Anderson was born in Yorkshire and obtained degrees in Mechanical Engineering and the History of Technology at Manchester University. He has worked in industry for over 30 years as a consultant in friction, lubrication and wear problems and on structural testing. He combines an interest in the history of technology and aviation with an enthusiasm for the novels and work of Nevil Shute and has been actively researching Shute's life since 2003. John is currently Vice President of the Nevil Shute Norway Foundation. He lives in Cheshire and is married with one daughter.

Lightning Source UK Ltd.
Milton Keynes UK
UKOW04n0756021214

242497UK00004B/72/P